Sacred Music, Religious Desire and Knowledge of God

Bloomsbury Studies in Philosophy of Religion

Series Editor: Stewart Goetz

Editorial Board: Thomas Flint, Robert Koons, Alexander Pruss, Charles Taliaferro, Roger Trigg, David Widerker, Mark Wynn

Titles in the Series

Freedom, Teleology, and Evil by Stewart Goetz
The Image in Mind: Theism, Naturalism, and the Imagination by Charles Taliaferro and Jil Evans
Actuality, Possibility, and Worlds by Alexander Robert Pruss
The Rainbow of Experiences, Critical Trust, and God by Kai-man Kwan
Philosophy and the Christian Worldview: Analysis, Assessment and Development edited by David Werther and Mark D. Linville
Goodness, God and Evil by David E. Alexander
Well-Being and Theism: Linking Ethics to God by William A. Lauinger
Thinking Through Feeling: God, Emotion and Possibility by Anastasia Philippa Scrutton
God's Final Victory: A Comparative Philosophical Case for Universalism by John Kronen and Eric Reitan
Free Will in Philosophical Theology by Kevin Timpe
Beyond the Control of God? edited by Paul M. Gould
The Mechanics of Divine Foreknowledge and Providence edited by T. Ryan Byerly
The Kalām Cosmological Argument: Philosophical Arguments for the Finitude of the Past edited by Paul Copan with William Lane Craig
The Kalām Cosmological Argument: Scientific Evidence for the Beginning of the Universe edited by Paul Copan with William Lane Craig
Free Will and God's Universal Causality by W. Matthews Grant

Sacred Music, Religious Desire and Knowledge of God

The Music of Our Human Longing

Julian Perlmutter

BLOOMSBURY ACADEMIC
LONDON • NEW YORK • OXFORD • NEW DELHI • SYDNEY

BLOOMSBURY ACADEMIC
Bloomsbury Publishing Plc
50 Bedford Square, London, WC1B 3DP, UK
1385 Broadway, New York, NY 10018, USA
29 Earlsfort Terrace, Dublin 2, Ireland

BLOOMSBURY, BLOOMSBURY ACADEMIC and the Diana logo are trademarks of Bloomsbury Publishing Plc

First published in Great Britain 2020
This paperback edition published in 2021

Copyright © Julian Perlmutter, 2020

Julian Perlmutter has asserted his right under the Copyright, Designs and Patents Act, 1988, to be identified as Author of this work.

For legal purposes the Acknowledgements on p. viii constitute an extension of this copyright page.

Series Design by Louise Dugdale
Cover Image © Aitor Diago / Getty Images

All rights reserved. No part of this publication may be reproduced or transmitted in any form or by any means, electronic or mechanical, including photocopying, recording, or any information storage or retrieval system, without prior permission in writing from the publishers.

Bloomsbury Publishing Plc does not have any control over, or responsibility for, any third-party websites referred to or in this book. All internet addresses given in this book were correct at the time of going to press. The author and publisher regret any inconvenience caused if addresses have changed or sites have ceased to exist, but can accept no responsibility for any such changes.

A catalogue record for this book is available from the British Library.

A catalog record for this book is available from the Library of Congress.

ISBN: HB: 978-1-3501-1496-8
PB: 978-1-3502-7795-3
ePDF: 978-1-3501-1497-5
eBook: 978-1-3501-1498-2

Series: Bloomsbury Studies in Philosophy of Religion

Typeset by Deanta Global Publishing Services, Chennai, India

To find out more about our authors and books visit www.bloomsbury.com and sign up for our newsletters.

For my family

Contents

Acknowledgements		viii
1	Introduction	1
2	Sacred music, longing and openness	3
3	Desire and knowledge	31
4	Music and affect	61
5	Sacred music and knowledge by desire: The account applied	83
6	Religious desire and contemplative prayer	121
7	General conclusion	149
Notes		151
Bibliography		181
Index		187

Acknowledgements

The author and publisher gratefully acknowledge the permission granted to reproduce the copyright material in this book:

© John Cottingham, 2009, *Why Believe?*, Continuum UK, used by permission of Bloomsbury Publishing Plc.

St Augustine, reissue ed. 2008, *Confessions*, Translation, Introduction, and Notes © Henry Chadwick 1991, pp. 207–208, reproduced with permission of Oxford Publishing Limited through PLSclear.

Thomas Merton, *New Seeds of Contemplation*, copyright ©1961 by The Abbey of Gethsemani, Inc. Reprinted by permission of New Directions Publishing Corp.

Extracts from The Book of Common Prayer, the rights in which are vested in the Crown, are reproduced by permission of the Crown's patentee, Cambridge University Press.

Except for when part of other quoted sources, biblical quotations are from The ESV® Bible (The Holy Bible, English Standard Version®), copyright © 2001 by Crossway, a publishing ministry of Good News Publishers. Used by permission. All rights reserved.

Every effort has been made to trace copyright holders and to obtain their permission for the use of copyright material. The publisher apologises for any errors or omissions in the above list and would be grateful if notified of any corrections that should be incorporated in future reprints or editions of this book. The third-party copyrighted material displayed in the pages of this book is done so on the basis of 'fair dealing for the purposes of criticism and review' or 'fair use for the purposes of teaching, criticism, scholarship or research' only in accordance with international copyright laws, and is not intended to infringe upon the ownership rights of the original owners.

Some of the material in this book was first published in Julian Perlmutter, 'Desiring the Hidden God: Knowledge Without Belief', *European Journal for Philosophy of Religion* 8, no. 4 (2016): 51–64.

Acknowledgements

This book owes its existence to more people than I can name here, but there are a few whose roles were especially significant. I would like to thank Sarah Coakley for her support and guidance during the writing of this project, and Tim Crane for reading a large amount of the material and raising important challenges that I was forced to meet. David Efird very kindly read the work at an early stage, and provided helpful comments. I am grateful to audiences at the 2015 conference of the British Society for the Philosophy of Religion, and the 2015 annual meeting of the American Academy of Religion, for providing valuable feedback on parts of the study at various stages. My thanks go also to Mark Wynn, who offered me support and encouragement in preparing the work for publication. Several people proofread chapters, including Patrick McKearney, Emma Wiggin and Barnabas Aspray, and I am grateful to them all.

The motivation for the topic of this study was due in large part to my time in the Chapel Choir of Trinity Hall, Cambridge. It was while singing Henry Purcell's *Hear My Prayer, O Lord* in concert that I realised there was something important to say about sacred music, non-belief and religious openness. Moreover, the weekly choral evensongs gave my time at Cambridge a rhythm and nourishment that could not have been provided in any other way. My thanks go especially to Andrew Arthur, for his expertise and passion in directing the choir.

I gratefully acknowledge funding received from the Arts and Humanities Research Council. Trinity Hall and the Faculty of Divinity at the University of Cambridge also provided generous financial support for research expenses.

Lastly, I thank my family and friends whose conversations and companionship helped in more ways than I can enumerate during the writing of this work. Above all, I thank my parents for their unfailing love and support, without which I cannot imagine this book having been written.

1

Introduction

This philosophical study unites three themes: religious non-belief, sacred music and religious desire. What primarily dictates this subject matter is the observation that sacred music – and specifically choral music in the Christian, Western classical tradition – has a peculiar capacity to strike a chord even in non-believers. 'In today's so-called secular society, sacred choral music is as powerful, compelling and popular as it has ever been', writes Jonathan Arnold in a recent study.[1] David Pugmire, meanwhile, has observed that 'sacred music seems to have a surprising power over unbelievers ... to ply them ... with what might be called devotional feelings'.[2] In newspaper articles we read of the continued popularity in Britain of choral services such as evensong, despite the country's low levels of church attendance in general.[3]

What are we to make of all this? For a start, there are non-believers and there are non-believers. Even the most hardened atheist may recognize the beauty that sacred music can possess, without being at all interested in the music's subject matter. On the other hand it is possible to be on the edges of religious adherence, neither believing nor disbelieving, yet retaining an interest in the teachings and practices of particular religious institutions. It is this sort of non-believer, whom I call the 'interested non-believer', that will be my concern in this study, although much of what I say will also apply to those who actively profess religious faith (and in any case, the line between the two can be blurry, with considerable variation in degrees of confidence, both between people and over the course of a single person's life). In short, I will argue that for an interested non-believer, the deep appeal of sacred music can be a way into growing in religious openness: engaged with in a particular way, sacred choral music has the capacity to shape profoundly a person's journey of religious inquiry. This is where the third of my key themes comes in: the way in which, I will argue, sacred music can do this is by helping the listener to cultivate religious *desires* of a certain kind. Religious desire, or more specifically the desire for God, is a natural focus for an investigation into 'non-believing openness', since a desire for God does not require a pre-existing belief that God is real. My central claim will be that through desiring God in response to sacred music in the way I shall describe, one can come to *know* something of what God would be like in satisfying the desire. Thus, if God is real and has (something like) this nature, then through the desire one knows about God, where this knowledge is imbued with a special, personal significance that shapes and sustains the religious quest. All this, I maintain, is possible for a non-believer.

The themes of sacred music and non-believing religious involvement have received increasing attention in recent philosophical literature, including the issue of their overlap: How, and to what extent, can a non-believer fully engage with sacred music?[4] The issue of religious desire has not seen as much explicit philosophical treatment, at least in the analytic tradition in which I am predominantly based. Yet the emotions more generally in religious life have been the focus of recent work – and the present study joins this emerging line of investigation. In particular, my underlying aim in what follows is to develop a religious 'epistemology of involvement', to use a phrase of John Cottingham:[5] a form of epistemology based on the recognition that religious understanding, if there is such a thing, requires one to be open and receptive, and that a programme of sustained religious praxis and affective response is needed in order to cultivate the receptivity in question. Hence, the epigraph at the start of Chapter 2 is quite deliberately placed: the whole study can be understood as picking up this thread of Cottingham's work and developing it in a particular way.

I have said that this study will be centred on desire for God in response to sacred music. However, only one chapter – Chapter 5 – discusses such responses in any detail in relation to the music itself. There are claims I need to establish in order for the arguments of that chapter to hold up, which I do in the first three chapters. Chapter 2 discusses the issue of sacred music and non-belief, the concept of interested non-belief that I will primarily be addressing and various aspects of desire that will be relevant in what follows. Chapter 3 establishes the epistemology of desire with which I will be working, in the context of more general considerations in the philosophy of emotion. Chapter 4 addresses the topic of music and affect, again with a view to the specific affect of desire that is my central concern. These chapters all feed into Chapter 5, which contains several in-depth musical illustrations of my central thesis. Finally, Chapter 6 examines the practice of Christian contemplative prayer in light of what will have gone before; in doing so, it provides both a theological context to the discussion and an account of how the form of religious involvement I will have articulated can be taken into a wider life of religious practice.

2

Sacred music, longing and openness

> *There is no promise that it will be easy. But this much, if we knew anything of human life, we knew already. There is no guarantee of the outcome … . But for some, as long as the music of our human longing calls us, … there will be no other path we can with integrity follow.*
>
> John Cottingham[1]

2.1 Sacred music and religious desire: A real-life story

In Alf Gabrielsson's *Strong Experiences with Music*, a collection of real-life accounts describing the effect of music on people's lives, we read the following story. One afternoon in the mid-1990s, Ella, a student in Sweden, decides to visit the cathedral near her home. Every so often she likes to come here to gather her thoughts and gain some perspective on her studies, and to take joy in the beauty and history of the building. This afternoon, on entering the cathedral, she pauses to remove her backpack. Just as she unzips her jacket, her attention is caught by the sound of a melody, faint yet distinguishable. She raises her head to hear more clearly. Is she imagining it? No one else seems to be listening; yet Ella is sure that she can hear a song. It is, she establishes, a male choir singing a Gregorian chant of some kind. She has never heard anything so beautiful, and in an instant the melody has captured her attention totally, filling and enveloping her. It seems to be coming from the very top of the building, almost merging with the stone walls.

As Ella continues to listen, sorrow begins to wash over her. She thinks of her loved ones who are now gone, and of everyone who has lost someone dear to them; she knows she is not alone in feeling sorrow, and there is now crying building in her chest. As she walks further into the church, the melody pursues her; she can now hear it loud and clear – simultaneously sad and consoling, and unbearably beautiful. Looking around, Ella still cannot see who is singing. She arrives at a set of candleholders, and tears now start to roll down her cheeks. She lights two candles for her loved ones and for all those who are in sorrow. Her emotions guided by the music, a feeling of dreadful loneliness fills her, a feeling of smallness, vulnerability and despair. Yet as her crying abates, a new feeling arises in her: a desire to kneel and pray, to ask God for help in coping, in finding answers to the loneliness, in helping others in distress. The strong need to kneel and pray is confusing and even embarrassing, but the music fills her so completely that there is no room for anything else.

Continuing down the aisle, Ella discovers a small altar. Stopping to look at it, she wrestles with her unwillingness and uncertainty. She wants to kneel and pray, but is not sure that she can. Suddenly, she puts her bag down, walks to the altar and kneels. The music has drawn her to this posture, convincing her that it is the only proper thing; it has peeled all her obstacles away. She abandons herself completely to the singing, and prays for help. During her prayer, something happens: Ella's loneliness and sorrow simply ease up and disappear, and a great calm settles in her. She becomes convinced that she is not alone, indeed, that she has never been alone. She rises slowly, filled with a completely new feeling of calmness and strength. After years of despair and seeking, Ella has a strong sense that she has arrived home.

The question of what it was that Ella heard remains unanswered. Yet it had a profound and lasting effect on her religious faith: she is now convinced of God's reality, manifest to those who truly want and need him. Ella gained a new self-knowledge and self-esteem that day, which she will carry humbly with her for the rest of her life.[2]

2.2 Statement of aims: Non-believing openness

Music has the power to move us as little else can; and in this real-life account of a transformative experience involving sacred music and religious desire, we can see many of the themes with which this study will be concerned.[3] Much of what I say in the following pages will apply to both religious believers and non-believers. However, my main goal will be to articulate a form of religious engagement that is possible and fruitful for what we might call 'interested non-believers' in relation to Christian theism: those who lack the belief that any of the theistic content in Christian doctrine is true,[4] yet who have felt at one time or another a longing for the sacred or transcendent as represented in the language, thought and cultural heritage of the Christian tradition. In other words, I will primarily be addressing those in the situation in which Ella seems to find herself in the first part of the story, before her experience in prayer; and I suspect such a situation is not uncommon in the 'secularized' West, or North Atlantic world, today.[5] Over the next five chapters, I will develop an answer to the following question: if one cannot believe that the God of Christian doctrine is real, how might one, nonetheless, remain open to the inestimable benefits that would be available if such a God *were* real – remain, that is, in a position that would conduce to one's eventually being able to receive and live out those benefits? My answer is twofold. First, *desires* of a certain kind for God can give the desirer knowledge about God if he is real, which guides and enriches the religious quest. Second, in order to cultivate desires of this kind, one can engage in a particular way with sacred music in the Western classical tradition, taking that engagement into the practice of Christian prayer.[6] However, although the desires in question can, indeed, be cultivated, I hope to show that they can also be manifestations of pervasive human longings and needs.

Ella's story hints at the greater detail I will develop in answering the question of how a non-believer may cultivate openness to God. At the start of the story Ella is either a non-believer or a 'half-believer'; at any rate, she is not a committed Christian. She is familiar and comfortable with aspects of her culture's Christian heritage; yet from her confusion and embarrassment at the desire to kneel and pray, we see that she is not accustomed to fully fledged religious engagement: her life is not centred on a religious outlook. As she listens to the Gregorian chant, she comes to feel a deep dissatisfaction at the human condition – dissatisfaction arising from a new, vivid awareness of human vulnerability and the resultant, ever-present possibility of sorrow, loneliness and despair. The music, in eliciting this feeling of deep dissatisfaction, leads to a desire to reach out to God in prayer – a sense that nothing in the world could satisfy the need for help that she now feels. The beautiful, insistent melody, as well as eliciting in Ella the desire to reach out to God, helps her to do so, stripping away her obstacles of unwillingness, uncertainty and embarrassment. Finally, her time of prayer, infused with the beauty of the music, leads to a radical, lasting transformation of outlook – from loneliness and sorrow to calmness, strength and a sense of homecoming. Vital to this transformation is a newfound self-knowledge, which consists centrally in a sense of self-worth that she carries humbly, as though she recognizes that its source and significance lie outside of her.

I said I will examine the capacity of sacred music to elicit desires of a certain kind for God, and the role such desires can play in one's life when taken into a sustained practice of prayer. More exactly, I will develop an *epistemology* of religious desire as experienced through sacred music in the Western classical tradition.[7] Chapters 3 and 4 will establish the groundwork: in Chapter 3 I will argue for an epistemology of desire more generally, and in Chapter 4 I will argue that music can combine with other aspects of the listener's experience to arouse emotions with extra-musical objects. Music's capacity to combine with words and to be performed in a particular context makes it apt for eliciting affective responses that contain enough conceptual content to be relatively specific: a key epistemic feature of desire, as Chapter 3 will have established. Then, in Chapter 5, I will apply this groundwork to several musical examples. These examples are intended to illustrate sacred music's capacity to elicit forms of desire for God that enable knowledge of the kind discussed in Chapter 3. Specifically, I will argue that *through* and *in* the musically elicited longing for God that I discuss, one can know in a personally significant way what God would have to be like in satisfying the desire. Thus, if God is real and is roughly as the desire characterizes him, then one knows something of what he is like in terms of his importance to oneself as the desirer – even in the absence of the desire's satisfaction, and *even without any belief that God is real*.[8] This may immediately raise the worry of wishful thinking: how can one know that God, if real, *is* roughly as one's desires characterize him? I will look briefly at the issue at the end of this chapter, and will return to it in Chapters 3 and 6. Chapter 6 – the final chapter – will examine how the kinds of desire discussed in Chapter 5 can lead into a long-term practice of prayer within the Christian contemplative tradition, as represented in the work of the twentieth-century Cistercian monk Thomas Merton. Like Ella's desire for God, the longing I shall discuss springs from sacred music's ability to elicit in the listener a deep dissatisfaction with aspects of the human condition, which cannot be met by anything the world has to offer. I will argue that having this dissatisfaction is a natural way of being led into contemplative prayer as Merton presents it. One can hope that if the God to whom all this engagement points is real, then one will be shaped in contemplative prayer to grow in love and knowledge of that God, whose nature is glimpsed in musically elicited desires such as the ones I will have discussed.

Thus, the kind of religious engagement for which I shall argue involves responding to sacred music with desire for God, and allowing the resultant desiring orientation towards God to be contemplatively refined and enriched. All this, I maintain, is possible without religious belief, and I will argue for this claim later in this chapter (it may be, then, that as far as the desirer is concerned, it is an open question whether the God 'whose nature is glimpsed in musically elicited desires' is real or imaginary). It can therefore take the form of *non-doxastic religious engagement* – available to those who do not believe in God's reality, but to whom it seems likely enough that a given theistic world view is true for it to be worthwhile to cultivate openness and receptivity in spiritual matters. The kind of religious involvement I will be proposing can aid this cultivation by establishing an *epistemic and affective framework* for seeking God. Through the desiring responses to the sacred music that I shall discuss, one knows something of what God would be like if he were to satisfy one's desire (the epistemic framework). The existential significance that permeates this knowledge and enriches one's concepts of the relevant divine attributes will draw one into seeking God more than a thinner understanding of those attributes would. That is, the religious quest will have personal import (the affective framework). This cultivation of openness would be aimed at being able, eventually, to recognize any truth that the religious world view in question might have – a point to which I will return later in the chapter. One cannot, then, engage with a religious outlook in this desire-centred way if one *disbelieves* it: one must see some non-negligible probability of the outlook's being true.

As mentioned already, I will be concerned in this study with the possibility of non-doxastic engagement with a *Christian* outlook. This is not based on any claim that Christianity is in some sense the most worthy of our engagement. Rather, the rich musical tradition within the church will provide the material for an extended example of how my overall claim might play out: an example of how the type of desire-based religious involvement I describe can help to cultivate religious openness in a non-believer. I hope, then, that much of what I say would apply at least to the other theistic religions.

In the rest of this chapter, I will clarify several key issues regarding the sort of non-believing situation and religious engagement I have outlined. First, I will make some comments on the capacity of non-believers to respond in a genuinely religious way to sacred music. Second, I will provide a detailed account of 'interested non-belief' regarding Christianity. Third, I will reply to the potential worry that the interested non-believer who follows my proposals for religious engagement is engaging in a programme of self-deception. And finally, I will relate the epistemology of religious desire developed in the following chapters to a number of philosophical issues pertaining to desire.

Let us turn first, then, to the subject of sacred music: in particular, what our musical focus will be, and the relationship between belief/non-belief and the appreciation of sacred music.

2.3 Sacred music and religious non-belief

As well as the desire for God, sacred music will be a central topic of this study. I am not too worried about providing a precise definition of sacred music, since I have no intention of, in principle, limiting what I say to music that is recognizably of any one type.[9] I take it that some music naturally lends itself to the label 'sacred'; other music's sacredness might be a source of contention. At any rate, I shall be concerned with choral music of the Western classical tradition whose text contains religious subject matter. In a common, everyday sense, such music is naturally called 'sacred', and it will offer a rich source of material for my discussions of desire for God, especially desire as experienced by those who are not fully fledged religious believers. For it is clear that sacred music of this kind has a peculiar capacity to strike a chord even in non-believers. As David Pugmire has observed, 'Sacred music seems to have a surprising power over unbelievers ... to ply them ... with what might be called devotional feelings.'[10] This apparently obvious truth has led to discussion over whether, and to what extent, religious music can be fully appreciated by a secularly minded person; and central to the issue is whether or not a secularist's emotional response to the music can be as complete as a religious believer's. David Pugmire has argued that through a certain kind of *imaginative* engagement with the subject matter of sacred music, unbelievers can genuinely emotionally engage with such music.[11] Daniel Putman, meanwhile, has rejected this claim, arguing that the believer's emotional response to sacred music is qualitatively different from that of the unbeliever. The believer's response will not stop when she leaves the music, but will be pervasive throughout her outlook on life. It will also have a depth that the unbeliever's imaginative response lacks.[12] For instance, 'imagining we are saved eternally is not even on the same plane as actually believing we are saved eternally and the emotions of the latter have a depth quality to them that affects the believer's entire way of life.'[13]

I maintain that non-believers can respond to sacred music with desire for God that has a powerful, lasting influence on the desirer. However, Putman's argument might seem to threaten my claim: Is belief really needed in order for an emotional response to sacred music to be deep and pervasive? Well, not all emotional responses are the same in this respect, and I want to claim that desire is one kind of response that does not require belief in order to be deep and pervasive.[14] Two points should suffice at this stage. The first thing to emphasize is that my concern is with the sort of non-believer who has not ruled out the possibility of God's reality,[15] whereas Putman's focus seems to be non-believers who, at least for all practical purposes, have ruled it out.[16] Quite apart from whether or not desire is compatible in some form with *disbelief* in the reality of the desire's object, God as a genuine epistemic possibility is likely to make some difference to the quality and power of emotions directed at him. And second (a point for which I shall argue in more detail later in the chapter), a desire for something or someone can be just as powerful when one is uncertain about the existence of that person or thing, as it is when one is sure of its existence. Indeed, the desire's power may even be heightened by the uncertainty, as one may be spurred on to try and find out whether the object of desire really does exist; and this will probably be especially true of desire for a person. The notion that desire for God – and, specifically, desire for God elicited by sacred music – seems readily compatible with non-belief is expressed by Jonathan Arnold in a recent study on the practice and reception of sacred music in a secular society such as that of the West today. 'In today's so-called secular society, sacred choral music is as powerful, compelling and popular as it has ever been', writes Arnold; and it seems that one reason for this is that 'the attraction of beautiful and profound harmony … appeal[s] to … desires deep in human souls. Those desires … still clearly exist whether an age is considered to be secular or Christian.'[17]

I have been speaking of the situation I want primarily to address as a kind of 'interested non-belief' in relation to Christian doctrine. Let us now turn to this notion in earnest and develop it in more detail.

2.4 Interested non-belief

The concept of an interested non-believer involves several elements. Rather than offer a characterization straight off, which would be unhelpful without any background, I will build the idea progressively through engaging with three themes: Charles Taylor's description of secularity, William James' notion of a 'live hypothesis' and the relations between different propositional attitudes that one might hold towards a religious world view.

Charles Taylor: Secularity and the phenomenology of (non-)belief

Taylor, in *A Secular Age*, distinguishes between three kinds of secularity that are present to various degrees in the West today, and identifies the kind that is the book's main concern:

> This would focus on the conditions of belief. The shift to secularity in this sense consists, among other things, of a move from a society where belief in God is

unchallenged and indeed, unproblematic, to one in which it is understood to be one option among others, and frequently not the easiest to embrace.[18]

We need to get clearer on what this means for the phenomenology of non-belief. If, as I claim, it is possible to desire God without believing in his reality, then the desirer must have a certain view of what a theistic outlook involves, such that it is centred on something desirable. This will go hand in hand with a view of what a secular outlook involves, such that the content of the theistic outlook is viewed as the more desirable of the two.

As a helpful guiding picture, we can consider Taylor's own characterizations of theistic and secular outlooks at the most general level.[19] Central to Taylor's conception is that theistic belief and non-belief go beyond mere propositional assent or theory: they are *lived conditions* that affect how we experience the moral and/or spiritual orientation of our lives. On this view, theistic commitment is to recognize a transcendent reality beyond the natural world, whence life at its fullest seems to come as a gift: 'I came that they may have life and have it abundantly', as Christ says in John's Gospel.[20] The best kind of life is thus defined by living in light of a good that is independent of human flourishing, namely, loving and worshipping God – even though such a life necessarily conduces to human flourishing. A secular outlook, in contrast, involves the opposite: there is no recognition of any transcendent reality beyond the natural world, and life at its fullest is seen as having an immanent source in the world – either within ourselves[21] or in something outside ourselves (for instance in nature). And we can complete the secular package with 'self-sufficient humanism', whose rise as a widely available option is, Taylor claims, coterminous with the secularity at issue. This humanism sees the best kind of human life as defined by the pursuit of human flourishing, rather than by anything beyond it.

These are the general pictures of belief and non-belief with which I shall work for the time being. The specifically Christian elements of the religious engagement I discuss will come into view later, especially in the context of the sacred music and contemplative prayer considered in Chapters 5 and 6. However, it is good to have a sense at this stage of what it is that someone, including the interested non-believer, might be desiring when she desires God. In later chapters, the various desires for God as he is portrayed in a Christian world view can all be seen as desires for aspects of the fullness of life to which Taylor refers: a fullness given by, and received from, a source not of this world. An interested non-believer, then, is someone who does not believe that there is any such transcendent source of fullness, but who nonetheless sees it as a possibility worth taking seriously. What does this latter aspect – the 'interested' aspect – involve? Here we come to the second and third themes involved in the concept of interested non-belief: holding something as a Jamesian 'live hypothesis', and the propositional attitudes thereby implied.

William James: Live hypotheses

In his essay 'The Will to Believe', William James characterizes a hypothesis as 'anything that may be proposed to our belief', and describes a *live* hypothesis as 'one which appeals as a real possibility to him to whom it is proposed'; it makes an 'electric connection with [one's] nature' and 'scintillate[s] with … credibility'.[22] This needs a little unpacking. James goes on to observe that 'deadness and liveness in an hypothesis are not intrinsic properties, but relations to the individual thinker'.[23] However, he is at pains to emphasize that it is rarely a cool, neutral judgement that makes a hypothesis live or dead for someone in the first place. Any number of non-rational factors are involved: 'Fear and hope, prejudice and passion, imitation and partisanship, the circumpressure of our caste and set'.[24]

Even with this clarification, I think there is the potential for misunderstanding the notion of a live hypothesis. For if we grant that the hypotheses we take seriously are often established as such through non-rational means, it is, nonetheless, tempting to think that a Jamesian live hypothesis is merely one to which the believing subject *attaches a fairly high degree of probability*: the more probable a hypothesis given one's evidence, existing beliefs and belief-forming tendencies (including the non-rational ones), the more live it is. However, I believe it would be a mistake to view a live hypothesis simply in this way. It is interesting to note James' use of metaphor: making an 'electric connection with one's nature' has a more visceral feel than a mere judgement of probability does. We see this illustrated when James goes on to discuss the notion in relation to Pascal's Wager. In this well-known fragment of the *Pensées*, Blaise Pascal argues that on the balance of probabilities, risks and gains, the rational thing to do is to wager one's life on the truth of Christian theism.[25] James points out that in order to view the wager, as applied to Christian belief, as something even worth thinking about, we must have 'some pre-existing tendency to believe' the hypothesis it offers. His illustration is instructive: he imagines someone who claims to be the Mahdi (an eschatological figure in Islam) using the wager's logic in order to urge us to confess him; but, of course, to James' audience from Yale and Brown universities, such a hypothesis would have been dead – 'No tendency to act on it exists in us to any degree'.[26]

In making this observation, James can be seen as commenting on the so-called 'many gods' objection to the wager, which points out that in the wager itself Pascal gives us no way of deciding which hypothesis to prefer out of the various hypotheses that promise an infinite reward.[27] However, rather than push the objection or reply to it, James is making a different point about the fact that the would-be wagerer faces a multitude of choices: namely, that since many hypotheses are dead to us, the question of whether we should wager for them *does not even arise* (if 'ought' implies 'can', then the mere fact that we cannot wager on a dead hypothesis means that in our current state we have no duty to do so – regardless of any other considerations that may be advanced). But what does it mean to say that the hypothesis of the Mahdi, or of an Islamic world view more generally, is dead to a person – to someone, for instance, who has been raised in a culture that has been shaped by Christianity but which is increasingly secular in Taylor's above sense? And what is it to say that the hypothesis of Christianity is live to such a person? It is, I claimed, not merely a matter of how much probability one attaches to the hypothesis. To see this, consider Ella from our opening story. We do not know whether she had undertaken any kind of investigation into the probability of Christian theism, or for that matter, any comparative study of the probabilities attaching to the other major religious worldviews. Moreover, we do not even know whether she had *any view at all* regarding these probabilities – even a view shaped by the non-rational factors James mentions. If we had asked her, before her transformative experience, whether Christianity was likelier to be true than any form of Islam or Buddhism, then for all we know she might have said that she had no idea. Nonetheless, if we were to discover that Christianity was her only live religious hypothesis – the only religious world view to make an 'electric connection' with her nature – then we would not be at all surprised. We would think it perfectly natural for Christianity to be the default locus of spiritual exploration for Ella, even if she had no view about how its probability compared with those of the other religions.

Why is this? In short, because it is clear from the story that Ella is familiar enough with Christianity for it to come naturally as a way of structuring her life. For instance, she is comfortable spending time in the cathedral, taking joy in its beauty and history; and she recognizes the music as Gregorian chant. Christianity's familiarity to her is, to some extent, an instance of what John Cottingham has recently called 'the phenomenon of pervasiveness'.[28] Citing as examples Chaucer's *Canterbury Tales* and a traditional Christmas carol, Cottingham argues that in the 'age of faith', Christian culture was woven into the fabric of everyday life: the examples in question are 'ineradicably dyed with the colouring of a religious outlook'.²⁹ While Ella's everyday life may not have been coloured to quite this extent by a Christian outlook, it is at least clear that she is at home in her culture's Christian heritage to the extent that it has shaped and channelled her emotions and thoughts,³⁰ meaning that the most natural setting for her transformative experience was a place of Christian worship, and the most natural way of interpreting such an experience would have been in Christian terms. Such a familiarity with, or being at home in, a religious tradition is a key factor in what it is for that religion to be a live hypothesis for someone. Of course, it is also true that intellectual barriers cannot be too great, and so rational argumentation undoubtedly has its place.³¹ But to treat liveness and deadness in a hypothesis – that is, whether or not someone can engage seriously with a hypothesis – as *simply* a matter of intellectual plausibility would be a mistake.

Let us take stock and return to this section's guiding question of how to characterize an interested non-believer. We said earlier, following Taylor, that this is someone who does not believe that there is any transcendent source of fullness, but who, nonetheless, sees it as a possibility worth taking seriously. We can now fill in what 'seeing it as a possibility worth taking seriously' consists in: it crucially involves being at home in aspects of some tradition that represents a transcendent source of fullness in a given set of ways. If one is familiar enough with the tradition then one will have some disposition to structure one's life, or aspects thereof, in terms of at least some of the tradition's elements, such as its concepts, language or cultural heritage. In other words, one will view the religious world view in question as a live hypothesis. For this to be the case, one must also attach at least some minimal degree of intellectual plausibility to the world view – although, in the case of an interested non-believer, this will still fall far short of any confidence that it is true.

It might be wondered how someone in this sort of situation could engage with and explore the religious outlook without engaging in self-deception or dishonesty. If one does not *believe* that the outlook is true, but merely sees it as a possibility worth pursuing further, what sort of attitude may one take towards it? More specifically, since we will be concerned with a form of religious engagement centred on desire for God in a Christian context, what sort of non-doxastic propositional attitude towards Christian doctrine could underpin *this* kind of engagement? We now come to the final theme in characterizing an interested non-believer: the kinds of propositional attitude towards the relevant religious outlook that would be appropriate for such a person.

Propositional attitudes and interested non-belief

I. Belief and desire

First, let me clarify my earlier claim that desire for God does not require belief that God is real. In general, a desire for something concrete – and in particular for a person – does not require a belief that the object of desire really exists. Here is an example. In an episode of the sitcom *The Simpsons*,[32] mischievous, ten-year-old Bart decides to play a trick on his teacher, Edna Krabappel. Using an alter ego named 'Woodrow', he responds to a personal ad of hers in a newspaper, writing her a string of love letters and eliciting in her a strong romantic desire for the fictional man. He even goes so far as to arrange a date with her, leaving her waiting alone at the restaurant. Eventually guilt gets the better of him, and he writes her a consoling letter as if from Woodrow, explaining that he must leave town and expressing his affection for her.

Now let us slightly tweak the events of the episode. Suppose that after being stood up at the restaurant, Edna read somewhere that there had recently been a number of hoaxes in response to personal ads. We might expect her suspicion to be aroused: the news might well cast doubt in her mind over the genuineness of her correspondence with Woodrow, and over the reality of Woodrow himself. Yet at this point she is uncertain either way: she *might* have been the victim of a hoax; but equally, Woodrow might have been somehow detained. Given this state of uncertainty, it would be entirely natural for Edna to continue desiring Woodrow, despite her doubt over his existence. After all, he seemed real enough in the letters: they vividly portrayed to her a sense of his character (Bart is an excellent hoaxer).

The same sort of reasoning applies to desire for God. One might experience what one takes to be a portrayal of God's character (in literature, music, art, liturgy, interactions with other people and so on), but, nonetheless, harbour doubts – even strong doubts – over the reality of the God thus portrayed (the Edna/Woodrow case shows that we can experience what we take to be portrayals of someone's character without believing in his or her existence). Yet in this situation, one may continue to desire God. What such a desire might involve will be the focus of Chapters 5 and 6, and I shall also say something about it later in this chapter.

It might be objected here that I have misrepresented the nature of personal desire, and that if it were represented correctly then it would be a merely trivial truth that the desirer need not believe that the desire's object exists. Some philosophers have maintained that all desires for concrete objects (including persons) are reducible to desires for particular propositions to be true, or alternatively, for the obtaining of the states of affairs that would make the propositions true.[33] One might think it obvious that a desirer *cannot* believe that a state of affairs exists/obtains when she desires it, since perceiving it not to obtain is a necessary condition of desiring it.[34] At any rate, clearly a desirer *need not* believe that a state of affairs obtains in order to desire it. Hence, if Edna's desire for Woodrow was really a desire that she be with Woodrow and do x, y and z with him, then – trivially and uninterestingly – she need not have believed that those states of affairs existed/obtained in order to desire them. Later in the chapter I will discuss the issue of desire in more detail. For now, though, even if the reader thinks that Edna's desire for Woodrow was really a desire that she be with Woodrow and do x, y and z with him, we can still ask the substantive question of whether *this* desire required her to believe in Woodrow's existence – that is, in the existence of the person on whom the desired states of affairs are centred. And my answer is no: if one desires a state of affairs that is centred on a person, one need not believe that the person in question exists.

A desire whose object is, or at least centrally involves, a person does not require a belief that the person exists. However, there is another sort of belief that *is* required for the desires I shall discuss in Chapters 5 and 6. This is *belief about*. The desires that will interest us are ones that characterize God in particular ways; and the desirer will therefore hold beliefs about God as he is characterized by the desires in question. Belief about, as Robert Audi has pointed out, does not entail a commitment to the reality of the belief's object(s); we can, for instance, hold beliefs about the relationship between Hamlet and Ophelia.[35]

II. Propositional faith: Audi and Alston

Even so, the interested non-believer, as I have been developing the idea, cannot simply hold beliefs about the content of Christian doctrine as she holds beliefs about the content of fictional works.[36] In the case of fiction, one engages with content one believes to be non-factual; but this is not the attitude one holds towards religious doctrine when in a state of interested non-belief. We are left, then, with the question of what kind of propositional attitude towards a religious outlook such a person could hold. What about a particular kind of *faith*, one that is *propositional* but *non-doxastic*? Audi, for example, describes an attitude he calls 'fiducial faith' as 'a certain positive disposition toward [a] proposition', involving a cognitive component stronger than that of hope, but weaker than that of belief.'[37] By this, I take Audi to mean that the level of confidence in a proposition's truth that fiducial faith bestows on the subject is somewhere between that of hope and that of belief. William Alston has characterized 'faith that' in a somewhat similar way, as involving a 'weak epistemic position' towards its propositional object, along with a favourable attitude towards that object.[38] Although Alston does not specify that faith of this kind involves a stronger epistemic position than hope, this is implied by the passage from the Epistle to the Hebrews that he uses as an illustration: 'Faith is the assurance of things hoped for.'[39] Though they can be held together, assurance is a stronger epistemic position than hope alone.

Because faith in Audi's and Alston's senses is stronger in its level of confidence than hope, it is 'incompatible with a pervasive or *dominating* doubt' over the truth of the proposition(s) towards which it is held.[40] This raises a problem for us: an interested non-believer will, of course, have just this sort of pervasive doubt over God's reality and the truth of Christian doctrine. The fact that such doubt is incompatible with the kind of faith at issue is reflected in the unsuitability of describing a non-believer, even an interested one, as someone who has faith. So it looks as though faith in this sense will not do.

III. Acceptance: Two kinds

Hope, in fact, is one key aspect of the attitude I want to outline as suitable for the interested non-believer engaging in Christian life in a desire-centred way. As Audi points out, one could hope that 'this is a world under God' while 'regard[ing] the evidence as giving the proposition only very low probability'.[41] The other aspect of the overall attitude I want to outline is *acceptance* of a proposition or set of propositions. However, there are different kinds of acceptance. For our purposes, we must distinguish between *truth-normed* and *non-truth-normed* acceptance – between acceptance that takes into account the question of a proposition's truth, and acceptance that does not.

Alston has articulated in detail a type of truth-normed acceptance.[42] On his account, acceptance is the voluntary adoption of a positive attitude towards a proposition (or set of propositions) *p* – an attitude that involves regarding *p* as true, and resolving thereafter to use *p* as a basis for one's thinking, feeling and behaviour. It is different from belief in two key ways: unlike belief, it does not engender a tendency to *feel* that *p* if the question arises of whether *p*; and unlike belief, it is voluntary. Acceptance that *p* does not require belief that *p*. Alston illustrates the idea with the following example:

> Consider an army general whose forces are facing enemy forces with a battle imminent. He needs to proceed on some assumption as to the disposition of those forces. His scouts give some information about this but not nearly enough to make any such assumption obviously true, or even overwhelmingly probably true. So what does he do? He *accepts* the hypothesis that seems to him the most

likely of the alternatives, though he realizes that he is far from knowing that this or any other such hypothesis is true. He uses this as a basis for disposing his forces in the way that seems most likely to be effective, even though he is far from believing that this is the case.[43]

Notice the truth-normed nature of the army general's acceptance: the question of whether his hypothesis is *true* matters to how acceptable he finds it. Specifically, he accepts the hypothesis about the enemy forces that seems to him to be the most likely.

In contrast, to get a sense of *non*-truth-normed, non-doxastic acceptance, consider *fictionalism* about various kinds of discourse. This is roughly the view that our attitude towards a discourse is not, or should not be, truth-normed or evidence-normed – even though the discourse is truth-*apt* (it could in principle be true, since it expresses propositions). Rather, our attitude towards the statements in the discourse is, or should be, non-doxastic acceptance of some kind, enabling us to commit to the discourse even though we do not believe it or may even disbelieve it – because such commitment is, or would be, beneficial in some way.[44] Richard Joyce, in his *The Myth of Morality*, gives an account of what this could look like with regards to *moral* discourse (having defended a moral error theory in the rest of the book). We should, he claims, adopt an attitude of 'disbelieving acceptance'[45] towards moral statements. More specifically, this is an attitude of *immersive make-believe*: just as we can immerse ourselves in a work of literary fiction by make-believing that its content is true, so we can do the same for moral discourse. In both cases, Joyce thinks, our non-doxastic, non-truth-normed commitment is instrumentally justified – at least in part by the effect it has on our emotions. Literary fiction gives us (perhaps among other things) pleasure and instruction, while engaging with moral discourse in a make-believing way can elicit emotional responses in us that are beneficial for our decisions and actions.[46] Similar proposals have been advanced with regard to religious discourse. For instance, Robin Le Poidevin and Natalja Deng have each defended a kind of make-believing religious engagement that is analogous to immersion in a work of literary fiction. The purpose of this might be to engage our emotions, heighten our awareness of our moral responsibilities, or instil a sense of purpose or community.[47]

IV. My proposal: hoping acceptance and an 'epistemology of involvement'

Having the truth-normed/non-truth-normed distinction in mind is useful for appreciating the nature of the attitude towards Christian doctrine that I propose for our interested non-believer. That attitude is *truth-normed acceptance combined with hope*. As a way into understanding this, consider the following suggestion of Robert Audi's:

> One might [have] acceptance combined with hope. One could resolve to act as if this is a world under God even if one only hopes this is so and regards the evidence as giving the proposition only very low probability. One's behaviour would be largely like that of someone with fiducial faith, but it would not be true that one trusts that the world is under God; one's attitude would be only a hope.[48]

This succeeds for our purposes where Audi's and Alston's versions of propositional faith failed. Our account (appropriated from Alston) of truth-normed acceptance does not specify any minimum level of confidence that the accepter must have towards the target proposition. It simply specifies that the question of whether the proposition is true matters to how acceptable one finds it. The army general accepts the hypothesis about the enemy forces that seems to him to be the most likely, but nothing in Alston's account of acceptance implies that he *had* to think the hypothesis the most likely in order to accept it – although, in his situation, this policy was clearly the most prudent. As I will show in a moment, there is a way of truth-normedly accepting the doctrinal content of Christianity even if one does not think it very likely to be true. *Hoping* that a proposition is true, on the other hand, does plausibly require a minimum level of confidence in the proposition; but this level is very low, as Audi points out. The confidence level required for hoping acceptance is thus determined by the hope, rather than by the acceptance; and because this level is very low, hoping acceptance (unlike propositional faith) is compatible with pervasive or dominating doubt.

How may one truth-normedly accept a Christian outlook if one strongly doubts that it is true? The question of whether or not it is true would have to matter to how acceptable one finds it, in some way other than the *likelihood* of its truth playing any role. Here is another way in which its acceptability can depend on a concern for its truth. One may accept Christian doctrine and discourse – including 'resolv[ing] to act as if this is a world under God' – in order to recognize any truth the discourse may contain. This brings us to the key theme of the current chapter, and, indeed, the binding principle of this whole study. In order to get a better handle on the idea, we can turn to a notion that John Cottingham has developed in much of his work: that of an *epistemology of involvement*.[49] Cottingham argues that religious understanding, by its very nature, requires one to be open and receptive rather than detached and purely intellectual, and that a programme of sustained religious praxis can help to cultivate – indeed, is *required* in order to cultivate – such a state:

It is precisely because the great truths of religion are held to be in part a mystery, beyond the direct comprehension of the human mind, that an attempt to grasp them head on via the tools of logical analysis is, in a certain sense, to evade them. A different strategy, the strategy of involvement, the strategy of praxis, is required by the nature of the material.[50]

The general idea is not new, of course, and Cottingham draws on various strands of the Christian tradition – as well as other traditions that could broadly be called 'spiritual' – to make his case.[51] Notable among these is a treatment of Pascal's Wager emphasizing the journey of personal transformation, brought on by long-term involvement in religious practice, that Pascal envisages for the wagerer. 'You want to find faith and you do not know the road', he writes. 'Learn from those ... who know the road you wish to follow. ... They behaved just as if they did believe, taking holy water, having masses said, and so on.'[52] Importantly, this long-term investment in religious practice does not, for Pascal, result in self-deception, since the outcome is not simply *belief*, but a whole moral and epistemic transformation of the subject.[53] On the moral side: 'You will be faithful, honest, humble, grateful, full of good works, a sincere, true friend.' And on the epistemic side: 'At every step you take along this road you will see that your gain is so certain and your risk so negligible that in the end you will realize that you have wagered on something certain and infinite for which you have paid nothing.'[54] The promise of eternal life comes into view more and more clearly as the wagerer journeys along the path of religious involvement.

However, although the idea of an epistemology of involvement is by no means new, Cottingham develops it in an interesting, multifaceted way. Central is the notion that there are 'some truths the *accessibility conditions* of which include certain requirements as to the attitude of the subject': the evidence for such truths is 'available only as a result of certain inner transformations'.[55] More specifically, our *affective* responses can 'involve transformative ways of perceiving reality'.[56] Cottingham stresses that this is not a case of special pleading for religious adherence: there are 'many cases of perfectly ... objective facts which nevertheless can only be detected by those who are, in virtue of internal transformations, in an epistemically privileged position'. For example, appreciating the properties of a complex work of music, or recognizing a good friend's qualities of character, both require a certain amount of attunement or habituation.[57]

How may this apply to *religious* understanding? As we have seen, the general idea is that 'intimations of the divine presence might be available, not universally, ... but only to those in an appropriate state of ... receptivity'[58] – a state whose cultivation requires sustained involvement in religious praxis. For specific applications of this principle, we can look, for instance, to Cottingham's discussion of (what he argues are) several distinctively theistic attitudes: humility, hope, awe and thankfulness.[59] These attitudes find natural expression in the 'rich tradition of parables and poems and hymns and prayers' of the theistic religions,[60] incorporated into regular patterns of praxis such as morning and evening prayer, and saying grace at meals.[61] Such practices can play a vital role in the cultivation of the receptivity that is necessary for catching intimations of the divine presence. They can prepare and train one to

> approach God in humility and awe, to risk the vulnerability of trust and hope …, to express that thankfulness and praise for the gift of life which would be out of place were there no one and nothing to thank, to live one's life in the faith that such thankfulness does find a response, and is returned in joy and blessing.[62]

The situation being described, then, 'is less like that of one who has items of doxastic baggage carefully secured and stowed prior to the voyage, than of one who embarks on a journey of hope'.[63]

It seems to me eminently plausible that Cottingham is correct in his epistemological emphasis on religious involvement. Religious truth, if such there be, is, indeed, 'beyond the direct comprehension of the human mind'; *theistic* truth, if such there be, centrally concerns something like a personal relationship. And if, in seeking to grow in religious understanding, our interested non-believer involves herself practically and affectively in the Christian tradition, she will truth-normedly accept a Christian outlook even though she might attach a low probability to its truth. The acceptance will yield the practical aspects of embarking on a journey of hope.

Again, let us sum up the argument of this section. I have been progressively clarifying the notion of interested non-belief, the situation that this study will primarily address. First, following Taylor, an interested non-believer is someone who does not believe that there is any transcendent source of fullness, but who sees it as a possibility worth taking seriously as a live hypothesis. Second, this 'taking seriously' involves being at home in a religious tradition that is oriented towards a transcendent source of fullness under a given set of representations; additionally, to take that tradition seriously, one must find it intellectually plausible to some degree, even though, as a non-believer, one falls far short of any confidence that it is true. And third, the propositional attitude towards a Christian outlook that I propose for an interested non-believer is truth-normed acceptance combined with hope – an attitude compatible with the pervasive doubt that will characterize any non-believer. The truth-normed aspect lies in the fact that one takes on the acceptance, involving oneself in Christian praxis and affective response, in order to grow in knowledge of whatever theistic truth there might be in the Christian world view with which one engages.

Of course, as I have mentioned, although such a stance towards Christian theism is compatible with pervasive doubt over its truth, it is incompatible with *disbelief*. Because hope logically requires at least the epistemic possibility that the hoped-for outcome will materialize, there must be for an interested non-believer the epistemic possibility that Christianity is true, at least in its core aspects. As we shall see in Chapters 5 and 6, this centrally involves the possibility that God is real, that he is characterized somewhat accurately – if incompletely and obscurely – by the desires for him that are cultivated through sacred music and contemplative prayer, and that he will (ultimately) satisfy those desires.

Still, because the attitude and religious involvement I am describing are compatible with attaching a low probability to Christianity's truth, one might have an objection to make: namely, that I am simply advocating a programme of self-deception or brainwashing. Let us now consider this objection.

2.5 Self-deception?

If one attaches a low probability to Christian doctrine, but, nonetheless, engages in a pattern of action and response that may result in at least some of that doctrine becoming more plausible, is one not simply trying to brainwash oneself? This spectre will rear its head at several points in this study. The answer will ultimately come in Chapter 6 when I discuss contemplative prayer, that Christian practice and spirituality which, through 'dark nights' of ascetic detachment, is supposed to result in a radical change in orientation towards the physical and the spiritual. Contemplative spirituality, in other words, is not aimed simply at cementing a view of God that is based on how one would *like* God to be. Thus, contemplative experience is sufficiently different from what someone – believer or not – will initially have been seeking, for it to be deeply incompatible with the possibility of brainwashing oneself into feeling that God is just so, according to one's 'pre-contemplative' hopes.

However, the fact remains, as I shall also stress in Chapter 6, that there is a marked *similarity* between contemplative experience and the 'pre-contemplative' religious orientation that I shall articulate. One would not undertake the kind of religious engagement whose apotheosis is contemplative prayer unless contemplation offered the prospect of fulfilling *something* in the hope and desire with which one approached the Christian outlook in the first place. Thus, although one will not be able to convince oneself in contemplative prayer that God is just as one would like him to be, perhaps there is still a danger – if one attaches a low probability to Christian doctrine – of entering a pattern of religious engagement simply in order to grow convinced that one will ultimately be spiritually satisfied. One hopes the outlook is true, and engages with it in order to recognize any truth it might contain, but according to one's *current* epistemic standpoint of attaching a low probability to the outlook, it is likely that if one ends up more convinced, one will have been duped.

In reply to this worry, I have two points to make. First, one might take William James' line and claim that in this sort of situation, being duped is not such a terrible thing.[64] It may look as though, in order to claim this, I must defend Pascal's view that the cost of false Christian belief is less than the gain of true belief.[65] But in fact this will not be necessary, because the attraction to a Christian outlook that I shall be exploring in the following chapters is, in a certain sense, *subjective*. By this I mean that it is not based on a careful calculation designed to persuade even the most hardened atheist of the potential gains and costs, but is, instead, a response to something apparently glimpsed: a greater experiential depth than usual, breaking through into certain moments, a depth possessing what Cottingham has described as 'a deeper resonance … somehow reaching beyond [our human struggles and needs] and engaging those indefinable and all-important longings that we call … "spiritual"'.[66] Indeed, this sort of depth is precisely the transcendent realm and source of fullness to which Taylor refers when he characterizes theistic commitment in terms of recognizing such a realm. Taylor provides a vivid example of an experience in which this depth seems manifest, an encounter with the beauty of nature from the life of the Benedictine monk Bede Griffiths.[67] Our opening story recounting Ella's experience of the mysterious Gregorian chant is another example. Of course, being attracted to a *Christian* outlook involves more than these glimpses in general terms: as we have already seen, it involves being familiar enough with Christianity for it to come naturally as a way of structuring one's life in general.[68] In Chapters 5 and 6, I will discuss desires for God that emphasize various aspects of God and of the divine-human relationship. That discussion will thus be concerned with various facets of finding oneself drawn to a Christian outlook in the way just outlined. And if one is in this situation, it starts to seem odd to demand a careful weighing up of the potential gains and costs of engaging in a pattern of Christian praxis. Someone in this situation will want to 'choose [their] own form of risk', in James' words;[69] and – provided they are not flouting clear epistemic or moral norms, such as entering a way of life that is based on views they actively *disbelieve*, or that includes morally reprehensible practices – it is hard to see how we could deny them the right to choose in favour of Christian involvement. If they end up duped, then so be it: 'Worse things ... may happen to a man.'[70] In any case, the non-doxastic involvement at issue is not aimed at cultivating a belief from which one thinks one will gain, as Pascal thought it should be,[71] but is, instead, a matter of open-endedly giving one's awareness the chance to grow. Consequently, at the very least, one could not be accused of engaging in a *deliberate* programme of self-deception.

The second point I wish to make on the danger of self-deception is that it actually seems fairly unlikely to happen, even unintentionally. Being open to, and involved in, a religious tradition need not mean losing the ability to assess it for indicators of truth, such as self-consistency and consistency with our experience in general, including our deepest intuitions about the human condition.[72] If this ongoing assessment does not alleviate one's intellectual misgivings over the outlook in question, then – barring severe fragmentation of one's psyche – one will not be in any great danger of coming to believe the outlook.[73] Of course, if the misgivings are not decisive, one may still continue to engage with the religious tradition for as long as one is drawn to it. And, importantly, for the purposes of the remaining chapters it is perfectly fine that one may not come to believe that Christianity is true, or even that God is real. As I said near the outset, the epistemology of desire that I shall develop does not *depend on* belief in God's reality, since – as I subsequently clarified – desire for God does not require any such belief. But I will argue that if God *is* real, which the interested non-believer entertains as a live hypothesis, then desiring him in the ways I shall discuss can aid one's openness to the benefits that are thereby available.

I have not discussed desire explicitly for much of this chapter, as other points have needed establishing. The desires at issue will get a full treatment in Chapters 3, 5 and 6. However, as a preliminary discussion, it is worth saying something about the philosophical context of my treatment of desire, and making some points that look towards my full epistemological account of desire developed in the next chapter.

2.6 Desire: Some preliminaries

The sort of desire that will concern us in what follows is the desire for God. However, this as it stands is highly ambiguous and needs sharpening. I certainly do not claim that the broad kind of desire for God, of which I shall be discussing four specific forms in Chapter 5, is the only kind. It is simply the kind that results in the forms of religious knowledge for which I will be arguing. With this in mind, I will now navigate some of the issues that bear on the discussion in later chapters. It will help to frame this navigation by engaging, first, with a recent account of desire by Talbot Brewer, and, second, with key strands of Plato's discussion of *erōs* in the *Symposium*.

Earlier I touched on the question of whether desires for people are always reducible to desires for states of affairs. Here I will deny that they are: some desires for people involve aspects that cannot be captured in a re-articulation as a desire for a state of affairs (or, alternatively, for the truth of a proposition describing that state of affairs). However, I want to provide a treatment of the issue that is more nuanced than simply coming down on one side of it. I will maintain that the desires that concern us – especially in Chapter 5 – *are*, in large part, desires that would be satisfied in states of affairs: that is what gives them their epistemic weight. Importantly, though, they are given full significance only when they come to be seen as manifestations of an underlying desire for God: an underlying desire that *cannot* be translated into any desire for a state of affairs. We can look at this proposal in a little more detail; and I shall do so through a detailed engagement with an especially rich account of desire that has been offered recently by Talbot Brewer.

Desires for persons and for states of affairs

Brewer takes issue with what he calls the 'three dogmas of desire' in contemporary analytic philosophy: that desires are propositional attitudes; that they are distinguished from other propositional attitudes by having a 'world-to-mind' direction of fit; and that any action can be explained as the product of a belief-desire pair.[74] For the matter currently at hand, it is the first one of these that concerns us: Brewer rejects the view that desires are propositional attitudes. The rejected view is really the disjunction of two views: according to one ('strong propositionalism'), 'the real intentional object of a desire is always a proposition', all desires taking the form 'S wants p to be true';[75] according to the other ('weak propositionalism'), 'the object of any desire is *capturable* in propositional terms, in the sense that the truth of the relevant proposition is a necessary and sufficient condition for the attainment of the desire's end'.[76] From here on in, I will not distinguish between these two, since they share the notion that concerns us most, namely that the obtaining of some state of affairs is a necessary and sufficient condition of a desire's being satisfied. I will therefore speak of this view as the propositionalist view, or the view that desires are all reducible to desires for states of affairs.

Brewer's reasons for rejecting the propositionalist view are, to my mind, persuasive. He argues that interpersonal desire as we typically think of it can remain, and, indeed, be intensified, even after any given desire for a state of affairs is satisfied; hence, the desire for the person cannot be identical with any desire for a state of affairs. Take, for instance, Dorothy's love for her beloved: 'Being with him, dwelling on his words, and touching and kissing him might all figure as propitious conditions for the intensification of her desire for him rather than as satisfactions of that desire.'[77] Indeed, even if we were to make the state of affairs very general, it would still not suffice as the object of a desire for a person. If, say, we try and translate the object of Dorothy's desire into the state of affairs consisting in her enjoying an intimate, constantly deepening relationship with her beloved, we have still failed to capture what her desire for the beloved himself involves. For the desire for the state of affairs could be satisfied – indeed, satisfied continually and at length if the relationship is a long, steady one – yet her desire for the man himself may never be totally satisfied: the lack of total satisfaction, after all, is what draws her further into a relationship with him in which aspects of each are revealed to the other in ever-greater depth.[78] The conclusion is that the object of a desire for a person 'is not a state of affairs to be brought about, but a [person] already wholly present if not wholly appreciated … . The attraction is not itself a call to world-making, but rather a magnetic attraction to someone already there to be vividly appreciated.'[79] Moreover, the propositional, state-of-affair desires that pertain to a personal desire make sense only by reference to the more primitive personal desire.[80]

Brewer applies his conception of personal desire to both the desire for human persons and the desire for God.[81] How does this relate to the forms of desire for God that will concern us later on, particularly in Chapter 5? Those desires will characterize God in a given set of ways, each directed towards God *in a given capacity*. I will develop this idea in detail in Chapter 3, and apply it to several desires for God in Chapter 5; for now, suffice to say that the desires will be of the following sort: a desire for God in the capacity of compassionately hearing and supporting one when in distress; a desire for God in the capacity of providing intimate protection in the dark aspects of our lives; and so on. The capacities in which one desires God will naturally imply certain divine characteristics: for instance, in order to be a compassionate support to someone in acute distress, God must be deeply resourceful and have the power to convey lovingly a sense of broadened possibilities. The very epistemic import of these desires stems from their enabling the desirer to grasp with a special, personal urgency something of what these divine attributes would have to be like in order to fulfil the desires in question. We can see, then, that the desires for God to be considered in Chapter 5 are, indeed, desires that would be satisfied in states of affairs. For instance, if one desires God in the capacity of providing compassionate support when one is in distress, then in order to satisfy the desire, it must be the case that God gives one a profoundly changed, hopeful perspective, a sense of widened possibilities. The desire for God in that capacity would be satisfied in that state of affairs; moreover, such a state of affairs is to some extent propositionally articulable. I said just now that through the desire, one knows with a special, personal significance something of what God would have to be like in order to satisfy it. We will see in the next chapter that this depends crucially on having a projected sense of the state of affairs that would constitute satisfaction: in general, the aspects of the desire's object that one knows about through the desire are those that would bring about the projected satisfaction.

However, by no means does it follow that Brewer's account is irrelevant to our concerns. For the desires that are satisfiable in particular states of affairs can still be manifestations of an underlying, non-propositional desire for God himself, and have their full significance by reference to that desire. Indeed, that is why I have chosen to describe the desires of Chapter 5 as desires for God in a given capacity – the capacity of bringing about a given state of affairs – rather than as desires *for* those states of affairs. This is a perfectly familiar phenomenon of personal desire more generally: my desire for someone may take various manifestations, and highlight various capacities possessed by the person, depending on the circumstances. For instance, my desire for a loved one might take the manifestation of wanting her to celebrate an important occasion with me, or of wanting her to lend a supportive ear and offer advice. I do not simply want the shared celebration, or the support and advice; rather, I want *her* in these capacities. The more specific desires have their full significance only in the context of my desire for my beloved tout court, and the relationship that this desire underpins. And it hardly needs adding that, as Brewer claims, the satisfaction of the state-of-affairs desires would not be the satisfaction of the underlying desire for the person herself. Note, though, that I am not committed to any claim, in psychology or theological anthropology, that humans by nature have an innate, underlying desire for God that subsequently finds manifestations in state-of-affair desires. It might be the other way round: one might come to have desires for God in particular capacities, such as the ones I shall describe in Chapter 5, and *thereby* come to recognize a fundamental dissatisfaction with one's condition (as Ella did in our opening story) that calls out for something beyond what the world has to offer. The initial, state-of-affair desires would thus come to have a greater depth and resonance once placed in the context of an underlying desire for God himself.

Desire as having mind-to-world fit

As a second point to consider in prefacing our full discussion of desire, we must address the *direction of fit* of the desires to be discussed – the point at issue in the second of Brewer's 'three dogmas'. According to the view Brewer rejects, desires are 'propositional attitudes with a world-to-mind direction of fit. A desire is an attitude towards a proposition that typically prompts one to adjust the world, where possible, in ways calculated to make it correspond to the proposition.'[82] Contrary to this, Brewer insists, desires represent their objects as good or worthwhile in some way, and hence have a *mind-to-world* direction of fit.[83] Likewise, I claim that the desires for God to be considered here have a mind-to-world fit. If such a God is real, then the desires track truths about the way things are – specifically, about the way God is in relation to oneself. My proposal is, in a sense, a development of one way in which Brewer's point could be true – one way in which a desire for God could represent God as good. Specifically, the desire represents God as having the qualities needed in order to satisfy one's desire for him, where these qualities are grasped in terms of their significance to oneself as the desirer. The goodness that the desire tracks, then, is not so much God's goodness *in itself* as God's goodness as it matters to the desirer in a particular circumstance. Still, as I will go on to argue in Chapter 6, if God is real then knowledge of this kind is a way of being led eventually into contemplation of God in himself, through a long-term practice of contemplative prayer as found in the Christian tradition. The musically elicited desires of Chapter 5 are thus a way of being shaped to depend on God in various ways, so that one might gradually come to love God for who he is, beyond any focus on specific divine attributes.

In this general line of thought, I am taking my cue partly from Plato's discussion of *erōs* in the *Symposium*. *Erōs*, as a human state (in contrast to its personification, for instance as a 'great spirit'[84]), is often rendered in English as 'love' but has connotations of strong desire, including sexual desire but not limited to it.[85] Plato describes it as being between lack and fullness: it lacks that for which it is a desire, yet is aware of that lack.[86] The *Symposium* is concerned with the desire for, and pursuit of, *beauty*, an exemplar of which, for Plato, is wisdom.[87] *Erōs*, then, is what drives the search for wisdom, and for beauty more generally; and thus, crucially for my account in the next chapter, in the perceived lack there must be a *sense of what one lacks*. We can see this in Diotima's account of the ascent to the Form of beauty, central to which is *erōs*: at each stage, the seeker has a purer sense of the beauty he seeks, as he progresses through levels of increasing abstraction from the physical.[88] The idea, then, is that through a desire for something metaphysically exalted, one comes to have an increasingly refined sense of what one is seeking; and as such, the desire plays a crucial role in shaping one's journey towards that apparent metaphysical reality. My account of the epistemic import possessed by certain forms of desire for God can be understood as a specific working through of this idea.

I have clarified where my account of desire will stand in relation to two of the issues Brewer raises: that of the desires' proper object, and that of the direction of fit with the world, or with (apparent or epistemically possible) reality more broadly. We now have one final point to address in our preliminaries on desire: the question of theological framework.

Desire for God and theological framework: The danger of wishful thinking

The notion of desire for God as drawing one continually into a deeper relationship with God is pervasive throughout the Christian tradition – found in, among other places, the work of Gregory of Nyssa, Augustine, Aquinas and various medieval mystics.[89] The question may arise, then, of what my theological framing and presuppositions will be in the following chapters, especially Chapters 5 and 6. The theology of desire with which I work will initially emerge organically from my discussions of particular musical works. I will be arguing for certain characteristics God would need in order to fulfil the desires in question; thus, a multifaceted characterization of God will emerge. The pieces I discuss are all musical settings of biblical texts, composed out of the Christian tradition and sung in the church. There is therefore good reason to think that the desiring response I describe in each case is, at least to a degree, rightly ordered towards God as he is represented in Christian tradition (including its roots in the Hebrew Bible): that is, ordered towards things that such a God could be hoped to grant if he were real. As I shall show in Chapter 4, music can shape the listener's response both with a specific affective colour and with the conceptual content of extra-musical factors; thus, it is well placed to elicit a desire precise enough to be ordered in this way. It is also important to emphasize the communal context in which these pieces are sung, a context both synchronic and diachronic. Responding to the music as part of a living tradition involves sharing it with a community: one whose members align themselves with a common vision of where life's deepest significance lies. Through participating in such a community, and having one's ideas about God shaped by its liturgy and the experiences of its 'cloud of witnesses', one's desires can be further shaped and refined according to how the tradition characterizes God. And listening to or singing the music in a corporate setting, especially in a liturgical service, can illuminate especially clearly the form that one's desire for God in response to the music should take, if that desire is to conform to the tradition's conception of God.

However, the danger of projection and wishful thinking is ever present in the desire for God. As Rowan Williams has put it, there is an ever-present risk of '[using] God to fill the gaps in our needs and preferences'[90] – a risk of forming ideas about God based on what we *think* he ought to do for us. In the coming chapters, I will develop an account of how desiring God can give the desirer knowledge, in terms of God's importance to herself as the desirer, of what God would be like in satisfying the desire. But could this not simply be a matter of knowing how one would *like* God to be in satisfying one's desire, with no correspondence to God's actual nature if he is real?[91] Given this, one might worry that projection and wishful thinking may seep into the discussion in Chapter 5, in spite of the weight of tradition behind the music and the texts that are set to it. How should we decide whether these desires for God are rightly ordered? In other words, what 'theology of desire' are we presupposing when we take it that the desires of Chapter 5, in characterizing God in a given set of ways, have the potential to be spiritually fruitful? What is the content of the 'live hypothesis' of God's reality with which we are working?

I do not claim that there is only one theological framework that is consonant with the characterizations of God developed in Chapter 5. However, in Chapter 6 I shall argue that the Christian contemplative tradition provides an especially fruitful way of taking those desires further. For in that tradition, with which I shall engage through the writing of Thomas Merton, we find a stringent test of how rightly ordered one's desire for God is. This is measured by how closely the desire resembles a completely un-self-centred desire for loving *union* with God – a desire possible in its purest form only after one has been purged of one's idolatrous conceptions of, and projections onto, God. In contemplative spirituality, then, we have a clear standard against which we can judge the desires of Chapter 5 – and I will argue that the view of God that will have emerged in that chapter can combine fruitfully with Christian contemplative practice as Merton presents it. The desires of Chapter 5 *are* conducive to cultivating, eventually, desire for God that is rightly ordered by the lights of contemplative spirituality. Our theology of desire will turn out to be consonant with that of the Christian contemplative tradition.

We have now completed our preliminaries – on sacred music and non-belief, on the concept of 'interested non-belief' that I will primarily be addressing and on aspects of desire that will be relevant in what follows. In the next chapter, I will examine desire in the context of emotion more generally, and argue that desires of a certain kind can give the desirer a special sort of knowledge about their objects. This will set the scene for our religious applications of the idea later on.

3

Desire and knowledge

> *There can be no knowledge without emotion. We may be aware of a truth, yet until we have felt its force, it is not ours. To the cognition of the brain must be added the experience of the soul.*
>
> Arnold Bennett[1]

In order to develop an account of religious knowledge centred on desire for God as elicited by sacred music, we need to establish that desire can, indeed, contribute to one's knowledge. In this chapter I will explore how desire can do this. Specifically, I will argue that desire can enable one to know what its object would be like in bringing about satisfaction; thus, if the object of desire does exist and would satisfy the desire in something like that way, then one knows about it in respect of the attributes through which it would do this. Such knowledge will be the focus, in a religious context, of Chapter 5.

If desire is to play the role in one's knowledge that I will argue it plays, it must have certain features – features that, I will urge, are to be found in the emotions generally. I will begin this chapter by discussing these features in this more general context. I intend in this way to locate the epistemically interesting features of desire within a wider picture of the philosophy of emotion. Once I have done this, I will turn to desire in particular. I will distinguish between three broad kinds of desire, and clarify which kind interests us for our religious purposes. I will argue that unlike the other kinds of desire, this kind is, indeed, a type of emotion, since it possesses the features that I will have discussed, in the guise they take in the emotions. I will then be in a position to draw on these features in proposing an account of the role desire can play in our knowledge. However, some readers might feel that the non-religious desires I discuss in building my account are a long way from desire for God. To allay this worry, I will make explicit the similarities between the religious desires to be considered in Chapter 5, and (in particular) one kind of non-religious desire considered here, namely, romantic desire. As I shall argue, romantic desire functions in the same general epistemic capacity as the other non-religious desires I consider, but its similarity to the desires for God in Chapter 5 is more marked. I hope to show, then, that as long as the desires for God in Chapter 5 share enough of the phenomenological structure possessed by the romantic desire in *this* chapter, they can both function in the same kind of epistemic capacity.

3.1 Emotion, thought and affect

When we are subject to an emotion, what is the relationship between 'the cognition of the brain' and 'the experience of the soul', in Bennett's words? How is thought related to feeling in emotional experience? This has been one of the main guiding questions in the theory of emotion, and the landscape can be carved up according to the various answers that have been given. I cannot cover the whole history of these theories in a single chapter, so I will be selective, focusing on the issues that have the largest bearing on my epistemology of desire. With this in mind, my focus will keep us comfortably in the philosophical armchair. I will concentrate, following analytic philosophy in general, on the concept of emotion: by virtue of what do we call something an emotion? This question has a phenomenological dimension – not so much regarding the precise quality of experience involved in this or that emotion (which is too specific to count as an aspect of the general concept of emotion) but, rather, regarding the elements of our overall experience that are incorporated into having emotions in general.

Any answer to the question of how thought and feeling figure in emotional experience will include an answer to the question of whether the emotions at issue are *cognitive* or *non-cognitive*; and theories of emotion generally fall into one of these two camps. For emotions to be cognitive is for them to involve thoughts, or cognitions, in some capacity. But this is just the start: if an answer to the question of whether emotions involve thoughts is to tell us much about how emotions are being construed, we need to know what concept of thought is in play. John Deigh has distinguished between two such concepts that have each enjoyed prominence in theories of emotion within the last hundred years or so. The first is broader, and applies to states of mind 'the realization of whose content implies the existence of some object',[2] including not only propositional attitudes but also states such as sensings, imaginings and memories.[3] The second is narrower, and applies to 'propositions, that is, thoughts of the kind expressed by complete, declarative sentences'.[4] The first is entailed by a theory of emotion that was prominent in roughly the first half of the twentieth century, for example in the works of Broad,[5] Stout[6] and Price,[7] who classified emotions as mental states in which the subject is cognizant of some object.[8] Broad, for instance, conceived of emotions as cognitions (thoughts in the wide sense) possessing a 'felt quality or tone'.[9] Meanwhile the second, propositional concept of thought is the one that concerns much contemporary cognitivist theorizing, which often construes emotions as necessarily involving propositional judgements or evaluations in some capacity:[10] my anger towards someone involves evaluating the situation as one in which they have wronged me, my fear of a dog involves evaluating it as dangerous, and so on. I will consider one such cognitivist theory a little later, that of Martha Nussbaum.

Deigh argues that the concept of emotion in general does not dictate that emotions include thought in the narrower, propositional sense. For instance, when we look down from a great height and are frightened despite the fact that we know we are not in danger, our fear need not include any thought that we are in danger. Even if we accept that in this situation we hold no *belief* that we are in danger, might we not *imagine* that we are? No, says Deigh; this would involve imagining something that poses a threat, such as a gust of wind that catches us off guard; and feeling frightened at a great height does not require us to imagine such a threat. 'The thought of danger, propositional or otherwise, is not a thread that runs through all experiences of fear.'[11] Rather, it is the property of being frightening of which one is aware when one looks down from a precipice,[12] and one can be aware of this property without that awareness being mediated by propositional thought. This is especially obvious when we react to danger with 'fight or flight': we are frightened by something, but propositional thought would slow us down. Rather, we are 'cognizant' of the frightening object: our thought about it is a thought in the wide sense of a mental state with objective content, and would be expressed not by a complete, declarative sentence, but by something else – a loud expletive, perhaps, or a cry of terror.

These considerations cast doubt on the idea that the very concept of emotion is of a kind of mental state that involves propositional thought. However, we can still ask: Is the concept of emotion of something that involves at least thought in the wider sense, that of a mental state possessing objective content? Does the concept of emotion dictate that emotions are cognitive in at least this sense? The sort of fear just considered does seem to include within itself just such a mental state: in the experience of fear that is not propositionally articulable, there do not seem to be separate thought and feeling components. One is fearfully aware of the object of fear, in the way that Broad described: 'To be fearing a snake …

is to be cognizing something ... as a snake, and for that cognition to be toned with fearfulness.'[13] However, we should be wary of generalizing too readily, and I will shortly look at two examples in which the emotional experience as a whole necessarily involves thought (propositional thought, at that); yet, I maintain, the emotions in the two cases do not include within themselves the entirety of that thought's content. Indeed, in at least the first example the emotion does not seem to include any thought content at all. In these considerations, we will glimpse just how heterogeneous emotions are, and thus how generic and minimal a correct articulation of the concept of emotion must be.

In order to make sense of the examples, we must first turn explicitly to an aspect of our experience that does seem to be essential to emotions – namely, *affect*. I use this term to denote that domain of mental states in which we spend much of life, and which reflect the different (and often conflicting) things that we value: states whose 'tones' permeate our perceptions and behaviour,[14] such as happiness, sadness, jealousy, regret, excitement, anger, despair, hope and so on. Affects may be either latent or occurrent; when occurrent, they are experienced as *feelings*.[15] There are broadly two kinds of affect, which I call 'emotional affects' and 'mood affects'. Emotional affects are directed towards an object; they are about something.[16] Like affects in general, they can be either latent or experienced as feelings. I may be in a state of anger but not feel angry (I may have 'repressed' my anger); or I may very much feel it.[17] Mood affects, by contrast, colour our experience quite generally, and are not about anything in particular.[18] Having said this, they might be caused by something quite particular, such as a bad day at the office, and then spread into the rest of our experience; conversely, they can 'latch onto' particular objects and become fully fledged emotional affects, such as when my irritable mood leads me to feel annoyed with you even though you have done little wrong.[19] Occurrent emotional affect, or emotional affective feeling, is what Peter Goldie and Geoffrey Madell have both called 'feeling towards'. It is, in Goldie's words, 'an ineliminable part of the intentionality of emotional experience ... directed towards the world from a point of view'.[20] And Madell describes it as 'a state of consciousness which is *at one and the same time both intentional and affective*'.[21]

What, we might wonder, is the nature of the intentionality of feeling towards? Without becoming entangled in long debates about intentionality, we can note that in general it is the property of being about, or directed towards, something. But being about something does not require any intrinsic intentional *content*. For example, the beep of a smoke detector is about something, namely, the smoke that has been detected. But the beep certainly does not have any intentional *content* in the way that much cognition does: if I imagine, see or smell smoke, my experience has a smoky quality of one kind or another; some aspect of smoke is present to me. The smoke detector's beep, however, is about smoke simply because the beep happens reliably when there is smoke.[22] And this leads us to ask whether feeling towards requires intentional content in order to be intentional. No doubt it has this content in some cases; as we have seen, the feeling of fear in the kind of fearful experience considered earlier is phenomenologically indistinguishable from the cognition of the fear's object. But this is not true to the same extent in every case of feeling towards; and the following two examples will, I hope, illustrate this.

Some years ago, I was invited to a reunion of those who had been in my year at secondary school – to take place ten years after leaving. Before the invitation, I had not been especially aware that it had been almost ten years; the thought had barely crossed my mind. However, once I became aware of the fact I felt unsettled. Was it really that long since I had seen those people, attended those classes and spent a large amount of time in those grounds and buildings? I certainly did not feel as different from that version of myself as ten years seemed to suggest; I could point to each change in circumstance in my life since then, and I hardly seemed to have changed at all from one period to the next. Yet there I was, almost ten years on. My emotional experience was of being unsettled *at the thought* that it had been nearly ten years since that time. That is, I could identify my thought separately from my feeling unsettled. To be sure, the feeling was *about* the fact that it had been nearly ten years; it was not simply *caused* by that fact. But its intentional object was supplied by the thought. It was directed towards the state of affairs that was represented in the thought's intentional content, rather than having any content of its own. As a result of the feeling, the thought was thereafter affectively toned in much the way Broad describes: when I called to mind the fact that I had left school nearly ten years previously, the thought would have an unsettled quality. But the thought itself was not the emotion of being unsettled. If we grant that occurrent emotion necessarily involves intentional feeling, then given the fact that this intentional feeling was phenomenologically distinguishable from the thought whose content the feeling was about, the emotion cannot have been the thought – even though it required the thought. It was, rather, simply the intentional feeling.[23] This is not to say that I coolly entertained the thought and the feeling followed; as soon as I was aware of the thought it was toned by the feeling. But it is still true that I felt the feeling *at* the thought: I could distinguish them to a certain degree. Moreover, my feeling unsettled did not in itself include any judgement or evaluation; as we shall see, it may have been different in this respect from the feeling in the next example. Madell is aware of the sort of experience I have described – an emotional experience in which the emotion does not include any cognitive content of its own – when he writes of emotions' being distinguishable from each other not by evaluations that they involve, but rather (at least in many cases) 'by a particular complex of intentional but affective states of consciousness'.[24]

The second example is Martha Nussbaum's, and is more complex. Nussbaum writes of the grief she felt when her mother died, concluding that 'emotions can be defined in terms of judgement alone'[25] – and specifically, that her grief was identical with her judgement that someone she loved dearly had died:

> If I embrace the death image, if I take it into myself as the way things are, it is at that very moment, in that cognitive act itself, that I am putting the world's nail into my own insides. ... Knowing can be violent, given the truths that are there to be known.[26]

Furthermore, the 'rich intentional content'[27] of the grief-judgement that someone dearly beloved has died must involve a true sense of the love in question:

> Internal to the grief must be the perception of the beloved object and of her importance; the grief itself must quantify the richness of the love between us, its centrality to my life. It must contain the thought of her irrevocable deadness.[28]

So grief, according to Nussbaum, involves the judgement that someone dearly beloved has died, and this judgement involves a rich sense of that love. It is doubtless true that the *overall experience* of grief involves these aspects. But on closer inspection, the *grief itself* seems to involve only the latter (a rich sense of the love once shared) and not the former (the judgement that the person with whom one had shared that love is dead). When we grieve a loved one, we have the thought that he or she has died. We will in all likelihood spend time in denial, partly believing in the reality of the death and yet partly hoping that we may see the deceased again. But sometimes the full force of the death hits us, and the thought that we will never see the person again presents itself in all its devastating bluntness. This thought will be coloured by deep sorrow and distress. However, grief does not include within itself this and similar thoughts. What it does include is the affective colouring and shaping of the thoughts. This often takes the form of a feeling towards the thoughts' content; sometimes we might say, instead, that someone is in a long-term state of grief, which shapes the very thoughts that she has even if it is not always at the forefront of her awareness. But in both cases it is the affect and its influence on thought that fall under the concept of grief, and not the thoughts themselves: the thoughts affected by grief are no doubt different in each case, whereas it seems to be a feature common to all cases of grief that one's thoughts are patterned and coloured in certain distinctive ways.

The affective element of grieving, then, seems to be phenomenologically distinguishable from the thoughts that it colours and shapes. This phenomenological distinction is reflected in our conceptual division between thought and feeling, in turn reflected in phrases such as 'I felt devastated at the thought that I would never see her again'. Here, though, things become a little more complicated. It is not as though we love someone, realize that we will never see him or her again, and feel a devastation that can be distinguished from our love. Rather, *in* our devastation we feel our love perhaps most intensely of all. The devastation itself, as Nussbaum urges, includes a feeling of the 'richness of love' that the griever once shared with the deceased; it is that love subject to the most ultimate and brutal frustration. And there might be a case to be made for the view that this love *itself* is a way of valuing the deceased, rather than being simply the result or the basis of such a valuation. After all, at least with family members, we do not value someone for reasons independent of our love, and love him or her on this basis; nor, it might be said, do we love someone and ascribe value to him or her on *this* basis, as a separate act. If love were, indeed, to incorporate a value-ascription, then love would have its own cognitive content; and from this it would follow that grief has its own cognitive content in the form of a value-ascription – for love, as we have seen, is part of grief. This is certainly Nussbaum's view: 'My grief saw [my mother] as valuable and as irrevocably cut off from me.'[29]

For our purposes (mindful of the relationship between all this and the epistemology of desire), it does not matter whether love, and therefore grief, possesses its own cognitive content in a value-ascription. Instead, I would like to use this and the other two emotion examples to highlight two points. The first I have touched on already: emotions vary widely in how they combine elements of our general experience, including propositional thought, non-propositional thought and affect. In the examples of fear, the affect was itself non-propositionally cognitive. In my experience of unsettledness, the affect did not include any thought content of its own, but 'borrowed' its content from the propositional thought that I had left school nearly ten years ago. And Nussbaum's grief lies somewhere in between the two. Like my unsettledness, her grief borrowed propositional content from a distinguishable thought: that someone she loved dearly had died. But unlike the thought content appropriated by my feeling unsettled, the content appropriated by grief is inherently affective, since it includes reference to love and loss; and the extent to which this content can be articulated propositionally is thus limited. In this respect, the thought content involved in an experience of grief is like that of the fear that I considered – even though, unlike that fear, the thought is not itself the emotion. The conclusion to draw from all this is that any articulation of the concept of emotion that has any chance of being correct cannot construe emotion *in general* as either cognitive or non-cognitive. Our examples of fear were cognitive if thought is not limited to the propositional; my unsettledness was non-cognitive even though intentional; and grief might, for all I have said, be either – depending on whether love itself is a way of ascribing value. We must stick to the generic, and I therefore suggest *intentional affect* as a concept of emotion, with all that those two terms imply. This incorporates the features that emotions simply cannot do without, but leaves enough room for the wide variety of forms that emotions take.[30]

The second point to draw from all this acts as a bridge into our considerations about desire in particular. I said at the outset that the epistemic capacity I shall argue that desire possesses stems from features that it shares with the emotions in general. We can now say that these features are intentionality and affectivity. However, like emotion in general, the sort of desire that, I shall argue, is an emotion can vary in how propositionally articulable it is: the desirer might, to some extent, be able to articulate propositionally the cognitive content that she grasps about the desire's object, or this content might for her be more analogous to that of the fear expressed in a primal cry. But the key claim that will run through the rest of this chapter is that under certain conditions, desire's very affectivity can contain cognitive content of its own that is not propositionally exhaustible – content that contributes to the desirer's knowledge, at the time of the desire and even in the absence of satisfaction, about what she desires.

3.2 Three kinds of desire

Melinda Vadas, in her paper 'Affective and Non-Affective Desire', distinguishes between two kinds of desire: affective and non-affective (as the title might lead one to expect). Of affective desire she writes:

> 'Desire' (as a noun) may refer to an affect, that is, a feeling, emotion, or mood, such as a desire to eat pizza, have children, or run in a marathon, and 'to desire' (as a verb) is, in this sense, to be in a certain affective state, that is, one involving the feelings or affections.[31]

Importantly, affective desire includes both a present aspect and a future-oriented one, which are phenomenologically inseparable. Such desire is

> both a *present* affect ... as well as a projection of affect; that is, I in a sense 'predict' that I will feel a certain way in the future .... Part of my *present* feeling of 'desiring a pizza' is the affective projection 'a pizza will satisfy me'. ... A necessary and sufficient condition of affectively desiring some state of affairs is the present and projected affective relationship of the agent to that state of affairs.[32]

Meanwhile, the word 'desire' in its non-affective sense '*has no referent, mental or non-mental*'.[33] It is simply used to indicate that a certain action is a goal-directed one. When I say, for instance, that I used modus ponens in my argument because I desired to shorten the proof, I need only mean that my using modus ponens was directed at the goal of shortening the proof (I *may* have affectively desired to shorten the proof, but this is not entailed by my saying that I desired to do so). In this sense of the word, I desire whatever goals I intentionally pursue.[34]

Let us sharpen Vadas' observations slightly. Under 'affective desire', she includes physical desires such as the desire for food. But is this kind of desire really affective? It does satisfy the descriptions of affectivity offered earlier (it reflects our valuing something, its 'tone' permeates our perceptions and behaviour and it may be either latent or felt). And yet there seems to be an important difference between, say, the hunger I feel just before lunch and a desire that is obviously affective, such as the desire to have children. The latter, especially with regards to whether it is satisfied, has much more of a bearing on the desirer's emotional well-being than the hunger I feel just before lunch. This is not to deny that eating lunch has *some* bearing on my emotional well-being; but clearly its effect will be negligible compared with that of having children. The hunger is mainly a physical desire. However, hunger for food can be more affectively toned under certain conditions. If I am starving and do not know where my next meal is coming from then my hunger will have a clear affective quality, since it is more immediately concerned with my continued survival, the assurance or non-assurance of which affects my emotional well-being. Likewise, my hunger may be affectively toned for other reasons – for example, if for me food symbolizes being part of a community or has a nostalgic hue. Having children, meanwhile, seems to be something for which a desire would be clearly affective under *any* condition: the desire for children, and its satisfaction or lack thereof, will always have a bearing on the desirer's emotional well-being. Not all affective desires, though, need be as profound as the desire for children. An example to which I will return later is the desire for the resolution to musical tension. Such a desire, and its satisfaction or lack thereof, will always have *some* effect, however trivial, on the desirer's emotional well-being. But although mundane hunger is largely non-affective because of the triviality of *its* effect on the desirer's emotional wellbeing, this kind of triviality does *not* make the desire for musical resolution largely non-affective. And this is because the emotional aspect of one's well-being is the *only* aspect that is affected by the desire for musical resolution; one's physical well-being, for example, is not affected. The affective element is all there is to the desire; so it is an affective desire.

With these considerations in mind, we can distinguish between three broad kinds of desire. There is Vadas' 'non-affective desire', which is a 'logical fiction'[35] (and thus has no felt quality), since the word 'desire' used in this sense has no referent. There is the sort of desire that can be felt but which is not affective, such as the hunger I feel when the food that I desire has no special significance for me. This is on a sliding scale with fully fledged affective desire: a felt desire is more or less affective depending on how much it and its satisfaction affect the desirer's emotional well-being. Affective desires can be physical to a greater or lesser extent: sometimes a desire's physicality will be intimately bound up with its affectivity (such as the state of being literally starving); other affective desires have practically no physically felt element (such as the desire for musical resolution – although our capacity to feel this desire and be satisfied depends on physical elements of ourselves, we can imagine having these experiences without our bodies).

It is, of course, affective desire that is my main concern here. As I hope to show shortly, both sorts of *felt* desire (affective and non-affective) can have epistemic importance. However, it is only affective desire that humans can feel for God, since God is not physical. Desire for God may sometimes have a physical element, but it is not one's physical well-being that is at stake: this desire is clearly affective in having a bearing on the desirer's *emotional* well-being (in particular with regards to the desire's satisfaction). I should clarify here that I am not making a claim that is problematic in the contemplative spirituality at which this study is ultimately aimed, namely, that the Christian life is aimed at cultivating feelings of happiness. Rather, as I shall explore further in Chapter 6, such a life is aimed at love and knowledge of God, which is supposed to bring with it the deepest possible joy. This love and knowledge can be attained only through letting go of what we *think* makes us happy in our ordinary ways of seeing ourselves and the world.[36] However, in order to present itself as worth inhabiting, the spiritual joy that comes with a progressively deepening knowledge of God must correspond in *some* way to our ordinary emotion of joy: spiritual joy must be recognizably an emotion – even if in analogous form. Thus, desire for God is affective: it affects what we can recognize as the desirer's emotional well-being, in particular with regards to its satisfaction.

But, we might wonder, are affective desires really emotions at all? At first glance it may seem obvious that they are: they are affective and intentional like emotions in general; and more specifically, like emotions in general, they have a felt quality when occurrent, reflect our ascribing value or disvalue to something and permeate and influence our thoughts, perceptions and behaviour. Some philosophers, though, have contrasted desires – even affective desires – with emotions in general. Justin Oakley, for instance, has argued that emotions necessarily involve desires as *components*: two examples are anger, which, he suggests, requires an (affective) desire to retaliate at whoever has made us angry, and jealousy, which requires a desire (again affective) to 'keep what it is one thinks one is in danger of losing'.[37] Peter Goldie, on the other hand, denies this: 'feeling towards', which we have seen is a key element of emotion for Goldie, is neither reducible to desire nor necessarily involves desire as a component. He cites pride as an example: pride is directed towards the way things are rather than towards how I want them to be; and any desires I might have while feeling proud are not necessarily directed at the object of my pride (I might, to use Goldie's example, desire to hug and kiss my daughter when proud of her for performing in a school concert, but it is not hugging and kissing her of which I feel proud[38]). Thus, it is not the case that emotions necessarily have desire as a component, let alone as the only essential component.

Although Oakley and Goldie disagree here, the presupposition underlying both their positions is that desire – even affective desire, for the desires they mention clearly *are* affective – is not really a kind of emotion, but is rather a state that may or may not be involved in emotions. But what if Oakley were right, and desire *were* a necessary component of all emotions? Would this stop affective desire from being a species of emotion in its own right? I do not see why it would. Affective desires would then be like lots of emotions insofar as *they* are components of other emotions (for instance, anger, confusion and devastation can all be components of grief). While no emotion other than desire is a component of *all* emotions, there is no reason to think that being the only emotion that *is* a component of all emotions would stop desire from being an emotion in its own right. Of course, if Goldie were right, and desire were *not* a component of all other emotions, then it would be like any other emotion in that respect. It seems, then, that regardless of affective desire's precise relationship to other emotions, there is no reason to treat as deceptive its appearance as an emotion in its own right.

3.3 Desire as knowledge about the desired: The 'Wynn-Madell' account

Let us take stock. I first argued that the essential features of emotion are intentionality and affectivity, and that emotions vary in the extent to which one can propositionally articulate their intentional content, whether or not that content is 'borrowed' from a distinguishable thought. I then turned to desire, distinguishing between three kinds and identifying affective desire as the kind that primarily concerns us. And most recently, I argued that affective desire is a kind of emotion, as, indeed, it first appears to be in virtue of sharing certain features with emotions in general, including intentionality and affectivity. We come at last, then, to the main point of this chapter: to show that, and how, affective desire can have epistemic importance, based on the features it shares with emotions in general. I will then apply the conclusions here to religious considerations in later chapters, especially Chapter 5.

We can start with an idea that Mark Wynn, drawing on an observation by Madell, has articulated. We have already encountered the notion of 'feeling towards' in Madell's work: 'A state of consciousness which is *at one and the same time both intentional and affective*.' On my account of emotion and definitions of terms, feeling towards is occurrent emotion, since an emotion is an intentional affect (or an 'affect towards') and an occurrent affect is a feeling. In discussing feeling towards, Madell observes that *desire* in particular is a state of consciousness that is at once affective and intentional. He makes this observation through considering the desire for a resolution to musical tension:

> Hearing the dominant seventh evokes a desire, and sometimes something akin to a longing, for its resolution. That is a state of consciousness directed to an intentional object; it is also an affective state of consciousness. ... It is a mode of 'feeling towards' its intentional object.[39]

Wynn points out that in this kind of case, the desire itself enables a kind of knowledge of its object's character, by casting the mind forward to an as-yet-unrealized resolution or consummation:

> On account of its felt recognition of the tension, the mind is cast forward, in desire, to an anticipated moment of 'resolution'. In [Madell's] example, the character of this resolution is grasped not musicologically, or in purely auditory terms (after all, it is not available to be heard as yet), but *by way of the felt yearning or longing* which points more or less precisely towards what is required

if a resolution of this particular musical tension is to be achieved ... the object of the affect is only anticipated, and not directly perceived.[40]

This phenomenon of the mind being 'cast forwards' in desire seems to be precisely what Vadas has in mind when she notes that affective desire involves a 'projection of affect': modifying Vadas' example, part of my *present* feeling of 'desiring a musical resolution' is the affective projection 'a musical resolution will satisfy me'. In feeling the desire, one is made vividly aware of what the musical resolution would have to sound like in order to provide satisfaction. The desire for the resolution is therefore not just feeling towards, as Madell claims: it enables a kind of knowledge of the resolution's nature even if that resolution has not happened yet – indeed, even if it will never happen. If the resolution is forthcoming, then through desiring it one grasps something of its nature in advance; if it never comes, then one knows through the desire what it would have to have been like.

Wynn's suggestion is certainly interesting; however, in order to see how it plays out in the religious context to be considered later, we must draw out more explicitly the nature of desire-based knowledge as he describes it. To this end, I will discuss desire-based knowledge in a number of non-religious cases. This discussion, I hope, will show that desire-based knowledge about the desire's object is a phenomenon familiar enough to be used in religious contexts without seeming inherently suspicious. It will also mean that my account, both of the conditions of this knowledge in general and of what determines the content of particular cases of such knowledge, is based on instances that (I assume) would be widely accepted as instances of knowledge. For my analysis will be plausible only if the reader accepts that the examples I analyse *are* examples of knowledge in the first place. Once I have established that there is such a thing as desire-based knowledge, and presented an account of its conditions and phenomenology, I will apply the notion to a religious context in later chapters – especially Chapter 5.

3.4 Developing the account: An analysis through three examples

Desires come in varying degrees of generality and specificity. Sometimes they are fairly ill defined, as when one has a general restlessness in life without knowing how one would like the situation to change. At other times a desire can take more of a specific form; and it is these kinds of desire – for something in a particular capacity – that interest us. For the knowledge that a desire can enable in the way that Wynn suggests is knowledge of what something would be like in the capacity of satisfying that desire.

Food

Consider first the experience of desiring food. As several biblical passages highlight, this can be phenomenologically similar to the desire for God, and it can thus help us develop an epistemology of desire applicable to God.[41] My concern here is the desire for some *particular* kind of food rather than general hunger, just as my concern in Chapter 5 will be the desire for God in particular capacities, rather than a general hunger for him. Although biblical hunger-based analogies for desiring God relate more to the general desire for sustenance or nourishment than to desires for particular foods, these need not be distinct. This is obvious in the case of food (a desire for a particular food can be a desire for nourishment), but it is also true of desire for God: desiring God in some particular capacity can be seen as desiring some particular aspect of his nourishment or sustenance. Thus, biblically depicted hunger for God, *in its more specific forms*, can be phenomenologically similar to the desire for specific kinds of food I use in developing my epistemology.

We have all found ourselves with this sort of desire – found ourselves especially in the mood for a buttery cinnamon bagel, or a juicy strawberry, or a steaming bowl of risotto. One way of describing this kind of experience is in terms of the food in question 'calling to us', as is nicely illustrated in one of A. A. Milne's *Winnie-the-Pooh* stories, in which Pooh, Piglet, and Rabbit are lost in the mist:

> 'If I walked away from this Pit, and then walked back to it, of *course* I should find it.'
> … 'Try', said Piglet suddenly. 'We'll wait here for you.'
> Rabbit gave a laugh to show how silly Piglet was, and walked into the mist. After he had gone a hundred yards, he turned and walked back again … and after Pooh and Piglet had waited twenty minutes for him, Pooh got up.
> … 'Now then, Piglet, let's go home.'
> 'But, Pooh,' cried Piglet, all excited, 'do you know the way?'
> 'No,' said Pooh. 'But there are twelve pots of honey in my cupboard, and they've been calling to me for hours. I couldn't hear them properly before, because Rabbit *would* talk, but if nobody says anything except those twelve pots, I *think*, Piglet, I shall know where they're calling from. Come on.'[42]

In desiring a given kind of food in this way, one has some sense of what it would take to be satisfied. This will include having certain sensations, such as tasting the exact kind of sweetness or savouriness of the food in question, feeling the texture of it in one's mouth and feeling its temperature in the mouth and going down the oesophagus. The sense of what it would take to be satisfied corresponds to the form the desire takes. In the sort of case under consideration, the form of the desire (hunger, or the desire to eat) depends on this sense: what makes a desire for a certain food the desire specifically to *eat* that food (rather than a desire for the food in some other capacity, such as making one's cupboards look well stocked) is partly the desirer's sense that satisfaction would consist in feeling the sensations just mentioned. Through feeling a strong desire for the food in question, combined with this heightened sense of what it would be like to consume that food, one can 'practically taste it'. In other words, one has desire-based knowledge of the kind Wynn describes: the aspects of the food that one knows about through desiring it are precisely the aspects that would bring about what one senses it would take to be satisfied (for example, its flavour, texture and temperature).

A vivid example of this can be found in Tolstoy's *Anna Karenina*. In one scene, the protagonist Levin has returned from a hunting trip 'tired and hungry', only to find that his companions have finished off all the provisions. The passage continues, 'Levin had been dreaming so specifically of pirozhki [stuffed buns] that, as he approached their quarters, he could already feel their smell and taste in his mouth.'[43] In the event, Levin does not have the satisfaction of tasting the pirozhki; yet his knowledge of their smell and taste is certainly heightened by his desire for them. We see, then, that desiring to eat some particular kind of food can give the desirer vivid knowledge of what that food would be like in the capacity of providing satisfaction. Thus, the desire and the knowledge it enables contain a characterization of what is desired in the capacity of providing satisfaction.

Now clearly one's sense of what would satisfy the desire is based on past experience: one cannot imagine eating a particular food if one has had no experience along those lines. For this reason, an important aspect of the desire-based knowledge I am describing is 'phenomenal knowledge', or knowledge of what something is like. That there is such knowledge as a distinct kind has been persuasively illustrated by Frank Jackson, using a well-known thought experiment in which Mary, a colour scientist who has never seen colour, leaves her black and white room for the first time and acquires knowledge of what it is like to see colours.[44] However, in order for a desire to function in the epistemic capacity I am describing, one need not have experienced anything *exactly like* the projected satisfaction; to imagine what it would be like, it is enough to have had experience *somewhat like* it. I have eaten mango, dark melted chocolate and solid mint chocolate all separately, but I have never eaten mango covered in melted dark, mint chocolate. Nonetheless, I desire this combination; if I think of it, I can form a sense of how it would taste and feel in my mouth. This sense of what would constitute satisfaction is based on my imaginative powers and an amalgamation of memories. Admittedly, my desire-based knowledge about this delectable dessert is not as vivid as it would be had I actually eaten it in the past. Nonetheless, the example shows that desire-based knowledge can to some extent be rooted in experience that is merely analogous to that which would constitute satisfaction: one only needs phenomenal knowledge of something sufficiently similar to the object of desire to enable one to form a sense of what satisfaction would be like. I will have a similar point to make with regard to romantic desire a little later. And as we shall see, this is important for our capacity to know about *God* through desiring him: in many, perhaps all, cases, one will not have fully experienced the satisfaction from him for which one longs.

Musical resolution

Consider a second example of the kind of desire-based knowledge that Wynn highlights: the sort of case through which he introduces the notion, namely, desiring a resolution to musical tension. This example illustrates especially well some of the aspects of the relationship between the *affective* and the *conceptual* in desire-based knowledge about the object of desire. I pointed out earlier that in enabling knowledge about its object, a desire takes a particular form that corresponds to one's sense of how it would be satisfied. However, for a desire to take a particular form, the desirer need not consciously *recognize* what that form is, as we can see from the desire for a resolution to musical tension. Because we have become used to certain harmonic progressions in Western music, we expect certain harmonic sequences to be resolved in certain ways. This expectation can take the form of a desire for them to be thus resolved; for instance, we desire a dominant seventh chord to be resolved onto the tonic, and are left feeling frustrated if it does not. Such a listener will sense that in order for her desire to be satisfied, she would have to hear a given sequence of sounds and have a corresponding feeling of completeness. And the sequence of sounds in which she senses that her satisfaction would consist determines the specific form of her musical desire: that of desiring the dominant to resolve onto the tonic.

Through the listener's desire for the tonic and her sense of what would constitute satisfaction, she has vivid knowledge of the aspect of the tonic chord that, she senses, would satisfy her desire, namely, its aural relation to the dominant. However, none of this presupposes that the listener *recognizes* her desire as being for a resolution from the dominant to the tonic. This would require knowledge of music theory; and clearly one can, without any music-theoretical training, respond to a dominant seventh chord with a desire for the tonic (which is why so much popular and classical music contains this progression: it sounds satisfying) – a desire that enables knowledge about the tonic in the way I described. In other words, one need not always have in mind any *concept* of what one desires in order for the desire to enable knowledge about what is desired.

It is worth spending a little more time on this relationship between the affective and the conceptual in the kind of knowledge I have been considering. Conceptual understanding can play a variety of roles in the knowledge a desire enables about its object – or no role at all. As we saw in the musical case just considered, the desirer need not always have a concept of what she desires in order for the desire to enable knowledge, since she does not always need this conceptual understanding in order to have a sense of what would constitute satisfaction. The listener's affective state, comprising the desire and the sense of what would constitute satisfaction, is non-conceptually formed; it is also cognitive and a way of registering the nature of something, just like the non-propositional fear we encountered earlier.

This affective, non-conceptual knowledge can become fused with conceptual understanding if the desirer learns how to conceptualize the object of her desire (as, say, the tonic and musical resolution) and the properties it would need in order to provide satisfaction (as, say, the tonic's aural relation to the dominant and therefore to the preceding musical tension). In this way, desire is like a number of other emotions. Wynn draws on the considerations of Deigh's that we have already encountered regarding the absence of propositional thought from some emotional experiences, and suggests that 'affects may constitute a mode of perception which operates independently of any conceptual articulation of the world's character'.[45] The sort of fear I have already considered is one example Wynn cites: 'Sometimes (I would say, typically) the recognition of a thing's scariness is realised in an affectively toned perception of its character (in the feeling of being scared by it).'[46] However, Wynn goes on to emphasize that such 'primal' responses can be infused with conceptual understanding to form a 'unified, affectively toned perception'.[47] For instance, an appreciation of female beauty can involve an affectively toned response that does not rely on conceptual elements; but this response is typically mixed with various culturally conditioned notions of what constitutes female beauty, together with what such beauty signifies.[48] While desiring musical resolution may not be as complex as affectively appreciating female beauty, the essential point here is the same: the knowledge involved in the affective experience of desire could be entirely non-conceptual (as it would be for one who desired musical resolution without knowing anything about music theory), or it could be conceptually formed while still involving an irreducibly affective element (as for someone who desires musical resolution and is competent in music theory, or, indeed, someone who desires a food of which they have a concept).

Romantic desire

I. *Affective and conceptual elements*

Another way in which desire-based knowledge can be conceptually formed is for conceptual understanding to help one arrive at such knowledge in the first place by shaping the content of the desire itself. To see this, we can look at *romantic* desire: another kind that can give the desirer knowledge as I have been describing it. Romantic desire especially is like desire for God in a number of respects, which I will consider shortly. In romantically desiring someone, it is not always immediately obvious what it would take to be satisfied. It is not, as it were, always part of the surface phenomenology of the desire, as it is in the two sorts of cases I have already considered. Because of the complex web of emotional significance and personal history involved in our romantic affections, there may be a number of things we seek in a romantic relationship that are unclear to us. And to be sure, what would constitute satisfaction may vary from person to person and from one time to another in one's life, depending on history, character and so on. In fact, if Talbot Brewer's discussion of romantic desire, which we saw in Chapter 2, is on the mark, then nothing can ever *finally* satisfy a romantic desire. However, there are clearly states of affairs that can constitute *partial* satisfactions of that desire; and it these that I am concerned with here.

In order, then, to recognize what it would take for a romantic desire to be satisfied, one may have to reflect on the matter, and this reflection will unavoidably involve conceptual elements. As an example, suppose the desirer came to recognize on reflection that her satisfaction would consist at least partly in being involved in a relationship of intimate love, acceptance and understanding. From there, the desirer would be able to form some idea of the attributes that the person she desired would need in order to contribute to that satisfaction – such as being intimately loving and supportive. These conceptual thoughts would shape the desire itself: through this process, the attributes in virtue of which someone would satisfy the romantic longing can become enmeshed in how the desirer perceives the one for whom she longs.

Consequently, the influence between conceptual and affective will also work the other way round in a case like this: the desire's affectivity permeates our concepts of the attributes through which (we sense) we would be satisfied. For instance, the desirer's notion of 'intimately loving and supportive' acquires a hue of emotional significance in light of her desire and her sense of what would constitute satisfaction: she knows how these attributes matter to her in the context of romantic love. And the desirer's knowledge of what the attributes would be in contributing to her satisfaction is thus deepened. We see especially clearly in this case, then, that the knowledge a desire can enable has a *relational* aspect: because the knowledge is of what someone would be like in the capacity of fulfilling one's desire, what one knows is not just the nature of certain personal attributes, but *how* those attributes matter to oneself.

This ability to deepen and enrich an existing conceptual grasp is something desire shares with other emotions. Goldie has shed some light on what this involves by imagining someone who has fallen on ice. Before the fall, the person has a purely conceptual grasp of the danger of ice; afterwards, his knowledge of the danger has new content.[49] That is to say, he now knows more about ice's danger, and this knowledge consists in an unfortunately intimate sense of what is in danger of happening in connection with ice. This deeper knowledge of ice's danger resides in a new kind of conceptual grasp of the harm that can befall one on ice – a grasp that is shot through with feelings concerning the ice, such as pain, embarrassment and wariness. The feelings here do not just attach to the same conceptual understanding; rather, they build on the content of this understanding, changing it in the process – 'although it might be that this difference cannot be captured in words'.[50] Just as, after my fall on ice, 'I think of its dangerousness as emotionally relevant in a special way',[51] someone with a romantic desire conceptualizes as emotionally relevant the attributes in virtue of which her desire would be satisfied. As Wynn puts the point, affect can draw on the content of conceptual thought 'so as to bring out its deeper existential sense'.[52] One is thus vividly aware of the attributes in question *through* the desire in something like the way we have seen in our other two examples, resulting in the aforementioned deepened knowledge of what the attributes would be in contributing to the desire's fulfilment. Thus, if the person who is the object of the romantic desire really does have those attributes, one comes to know about her in those respects in terms of her importance to oneself as the desirer. Even if one has not become well acquainted with her, one still knows, through the desire, the sort of person with whom a relationship would prove fulfilling. And this will mean that one knows, to an extent, what one is looking for: one will be able to recognize such a person if one gets to know her. In such an eventuality, one will grow in knowledge of the person whom one desires, becoming more intimately acquainted over time with her, and thus with the attributes that one initially knew about through the desire; only now, one will know those attributes in the context of a relationship with a particular person.

II. Romantic desire and desire for God: Three similarities

Three aspects of romantic desire provide useful illustrations of similar aspects of desire for God, and it is worth considering these now. First, romantic desire shows that the overall kind of desire-based knowledge for which I am arguing does not require the projected satisfaction to be merely some kind of sense experience, as it was in the food example (and perhaps in the musical example). Even though romantic satisfaction might come *through* sense experience, a romantic desire for someone involves more than just the desire for a particular kind of sense experience: complex affective and cognitive states are involved in the desire's ongoing satisfaction, or striving towards satisfaction.

Second, as in the food case, the sense of what would constitute satisfaction of a romantic desire need not be based on past experience of precisely that kind of satisfaction. It would be strange to claim that if someone had not yet been in a romantic relationship, she would have no idea as to what would constitute satisfaction of any romantic desire she might feel. Such a person plausibly *would* have a sense of what it would take to be satisfied, since that is partly what would guide her search for a suitable partner. This sense may be drawn from other relationships that share important features with a romantic relationship – for example, family relationships involving close personal trust and shared interests. Hence, in the case of desire for a *person*, the knowledge thereby enabled depends not just on phenomenal knowledge as Jackson describes it, but on a particular kind of phenomenal knowledge, namely, personal knowledge. Eleonore Stump has argued that this is a particular kind of knowledge – albeit a subset of phenomenal knowledge. Stump imagines that Mary, our colour scientist, has just been released from prison and meets another human being, her mother, for the first time. In that second-person experience, she thereby comes to know things that she did not know before, for instance, what it is like to be loved.[53] In order to form a sense of what it would be like for one's romantic desire to be satisfied (or, as I said earlier, partially satisfied) one must have had prior experience that was at least analogous to that satisfaction – and this will have given one knowledge of what it is like to relate to persons in various ways. Of course, a romantic relationship also differs in important ways from family relationships: it has its own kind of sharing and closeness, and in general its own kind of love.[54] But based on experience of the partially analogous relationships, and on what one knows about the sort of love appropriate to romantic relationships, it is possible, through an imaginative leap, to know something of what it would be like for one's romantic desire to be satisfied; hence it is possible to know, with the personal significance already mentioned, something of what a person would be like in satisfying that desire.

In virtue of these two features as they manifest themselves in romantic desire – not being satisfied in mere sense experience, and involving a sense of what would constitute satisfaction that need not be based on past experience of that same satisfaction – such desire is especially apt for illustrating how desire can enable this sort of knowledge about God. Desire for God would also, of course, be satisfied in something more than sense experience; and as I have said, one might well lack any past experience of the satisfaction of a desire for God, meaning that a sense of what would constitute that satisfaction would have to be based on some analogous experience. This should be borne in mind for Chapter 5.

There is one more respect in which romantic desire is a good model for thinking about desire for God. This is that both are prone to wishful thinking – a danger I raised at the end of Chapter 2. Suppose I desire someone romantically, along with a sense of what would constitute satisfaction and resultant knowledge of what she would be like in granting that satisfaction, in terms of her importance to me in respect of those attributes. Could this not simply be a matter of knowing how I would *like* her to be in satisfying my desire, with no correspondence to her actual nature?

In order for a romantic desire to enable the kind of knowledge about someone I have described, that desire's satisfaction would need to be something that the beloved would bring about: in other words, the desire would need to be rightly ordered towards her. There are at least two ways in which one could come to have a desire like this. First, one could have the desire elicited by knowing the person in question to a degree. One might perceive attributes in someone that one finds attractive, and come to have a desire for her whose satisfaction would depend on those attributes. Returning to something like our earlier example, one might perceive in someone a capacity for intimacy and support, and come to have a desire whose satisfaction would involve a relationship of intimate love and support.

A second way, meanwhile, in which one's desire for someone could be such that the person in question would, indeed, contribute to its satisfaction, is as follows. One's interpersonal desires – including the sorts of things that one seeks in romantic relationships – may have been aligned with the sort of person that the object of one's desire is, quite independently of any contact with her. This would likely happen, at least in part, through one's development in relating to people: developmental psychologists have given detailed accounts of how various factors in one's early relationships can affect one's emotional development, which would, in turn, affect one's priorities when seeking subsequent relationships.[55] We can see, then, that the sort of satisfaction at which a romantic desire is aimed can be determined by things other than contact with someone whom one romantically desires. Consequently, the kinds of personal attributes in a prospective partner that one grasps through one's desire, in terms of their significance to oneself, can be determined by things other than contact with someone whom one romantically desires. Thus, if one encounters someone to whom one finds oneself attracted, the desire one feels for that person may have been – indeed, probably will at least partly have been – shaped in its nature by one's pre-existing dispositions. If the person whom one desires turns out to possess attributes through which the desire could be satisfied, then, because one knows something of those attributes through the desire in the way I have been describing, one thereby knows something about the person in a personally significant way.

These, then, are ways in which one's romantic desire may come to be rightly ordered to a particular person. What about desire for God? There are a number of ways within religious practice, and within Christian practice specifically, to shape one's desires to be satisfiable in certain states of affairs rather than in others – including states of affairs that God as conceived in a certain way could be hoped to bring about. As I have made clear, the methods with which I will be primarily concerned in Chapters 5 and 6 are, respectively, engagement with sacred music and with contemplative prayer. The desires can thereby be rightly ordered to a particular kind of God and enable openness to such a God. The kind of God with whom I will be concerned is the one characterized in the music, texts and contemplative spirituality that I will be examining: this is the content of the 'live hypothesis' of Christianity with which I shall engage. Thus, the shaping of the desires – at least in the context of sacred music – might look rather like the *second* way described previously in which romantic desire can come to be rightly ordered to a particular person. However, there is room, if one is so inclined, to hold that in these shaping processes one does encounter God, even if indirectly; and in this case, the shaping would be analogous to the *first* kind of romantic 'right ordering' described here.[56]

In summary, then, I have looked at three kinds of desire: for food, for musical resolution and for a romantic partner. They all illustrate that a desire, combined with the sense of what would constitute satisfaction, gives the desirer knowledge about the object of desire in the capacity of bestowing that satisfaction, where that knowledge is imbued with a special, personal significance. Thus, if the object of desire really exists, then the desirer knows in this way about it, him, or her, in respect of the attributes through which the satisfaction would be achieved. If the object of the desire does *not* exist, then one at least knows what something would have to have been like in order to satisfy one's desire.

3.5 Desire's contribution to the desirer's knowledge: A worry

Someone may object that it is not clear that a desire actually contributes anything to our knowledge about what is desired. Does, say, desiring to eat a cinnamon bagel add anything at all to our knowledge of the bagel's properties in virtue of which it would satisfy us, over and above the knowledge we gain from actually experiencing those properties? And surely the same point applies to the desire for musical resolution and to romantic desire.

In reply, I claim that desire does, in fact, add to the knowledge given to us by full experience of something – in at least two ways. First, desire can enable us to know about something with the vividness I have mentioned, even when we are not actually experiencing what we desire. For instance, as described earlier, and as was especially evident in the case of Levin's desire, we can long for a food so strongly that we can 'practically taste it'. When feeling the desire to eat a given kind of food, one's knowledge of the aspects of the food through which it would provide satisfaction is fuller than at any other time, except for when one is actually experiencing the food in question. It is true that we would not be able 'practically to taste it' through desiring it unless we had previously tasted it, or something like it. But desire, through its affectivity, can jog our memory of what it is like to eat something, and thus give us a vivid kind of knowledge that we had in the past: knowledge available through desire at times when full experiential knowledge is unavailable.

The second way in which desire can add to full experiential knowledge is something I have touched on already: by including an inherent sense of lack, the desire enables an especially clear recognition of the importance of the desire's object to oneself as the desirer. When we lack something important to us, we are often much more aware of its importance to us than when we possess it. In our age of year-round produce, I have access to strawberries every day for breakfast if I want them. However, if they were available for only two months each year, I would undoubtedly long for them at times during the remaining months, and I would thereby acquire a heightened sense of why I am so fond of them – that is, of their importance to me. An analogous point may be made about romantic desire ('absence makes the heart grow fonder'): the 'personal import' of desire-based romantic knowledge is the special feature of that knowledge. Hence, the knowledge in question is not simply of what something is like; nor is it simply knowledge of one's own preferences, values, or priorities. Rather, it is a vivid sense of how the desire's object would meet those preferences, values, or priorities were one to stand in the right kind of relation to it. Certain aspects of something are highlighted in one's awareness as especially salient. As we shall see in Chapter 5, this is a prominent feature of the religious, desire-based knowledge to be discussed there.

To this, one might object further that this sort of knowledge – knowledge of how something is important to oneself – *underpins* a desire for that thing, rather than being *enabled* by the desire. One might think that our having such knowledge is *why* we desire things.[57] I do not deny that we must already know that something is important to us, or that we would find it enjoyable, in order to desire it. But, as illustrated in the cases of the unavailable strawberries and the absent lover, a desire for something can give one an especially vivid, heightened sense of that thing's importance to oneself – and, specifically, a sense of the characteristics in virtue of which it is important, and through which it would satisfy the desire. Sometimes one's quest for the object of desire can be a long, drawn-out one, as it most likely will be in the case of desire for God. In this sort of context, such periods of heightened awareness of how something is characteristically important to oneself can provide added impetus to the search, strength in times of difficulty and guidance as to how one should let oneself be shaped to receive, eventually, the object of one's desire.

Of course, these times of heightened awareness depend for their intelligibility on a backdrop of standing, or non-occurrent, desire for the thing in question: there will be times when one's desire for something, or someone, is not currently affecting one's thoughts, feelings, or actions.[58] But even at these times, the desire will involve a sense of its object's importance to the desirer: aspects of one's experience will tend to be lit up as especially salient in virtue of how one associates them with the object of desire. For instance, if I love someone and desire them in their absence, I may not spend every waking hour *feeling* the desire; but certain things will remind me of my beloved (places we have visited, food we have eaten together), and will thus be lit up as especially significant for me. At these times, I will likely come to feel the desire consciously: it will become occurrent once more. Similar things can be said of desire for God. I may not spend every waking hour feeling such a desire; but there will be times when aspects of my experience are lit up as especially salient, and I come to feel the desire once more. In Chapter 5, I will be arguing that engagement with sacred music is one way in which this can happen. Because of the content of the musical pieces I discuss, the desires for God that come to the surface of one's awareness at these times will characterize God in particular ways; and the desires of Chapter 5 will be like the desires explored here – namely, for God in particular capacities – and hence able to function in the epistemic way I have described in this chapter.

As well as the ways in which the desire-experience *itself* can contribute to one's knowledge regarding the desire's object, a desire can, of course, *lead to* further knowledge. Desire, if allowed to develop, can lead one to experience the object of desire directly. There is more than one way in which this might happen. Desire can guide one's thoughts, feelings and actions, leading one to seek what one desires, which may result in one's finding or acquiring it. Alternatively or in addition, as St Augustine suggests in a religious context, desire for something may expand our capacity to receive it:

> The entire life of a good Christian is a holy desire ... God stretches our desire through delay, stretches our soul through desire, and makes it large enough by stretching it. Let us desire, then, brothers, because we have to be filled. ... Let us stretch out to him so that, when he comes, he may fill us.[59]

This is a familiar enough phenomenon; we need only look to romantic love for an example of something that we can receive more fully the more we desire it. A desire-experience of the kind I have been discussing, then, as well as giving the desirer knowledge about the desire's object, can lead the desirer to a still greater knowledge of that object. This idea should be borne in mind for the religious context of Chapters 5 and 6; Chapter 6, especially, will be concerned with the theme of attribute-specific desires for God leading to deeper knowledge of God in the context of contemplative prayer.

3.6 Summing up and looking forwards

I shall now draw what our three examples have shown into a cohesive account of desire *qua* enabling knowledge about its object. After doing this, I will make some anticipatory remarks about how our non-religious examples can lead us towards thinking about the kinds of desire for God discussed in later chapters, especially Chapter 5.

The kind of desire that enables knowledge about its object

Let us summarize the conditions for the desire-based knowledge I have described. First, the desire must take a *particular form*; that is, it must be for something in a particular capacity, since the knowledge involved is knowledge of what something would be like in the capacity of providing satisfaction. Second, one needs some sense of what would constitute satisfaction; and the aspects of the desire's object that one knows about through the desire are those that would bring about this projected satisfaction. Third, in order to have this sense of what satisfaction would be like, one must have experienced at least something like the projected satisfaction. What is important for us in this regard is that, as we shall see later, the desires for God to be considered in Chapter 5 can come with *some* sense, however incomplete, of what satisfaction would be like, based on merely analogous past experiences.

It is also worth once again emphasizing two points raised in Chapter 2, applied to what we have seen from the cases examined here. First, in order to enable knowledge in the way I have described, a desire must be satisfiable in a *state of affairs*. A sense of what the desire's satisfaction would consist in, which is crucial to the desire's epistemic power as I have described it, is precisely a sense of what state of affairs the desire's satisfaction would consist in. However, as I argued towards the end of Chapter 2, a desire's being satisfiable in a state of affairs is perfectly consistent with its being directed towards a concrete object, such as a person. The state-of-affairs desire can be a manifestation of an underlying, non-propositional desire for the person: it can be a desire for the person in a particular capacity that has its full significance only in the context of the underlying desire. It will eventually emerge, in Chapter 6, that the specific desires for God discussed in Chapter 5 can have just this role in one's wider spiritual life.

The second point to pick up from Chapter 2 is that *belief* in the existence of what one desires is not needed in order for a desire to satisfy the conditions for knowledge – or, for short, in order for it to be a 'k-desire'. One need not believe that a particular kind of food exists in order to k-desire it; for instance, I might k-desire wasabi-flavoured crisps, even though I do not know whether there are such things. Somewhat similarly, one need not believe that a particular musical resolution is forthcoming in order to k-desire it when one hears musical tension. And finally, I showed in Chapter 2 that one need not believe that the object of one's romantic affections exists in order to desire him or her; and, given the considerations here, such a desire could be a k-desire.

One might object that in all these cases, the desirer at least believes in the existence of the general *kinds* of things that she k-desires. Hence, although I am agnostic over the existence of wasabi crisps, my desire for them depends on my belief that there are such things as wasabi, crisps and wasabi-flavoured snacks. Similarly, in order to k-desire a dominant-to-tonic resolution, one must believe in the existence of such resolutions in general.[60] And in order to k-desire someone romantically, one must believe in the existence of romantic partners in general. But, the objector might continue, isn't *God* different? Assuming that one does not believe in anything of God's kind other than God himself, it follows that if one does not believe in God's reality, then one does not believe in anything of God's kind at all. And in this case, how could one desire God?

The question, I think, is this: if one lacks any belief in a given kind of thing, then how can one acquire the notion of that thing in order to desire it? And in the case of God, the answer is not far to seek; indeed, we saw it in Chapter 2. One might, without believing in anything of God's kind, experience what one takes to be a portrayal of aspects of God: for instance, through literature, music, art, liturgy, or interactions with other people.[61] One would need also to have learnt an idea of God that enabled one to think about such an experience in terms of God; or, indeed, one might simply have learnt an idea of God that one came to associate with aspects of one's ordinary experience. In any case, one would have the notion of God that one needed in order to desire God, even though one lacked a belief in anything of God's kind. And this applies to the specific, k-desires for God to be considered in Chapter 5. In short, the desires for God with which I shall be concerned are possible without belief in God's reality. The desire-based knowledge may therefore be expressed propositionally as 'if God existed, God would be such-and-such in satisfying my desire', where 'such-and-such' denotes attributes grasped in terms of their importance to the desirer.

Anticipating the desire for God

In Chapter 2, I introduced the idea of an 'epistemic and affective framework' for seeking God. Through desiring God in various capacities, one knows something of what God would be like if he were to satisfy one's desire; furthermore, the personal, existential significance that permeates this knowledge and enriches one's concepts of the relevant divine attributes will draw one into a personally invested search for God. This, in essence, is how desire-based knowledge of the kind described in this chapter can be valuable to a life of religious seeking. The affective aspect of the framework motivates the journey; the epistemic aspect guides it. Thus, the two aspects together can aid one's openness to the God whom one desires. I shall end this chapter by remarking on how this idea links up with a point raised earlier in the context of romantic desire.

I said earlier that even if one has not become well acquainted with another human person whom one desires, one can still know, through the desire, what sort of person would be a partner in a fulfilling relationship. This will mean that one knows, to an extent, what one is looking for. One will recognize such a person if one gets to know her; and if the person whom one desires *is* that sort of person, then through the desire one already knows something about her in terms of her significance to oneself. The same general idea applies to desiring God. If, through desiring God, one knows something of what he would be like in satisfying the desire (including how those aspects of God matter to oneself in virtue of one's desire), then one will be in a position to recognize God if he is indeed like that and becomes manifest in one's experience. Different forms of desire for God will enable this sort of knowledge about different divine attributes depending on what would constitute satisfaction, and will frame one's religious engagement accordingly. As in romantic desire, one may be guided by these initial desires to grow in knowledge of God, becoming more intimately acquainted over time with him, and thus with the attributes that one initially knew about through the desires in question. Only now, one will be growing in knowledge of those attributes in the context of a fuller relationship with God – a relationship that far outstrips anything one could have previously imagined. However, the initial desires will have been a key part of one's search for God: they will have provided impetus to that search, and guided one in seeking out the sort of God who would offer fulfilment.

Again, I will offer a fuller account in Chapter 6 of how the musically elicited desires of Chapter 5 may conduce to one's spiritual growth in contemplative prayer. Such growth would consist in coming to knowledge *of* God, rather than merely knowledge *about* him in certain respects. And, as Chapter 6 will make clear, growing in knowledge of God in contemplative prayer would involve growing in *love* of God, as one's attention is focused more and more on God himself, rather than on God in virtue of specific divine attributes. All this, of course, presupposes that the Christian tradition in which one involves oneself might be sufficiently true for there to be such a thing as the spiritual growth at which the tradition aims. As I explained in Chapter 2, this is a possibility our interested non-believer takes seriously enough to act on.

I have now established the general epistemology of desire to be applied to desire for God in Chapter 5. Before getting there, however, I must examine the other key theme in this study: musical experience, and specifically, the ways in which one may respond affectively to sacred music. Once I have argued for the conclusions in the musical domain that are needed for my religious discussion of Chapters 5 and 6, I will turn to that discussion in earnest.

4

Music and affect

All the diverse emotions of our spirit have their various modes in voice and chant appropriate in each case, and are stirred by a mysterious inner kinship.

St Augustine[1]

In this chapter, I shall explore some key aspects of musical affectivity – music's power to be expressive of, and elicit, affective states.[2] The relationship between music and affect has a long history of reflection in Western thought, going back to Plato and Aristotle, and even earlier to Pythagoras and his followers.[3] Again, I will concentrate on establishing the groundwork for the religious considerations in the following chapters, so I will be selective in the issues I cover. First, as a matter of ground clearing, I will address three issues that rear their heads strongly, and might appear to hinder the development of my overall argument. By clarifying why these issues need not disturb my central thesis, I hope to forestall any anxieties about them so that we can move forward with confidence. After this, I will turn to the chapter's main body of discussion, arguing for claims that will be necessary in the chapters that follow.

4.1 Issues on which neutrality is appropriate

The relationship between the experience of the composer and that of the listener

With regards to the instances of religious knowledge to be discussed, the key fact is that they are enabled by the listener's feeling of desire of one form or another for God, in response to sacred music. Therefore, it does not primarily matter for our purposes what the composer was feeling as he composed the music; nor does it primarily matter whether or not the composer *intended* the music to be expressive of, or elicit, the desire I describe in each case. All that matters in the cases I consider is that the music elicits a desire of a given form in the listener; this is enough for the music to engender the religious knowledge that I shall describe.

An example may help here. John Rutter, the well-known contemporary composer of church music, describes himself as an agnostic, albeit one who possesses 'a sense of generalised spirituality' and who is 'hugely sympathetic to the Church'.[4] In light of this, it is possible that whatever his affective states when composing any of his pieces, they were at least subtly different from the states to which a religious believer would be moved on hearing them. Furthermore, we may suppose that if he did not, while composing his pieces, experience the affective response to any of them that a fully fledged believer might experience, then he would not have intended for the listener to have precisely that response (since he did not know what such a response would be like). However, the listener might still respond to some of his pieces with a desire for God that has epistemic import in the way I articulated in Chapter 3 – whether that listener is a religious believer, or a non-believer who feels different affects on listening from those that Rutter felt while composing, or that he intended the listener to feel. As I established in Chapter 3, the epistemic import of a desire stems from its phenomenology. Thus, Rutter's compositional feelings and intentions influence the epistemic import of the listener's response only insofar as they influence the phenomenology of that response – which, of course, they might do if the listener knew about Rutter's stance regarding Christian belief. But his attitudes in composing are not *intrinsically* important to the response's epistemic import; nor are they *necessarily* important, since they will not *necessarily* affect the response's phenomenology.

We can put the point another way, by considering the difference between prominent attitudes towards music in the baroque and romantic eras. In the baroque era, music was rarely offered as a vehicle of self-expression – an expression of the composer's own experience and emotions. Instead, it was often intended to be expressive of, or arouse, some particular 'affection', perhaps by making audible the 'aesthetic essence' of a mood or emotion.[5] In the romantic era, by contrast, self-expression became central to music, which came to be considered 'a window on the soul and a medium by which the heart of the musician and that of the listener could somehow commune', with the specific feelings aroused seen as less important.[6] The epistemological position of subsequent chapters does not depend on the instantiation of the romantic 'window on the soul' ideal. For sacred music to engender the religious knowledge I shall describe, it need only perform the role envisaged for it in the baroque period of arousing some affective state – and in particular, it must arouse a desire of some form or other for God with something like the phenomenology described in the previous chapter.[7]

The means by which music is expressive of, and arouses, affective states

It does not matter for our purposes *how* music is expressive of and arouses affective states, as long as it does so. My own view on how music is expressive of affects, at least in regard to 'dynamic' music (in contrast to static chords), is what is known as the resemblance theory: music is expressive by resembling human expressive behaviour.[8] For instance, Aaron Ridley suggests that the expressive association between music and affective states can be grounded in the music's resemblance to the human voice and to the expressive movements of bodies.[9] Stephen Davies' account is similar: he thinks that music is expressive because it captures the 'looks' we associate with various affective states, and it does so on account of its dynamic character, and this character's resemblance to the gait, bearing, carriage and so forth of humans.[10] Meanwhile, I take the view that music's ability to *arouse* affective states is at least partly a matter of what James Young calls 'emotional contagion', which builds on the resemblance theory of musical expressiveness (and which I discuss briefly a little later). With all this said, however, it remains the case that no matter how music is expressive of, and arouses, affective states, it simply needs to be true that it *can* do these things in order for the following chapters to hold up.

How widely felt are the affective responses I describe

One more thing to note that does not affect my arguments is how widely felt are the affective responses to music that I describe in the following chapters, especially Chapter 5. What I say in those chapters does not require that everyone respond in the ways I describe to the musical examples I consider. In order for my arguments to have wide application and interest at the level of the specific forms of desire I discuss (i.e. the desires for God in the specific capacities that I discuss), it need only be the case that a great many people respond to *some music or other* with those forms of desire for God. If a piece that I discuss does not elicit in the reader (or in anyone else) the desire I talk about in connection with that piece, it will at least serve as an illustration of that kind of response. If there are other pieces that elicit the desire under consideration, my arguments can be applied to those pieces. But even if there were no other pieces that elicited in the reader (or in anyone else) the desire under consideration, this would still not render epistemologically unimportant the piece in question. For in this case, my discussion of that piece would still illustrate the phenomenon of *some desire or other* being elicited by music with text, and functioning in the epistemic capacity I described in Chapter 3. It is my hope that at least this more general epistemological import of desire will apply to a good many people on hearing *some* musical examples, even if they are not the examples I consider.

This raises the question of whether some kinds of music are intrinsically better than others at eliciting the kinds of desire considered in the following chapters: desires that give the listener knowledge about God that is spiritually fruitful if God is real. Is responding to some kinds of music with desire for God better than responding to other kinds with desire for God? Can some music elicit desire for God that is more deeply felt and more nuanced, and that takes in more of one's human nature, than the sorts of desire elicited by other music? This is a subset of the notorious question of musical, and indeed aesthetic, taste: What, if anything, justifies judgements of aesthetic merit or demerit? I do not propose to discuss such a thorny issue here. I said in Chapter 2 that my musical focus will be choral music of the Western classical tradition; and I will therefore not discuss other kinds of religious music in any detail. There is simply not the space to be exhaustive in this respect, and it is no part of my argument that the music on which I focus is intrinsically superior to other kinds in the capacity that concerns me.[11]

So much for the questions about music's affectivity whose answers will not make a difference to the following chapters. What about the aspects that are relevant? I start by considering a view of Peter Kivy's that, if correct, would threaten to undermine our whole endeavour. This will frame the discussion for much of the chapter. I shall then end by considering two additional points that will also prove important in the chapters to come.

4.2 Peter Kivy and the possibility of extra-musical emotion

Kivy's view and a related worry

If affective responses – and specifically, desiring responses – to music are to contribute to religious knowledge in the ways for which I will argue, then this responsiveness must be directed at something more than just the music. Kivy's view to which I referred is that the only kind of emotion music arouses in the listener is emotion about the music itself. This emotion can have different musical objects in each case; one might 'be moved by sheer beauty of sound', or by more complex features that the music might have, such as beauty and craftsmanship of counterpoint, masterful preparation of cadences, or whatever.[12] One might also be moved by the emotionally expressive qualities one hears in the music: 'Aroused to ecstasy by the beauty … of a particularly anguished passage … or impressed to the extent of being moved by the masterful way an aria is contrived to be expressive of … anger or joy.'[13] Importantly, though, Kivy denies that the listener's response in the latter sort of case mirrors the emotions she hears in the music.[14] He sums up his view thus: 'Great music in the Western, absolute music canon, moves us to a kind of enthusiasm, or excitement, or ecstasy directed at the music as its intentional object.'[15]

Kivy's main reason for holding this view on music's arousal of emotion is that it is, he claims, the only one that fulfils the requirements that he thinks any view on the subject *should* fulfil.[16] He contends that since emotional arousal is a common, everyday affair that we usually understand perfectly well in non-technical terms, and since music is also a common, everyday affair, an account of how music arouses emotion must include an ordinary, non-technical explanation of how it does so in order to be plausible. Music's arousing of emotion about itself in the way Kivy describes has just such an explanation: simply put, we are 'moved by the beauty or perfection of the music'.[17] But, says Kivy, there is no such explanation for how music could elicit *ordinary* emotions: music seems too far removed from the real-life things that *do* elicit ordinary emotions for us to be able say how it might do so in an ordinary, non-technical way. In addition to fulfilling this requirement, the account Kivy offers respects what he takes to be the nature of musically elicited emotions: object-directed and based on beliefs about their objects. On his account, the objects of musical emotion are the music or certain features thereof, and the accompanying beliefs are beliefs that the music has the qualities and features that elicit the emotion.

The general thrust of Kivy's view here can be traced back to Eduard Hanslick. Hanslick famously argued that when someone listening to music comes to feel emotions with extra-musical objects, this emotional arousal depends only on factors external to the music, and can therefore tell us nothing about the character of the music itself. Like Kivy's view, Hanslick's stems from a cognitive theory of the emotions: emotions necessarily involve thoughts or beliefs; but since music cannot be expressive of the thoughts or beliefs that ordinary emotions require, it cannot be expressive of those emotions. Music therefore cannot *elicit* ordinary emotions in virtue of any of its intrinsic features: any eliciting of emotion as one listens occurs simply because the listening is the *occasion* for the formation of that emotion.[18] The reply to Kivy that I develop, then, will also work as a reply to Hanslick if successful.

Kivy does specify that he is referring to *absolute* music – 'music unaccompanied by text, title, subject, program, or plot … music alone'.[19] Now the notion of absolute music is controversial: one might doubt whether we ever experience music in isolation, removed from anything else that could colour our experience of it.[20] But regardless of whether there is such a thing, it seems that Kivy's view, if true, would have consequences for 'non-absolute' music, or music combined with other factors. If music could arouse only Kivy's 'aesthetic' emotion, then it would seem to follow that when we experience music combined with *non*-musical thoughts and experiences, any emotion directed at something *other* than the music is aroused simply by those non-musical factors – not by the music.[21] For Kivy's purely aesthetic emotion is given its identity by its object – namely, the music or features thereof. Introduce an object and phenomenology that go beyond the music, and we are talking about a different (perhaps additional) emotion, not the one elicited by the music. Thus, it seems that the music itself would have no part to play in eliciting that other emotion. And if someone wants to say that music *can* elicit something other than Kivy's aesthetic emotion *when combined with other factors*, it remains on Kivy's view a mystery how music is supposed to accomplish this. If music's intrinsic emotional power is limited to arousing the aesthetic emotion, then how is it supposed to contribute anything towards the arousal of a different emotion? Hence Kivy's view, if true, would have the counterintuitive consequence that music plays no part in arousing explicitly *religious* emotions when combined with religious factors in the listener's experience.

This would render false the central claim of this study, since in order for a desire for God in response to sacred *music* to yield religious knowledge, music must be one of the factors in the listener's experience that helps elicit a desire for God – that is, an emotion directed at something other than just the music. Thus I must show that, plausibly, when a work of sacred music arouses an emotion directed towards God, the music itself plays an important role in eliciting that emotion. This is not to say that the music must give the emotion its religious subject matter; as we shall see, this can be done entirely by extra-musical factors. But it must play an important role in eliciting an *affectivity* of emotion directed towards God. In showing that music can do this, I hope also to make it clear that even when a piece's *text* does not play a central role in one's listening experience, one's affective response to that piece can still be directed at something more than the music itself. The affectivity elicited (at least in part) by the music can be given religious subject matter by any number of extra-musical factors. In essence, then, I shall argue in this section that music can combine with other aspects of the listener's experience to arouse fully fledged emotions with extra-musical objects.

Extra-musical subject matter and two kinds of intentionality

Before refuting Kivy's view, we should note that even if we could only respond to music with his aesthetic emotion, it would not follow that this emotion could have no religious significance. Intentionality is the property of being about, or directed towards, something; but being about something does not require being directed towards it. In order for an emotion to have something as its subject matter, it need not be *directed* at that subject matter. Even if I respond to music with excitement or ecstasy directed just towards the music, this emotion might still be tinged with religious feeling, however general. I suspect this is a familiar enough experience with regard both to music and to other things, such as features of the natural world: responding to something's beauty with a deep reverence that approaches awe – awe that anything so sublime could exist, with the vague notion that what one perceives hints at something greater. However, one's awe need not be *directed* at anything other than the immediate object of perception, since the intimation one has of a realm surpassing that perception may be too vague and implicit. Such a realm (be it real or imagined) shimmers in the background, without coming sharply enough into focus to be the object at which one's reverence is directed. Moreover, one way in which an aesthetic love of something can be religiously toned like this is through factors in one's experience that are additional to the object of aesthetic feeling. If one listens to a piece of music in a church, with sunlight streaming through the stained-glass windows onto a devotional painting, the experience takes on a religious hue that increases the likelihood of one's love of the music itself being religiously toned.

I make this point not because I think that religious affective responses to music are limited to a religiously coloured love of the music, but, rather, because this is an important aspect of the sort of affective response that will be our main concern: one that involves *more than* just a religiously toned love of the music. In the responses of desire for God that I describe in the following chapters, especially Chapter 5, there is a more complex interplay of music and extra-musical factors (especially words); yet, as we shall see, this interplay involves an aesthetic love of the music interacting with some definite religious subject matter or other in the listener's response. The aesthetic love of the music, I hope, will become clear in my detailed descriptions of the pieces I consider.

So, we can already see that when we experience music combined with extra-musical factors, it is *not* necessarily the case that any emotion that is about more than the music is aroused simply by those extra-musical factors. The aesthetic love of music that (as Kivy rightly claims) music can elicit can be *about* something more than just the music, even if it is not *directed at* this additional subject matter; and this extra intentionality can be given to the aesthetic emotion by extra-musical factors in one's experience. However, we must do more to establish that music can be one of the factors in the listener's experience that helps elicit a *desire* for God – and more generally, an emotion explicitly *directed at* more than just the music. We must address Kivy's view on musically elicited emotion.

Music can arouse objectless versions of everyday affects: Neutralizing Kivy's arguments

First, it seems far likelier than not that even without any overt extra-musical factors, music can arouse affects other than Kivy's aesthetic emotion – objectless versions of everyday affects such as joy, sadness, or anxiety or analogues thereof. I say without 'overt' extra-musical factors since I do not take any stance on whether 'absolute' musical experience is possible. But regardless, we often experience music without any extra-musical associations consciously in mind – and it is this sort of experience that is the subject of the following considerations. If this kind of listening can result in an objectless affective state whose identity is not fixed by being directed at the music, then the affect elicited will be free to be directed at something else, given the right associations in the mind of the listener; and these could, of course, include religious associations.

Kivy, remember, argues that because emotional arousal and music are everyday affairs, and because we usually understand emotional arousal non-technically, any arousal of emotion by music must have a non-technical explanation; and since, he claims, there is no such explanation for how music could arouse *ordinary* emotions in any form, it is implausible to think it does. Let us examine this reasoning. Three thoughts seem to drive Kivy's argument. First, most instances of emotional arousal have common-sense explanations: in ordinary life, we can usually explain why we feel angry, sad, happy and so on, without the need for technical psychology.[22] Second, the only exceptions are cases where a given emotional response to something does not seem like the natural response. Kivy mentions pathological emotion as an example, which could in theory include pathological emotion brought on by music: if someone became enraged every time she heard Brahms' Second Symphony, we might think she had 'a pathological condition that required psychoanalytic untangling'.[23] But – and this is the third motivating thought – most musical arousal of emotion is perfectly natural and common. Therefore, we do not need a special, technical explanation in order to make sense of it. Music's arousal of emotion (other than cases in which it arouses an emotion that is not a natural response) must have a common-sense, non-technical explanation – an explanation, Kivy claims, that is lacking for music's arousal of ordinary, everyday emotions, but that he argues is available for its arousal of aesthetic emotion.

To emphasize, I do not claim that music without overt extra-musical associations can arouse fully fledged emotions directed at extra-musical objects. But I do claim that this sort of music can arouse objectless affects, or moods, that are at least similar to those we feel in ordinary life. Positive reasons for this will follow shortly, but we must first clear the ground by refuting Kivy's argument that music could not in principle arouse such affects. Must there be a common-sense explanation for music's arousal of affect? Kivy's argument for this conclusion is valid; but is it sound? Are all the premises true? The first and third premises are fairly uncontroversial: in ordinary life, we *can* usually explain non-technically why we feel the emotions we feel; and most musical arousal of affect *is* natural and common. The second premise is the contentious one: Why think that the only affects that lack common-sense explanations are ones that seem unnatural given their circumstances? Kivy gives no reason for thinking this. It is true that unnatural affects, such as pathological affects, lack common-sense explanations; but that does not mean these are the *only* affects lacking such explanations. In particular, common, musically elicited affects may also lack common-sense explanations. This possibility becomes only more plausible when we consider that there are other examples of perfectly natural affective states that lack common-sense explanations. Depression and anxiety are not always about anything in particular, and so cannot always be explained in the non-technical way that Kivy has in mind. And yet we would hardly call these states 'unnatural' or 'unexpected'; on the contrary, they are relatively common. In general, there is nothing absurd about the idea of an affective state that is *both* natural in the sense of being such that anyone could plausibly imagine themselves in it,[24] *and* only explicable in technical terms. Thus, musically elicited affects, even though they are natural and common, need not have a common-sense explanation. And this means, of course, that if, indeed, there is no such explanation for music's arousal of ordinary, everyday affects (or analogues thereof) in objectless form, this does not count against the view that music arouses those affects.

I have addressed Kivy's argument against the view that music can elicit versions of ordinary affects in general. But we are not out of the woods yet: Kivy also specifically denies that music arouses *objectless* affects. Musically elicited affects, he thinks, are object-directed and based on beliefs about their objects – and those objects are purely musical. In order to defend the view that music arouses objectless versions of ordinary affects, we must address Kivy's reasons for denying specifically that it arouses objectless affects.

First, he maintains that we have no idea *how* music might do this. 'In the absence of such an explanation, I would have to have pretty overwhelming evidence that music does indeed arouse objectless emotions ... and I patiently await its as yet undreamed-of explanation.'[25] The 'overwhelming evidence' we will come to shortly – evidence that is strong enough, I suggest, to justify the view that music arouses at least analogues of everyday, objectless affects *even if* there were no explanation of how it might do so. But in any case, there are convincing explanations available. James Young draws on psychological and neuroscientific studies to present several of them; I will briefly describe just one, which Young calls 'emotional contagion'. Often enough we find ourselves adopting the emotions expressed by those around us; and moreover, as Young says, 'we can catch emotions from items that are expressive of emotions as well as directly from the expressive behaviour of others' (think of cheerful shades of yellow or dreary shades of grey).[26] These items plausibly include musical works, if, indeed, music can resemble human expressive behaviour, as suggested earlier.[27] One explanation of our 'catching' emotion from music is that music induces changes in facial expression and posture when listeners recognize (consciously or not) that it resembles human expressive behaviour (which also induces these changes). These changes lead to physiological changes, the proprioception of which leads to emotion.[28]

The other of Kivy's reasons for denying that music elicits objectless affects is that listeners do not behave as one might expect them to if they were in the affective states supposedly elicited.[29] The first thing to say in response is that music does not always elicit the same versions of affects as real-life events do, but often, instead, elicits analogues of real-life affects.[30] This explains why people choose to listen to music that elicits something resembling a negative affect: having an analogue of that affect elicited is not necessarily an unpleasant experience. One of the differences between musically elicited analogues of real-life affects, and the real-life affects themselves, is that we are less likely to feel the need to act in response to a musically elicited affect, since it lacks the life context that usually makes emotions action guiding.[31] Thus, a lack of action does not indicate a lack of affect. But in any case, musically elicited objectless affects do often manifest themselves in behaviour and in other physical signs. As Young points out:

> When we hear certain forms of music we are moved to dance for joy. ... Listening to other music that arouses more sombre emotions we become still. Perhaps we cry. Sometimes we are so moved that our appetites wane. The fact is that our emotional responses to music do have a behavioural aspect. They are not always precisely the behavioural responses we have when we feel emotions in the ordinary course of our lives, but the emotions are not precisely the same in other respects either.[32]

Contrary to what Kivy thinks, then, we do sometimes respond behaviourally to music – a sign of affective arousal. But even when we do not respond behaviourally we may still respond affectively, in which case the difference between these affects and their real-life counterparts robs them of their influence on our actions.

Music can arouse objectless versions of everyday affects: the positive evidence

We have now done enough, I think, to neutralize Kivy's arguments that music cannot, in its own right, arouse at least objectless analogues of ordinary affects. However, this does not in itself mean that music arouses such affects. It simply means that Kivy's arguments need not stop us taking at face value evidence that it *does* arouse them – rather than just arousing the aesthetic emotions he describes. There is a substantial body of experimental evidence to this effect: both evidence that music without overt extra-musical associations can elicit at least analogues of ordinary, everyday affects and evidence that music plays the bigger role in eliciting affects when combined with words.[33] Let us look briefly at these claims in turn.

First, there is evidence that music, independently of any overt extra-musical factors, can elicit the affects of which it is expressive, and not just Kivy's aesthetic emotion. A number of experiments have been conducted in which subjects were asked what affects they felt in response to music, explicitly distinguished from what affects they *heard* in the music – thus safeguarding against a worry Kivy has voiced, that the subjects confused the two.[34] In the experiments, there were many self-reports of affective responses to the music. In one experiment in particular,[35] pieces *expressive of* particular affects were likelier than other pieces to elicit in subjects two indications of those same affects as a felt response. The first indication consisted in subjects' *reports* that they felt the affects of which the music was expressive;[36] the second indication was the eliciting of distinctive *physiological* states that were associated with those affects, since they bore similarities to *non-musical* physiological states associated with those affects.[37] Hence, the affective responses tended to mirror what the subjects heard in the music, and thus seemed to be elicited by the music itself. This conclusion is strengthened by the following facts about the experiment, which strongly suggest that it was not extra-musical factors arousing affects in the subjects.[38] First, the music was instrumental: adagios by Albinoni and Barber, 'Mars' from Holst's *Planets*, Mussorgsky's *Night on Bare Mountain*, a movement from Vivaldi's *Spring* concerto, and Hugo Alfvén's *Midsommarvaka*. Second, titles do not seem to have played any part in the affects aroused: pieces lacking descriptive titles seemed just as conclusively to arouse affects; and of the descriptively titled pieces, most of the titles were unknown to most of the subjects. And third, cultural associations are unlikely to have played any part in the subjects' affective responses: most pieces had no associations for most of the subjects, since most were unrecognized by most of the subjects.

As mentioned, there is also experimental evidence that music plays the bigger role in eliciting affects when combined with words.[39] According to subjects' self-reports, melodies expressive of particular emotions, with no prior associations for the listeners, tended to arouse those emotions more intensely when lacking lyrics than they did when accompanied by lyrics.[40] In addition, again according to self-reports, when subjects heard a melody expressive of one affect set to lyrics expressive of different affects, the affect they reported feeling tended to be the one of the melody.[41]

There is, then, experimental evidence for music's ability to elicit objectless versions of ordinary, everyday affects. Some might even wonder whether experimental evidence is necessary for claiming that music has this capacity: surely, one might think, introspection when listening to music is enough to be sure of it? In any case, there is plenty of empirical evidence for this phenomenon. Kivy, of course, must maintain that those who *think* they feel such affects in response to music are always mistaken about their own inner states. Given the prima facie implausibility of this view, the burden lies on Kivy to argue for it. As we saw earlier, he has attempted to do just that by arguing that music does not elicit anything except a special, aesthetic emotion (which would entail that people are mistaken if they think it has elicited anything else in them). But given the difficulties those arguments face, we have no reason to think that people are mistaken in their self-reports of musically elicited affects; and there is also, of course, the physiological evidence. We can thus conclude with confidence that music does, in its own right, elicit objectless versions of everyday affective states.

Music and extra-musical factors: Combined affective response

I am arguing ultimately that when a work of sacred music arouses in the listener an emotion directed towards God (including a desire), the music itself plays an important role in eliciting that emotion. This is a subset of a more general claim: that music can be one of the factors in the listener's experience that helps elicit an emotion directed at more than just the music. Establishing that music can arouse objectless versions of everyday affects is an important part of seeing what can happen phenomenologically when music combines with other factors to arouse emotions with extra-musical objects. The musically elicited affective state will, in such a case, be free to be directed at something else, given the right associations in the mind of the listener; and these could, of course, include religious associations. As well as this, however, I shall argue that even when a piece of music does *not*, just in virtue of the music itself, elicit an affective response (other than Kivy's purely aesthetic emotion), the music can still have a vital role to play in combining with extra-musical factors to elicit emotions directed at extra-musical objects. Thus, whichever sort of experience a listener has in regard to the *desiring* responses considered in the next chapter, something of what I say in what follows will apply to that experience. Let us look at each of these cases in turn, then: first, in which the music itself elicits an objectless version of some everyday affective state; and second, in which it does not.

I. *Musically elicited objectless affects can acquire extra-musical objects*

Once again, Kivy is our target here. Kivy has claimed that even if music *could* elicit objectless versions of everyday affects, those affects could not acquire extra-musical objects. He considers the possibility that while listening to music, one could be led to think about real-life, or at any rate extra-musical, things that could become objects of a musically aroused affect such as joy or sadness.[42] This idea, he thinks, is 'bizarre', since it is incompatible with 'serious' listening: if the listener were to do this, she would lose her concentration on the music.[43] I must say, I cannot help thinking that Kivy's view is the bizarre one here. First, we must note that he does not argue for his claim that musically elicited affects *cannot* acquire extra-musical objects; only that if they do, the listener has become distracted from the music. But even this view is clearly implausible. It *is* possible for non-musical intentional objects to come to mind as one listens to music, thereby becoming *emotional* objects for the musically elicited affects that one feels, and for this to happen *as one concentrates on the music*. This is why music can be cathartic – an entirely familiar experience in which music enables us to feel our emotions about real-life events especially vividly and purely.[44] If something has happened in my life that is a source of joy, and I put on the first movement of Beethoven's Violin Concerto, my joy is given expression and thereby intensified. It would be very strange to say that in this process I have become distracted from the music: my attention to the music is precisely *how* my joy has become intensified.

It seems clear, then, that musically elicited, objectless affects can acquire emotional objects from extra-musical aspects of the listener's experience. A musically elicited affect can colour the listener's awareness enough to be directed at things outside the music, shedding a certain purified, or intensified, affective light on her view of at least parts of the world; and, of course, it helps if those parts of the world were already things towards which she felt that emotion. In particular, a *religious* extra-musical, emotional object (for instance, God conceived in a certain way) – and, indeed, the associations one has to that object – might come from any number of extra-musical sources: straight from the text that is set to music, or from a mixture of the listener's own experiences and thoughts, such as knowledge of the text's original context, experience of the sort of liturgical setting in which the piece could be performed and so on. What I now want to do is to show, through an example, how a musically elicited, objectless affect can combine with a text's religious subject matter – its religious emotional object and the religious emotion heard in the text – to form a deep, multilayered emotional response. The response is qualitatively toned by the extra-musical subject matter as a whole, and directed at that subject matter's intentional object.

The piece is Mozart's well-known setting of Psalm 117, 'Laudate Dominum', which forms part of his *Vesperae Solennes de Confessore*.[45] It is scored for soprano soloist, choir and orchestra, and is a setting of the Latin words of the Psalm, followed by the 'Gloria':

> Laudate Dominum omnes gentes
> Laudate eum, omnes populi
> Quoniam confirmata est
> Super nos misericordia eius,
> Et veritas Domini manet in aeternum.

> Gloria Patri et Filio et Spiritui Sancto.
> Sicut erat in principio, et nunc, et semper.
> Et in saecula saeculorum.
> Amen.

An English rendering is as follows:

> Praise the Lord all nations;
> Praise him, all people.
> For he has bestowed his mercy upon us,
> And the truth of the Lord endures forever.
>
> Glory to the Father and to the Son and to the Holy Spirit.
> As it was in the beginning, and now, and always.
> And for ever and ever.
> Amen.

Mozart's setting of the words is a true delight, with a melody of effortless, radiant joy. On 'Amen', the soloist's voice flows free in a melismatic ascent up the octave as it is liberated in praise, that act in which, as the Christian outlook has it, we humans are able to partake when we are at our freest. In Rowan Williams' words:

> The world [God] has made is designed to become a reconciled world, a world in which diverse human communities come to share a life together because they share the conviction that God has acted to set them free from fear and guilt. ... This reconciliation liberates human voices for praise, for celebrating the glory of the God who has made it possible and has held steadily to his purpose from the beginning.[46]

The words of the Psalm speak clearly of such praise, and yet even for a listener who does not understand Latin, a general knowledge of the theme – including one arising simply from knowing the meaning of the Latin title – would suffice for her listening experience to be religiously infused. Moreover, understanding the connotations of 'praise' or 'laudate' of which Williams writes can introduce a further dimension to the listener's experience of Mozart's piece: it can be heard as expressive of freedom – freedom from the aspects of our dealings with ourselves and others that lead to fear and guilt, and so freedom to recognize God's love, faithfulness and glory, and to respond with gratitude and joy.

Thus, even if the piece's exact text has no role in the listener's experience, her response can have religious content. The religious content of the response to 'Laudate Dominum' that I have begun to sketch involves both conceptual and affective aspects. The conceptual aspect is provided by what can be the barest understanding of the text's subject matter, and by a wider conception of the nature of praise; and this aspect informs how the listener hears and responds to the aesthetic and affective qualities of the music. For she can hear the sheer happiness of the piece as the state for which she and all other humans are made, a God-directed state whose naturalness is embodied in the utterly natural feel of the melody, which sounds as though it had always existed and Mozart had simply to uncover it. She thereby hears the beauty and joy of the music as having a particular religious significance, and her affective response to the music is religiously toned in the following way. Her musically elicited affect of joy combines with the religious subject matter of the text, or at least the text's general theme. The subject matter in question involves two main aspects. First, there is the text's religious emotional object, namely, God. And second, there is the religious emotion heard in the text and nuanced by the wider considerations Williams articulates: an attitude of praise that feels entirely natural and free. In this way, the resulting affective response on the part of the listener is multilayered, qualitatively toned by the extra-musical subject matter as a whole, and directed at that subject matter's intentional object: a joyful feeling of praise for God that is entirely natural and free.

This example, then, shows us one way in which religious associations can influence one's response to a piece of sacred vocal music – and in particular, how those associations can make that response a unified complex that is both affective and conceptual, and about something more than just the music, even if the listener barely understands the text of the piece. Of course, this is not a *temporal* sequence in one's actual experience of the piece, since one never actually feels the pure 'garden-variety' affect that the music can elicit without the text. But the description I have offered does, I believe, express one way in which music can combine with extra-musical subject matter to elicit an emotion directed at something extra-musical: because the music itself (for instance, sung wordlessly) would elicit an objectless, everyday affect and not an emotion directed simply at the music, this affect is free to be coloured by and directed at something else, given the right associations in the mind of the listener.

II. *Even when music does not intrinsically elicit objectless affect, it can combine with extra-musical factors to elicit emotions with extra-musical objects*

I used Mozart's 'Laudate Dominum' to illustrate the phenomenon of a musically elicited, objectless affect acquiring extra-musical content because the piece naturally lends itself to being heard in those terms. Now a piece of music that elicits *desire* for God may or may not work for the listener in the same way as the Mozart example. It may be that the music itself, like Mozart's music, would elicit some sort of objectless affect, which is given specific content by the extra-musical aspects of the listener's experience. Alternatively, the piece may be different from the first case, in *not* eliciting any objectless affect just in virtue of the music; yet I maintain that even in this sort of scenario, the music still has a central role in the desire that is elicited in the listener. Again, extra-musical factors in the listener's experience may bring to her mind extra-musical subject matter, including objects of thought that can also function as emotional objects, and perhaps a particular affective state. And the music can enable a deeply felt emotional response that is qualitatively toned by the extra-musical subject matter as a whole, and directed at that subject matter's intentional object.

To see that when the music does not intrinsically elicit any objectless, ordinary affect, it can still play a vital role in combining with other factors to elicit extra-musical emotion, consider the following. Music set to words is similar in an important respect to phrases spoken in particular tones of voice: in both cases, we experience the intonation and words as a single entity, rather than as two separate things. To claim that it is just the text, and not the music, that elicits an extra-musical emotion would be like saying that something uttered in a particular tone of voice elicits emotion just in virtue of what is uttered, and not in virtue of the tone of voice. But this is clearly wrong. We hear something uttered, and the tone in which it is uttered, as a single entity, that is, the utterance; and the emotion is elicited by this whole entity. Even when a tone of voice *without its accompanying words* would not elicit any particular emotion, it remains the case that the tone of voice *combined* with particular words can elicit an emotion about something other than the utterance itself. Similarly, even if some music abstracted from text would not elicit any affect (other than a purely aesthetic emotion), this does not undermine the view that when combined with text, such music can help elicit emotion directed at something beyond the music. We hear music and text as a single entity, and emotion is therefore elicited by the whole combined entity.

It is important to get clear on the structure of this argument. I am *not* arguing as follows: (a) tones of voice combine with words to be heard as single entities with those words; (b) music is like tones of voice; therefore, (c) music combines with words to be heard as a single entity with them, and thereby elicits emotion as a single entity with the words. This is obviously invalid: the premises leave open the possibility that music is like tones of voice in some way other than combining with words to be heard as a single entity with them. Rather, I maintain that the first part of the conclusion to that argument stands without any need of justification: it is just obvious that music and text can at least sometimes be heard as a single entity. As the philosopher R. G. Collingwood once put the point:

> Words and music [should] form an inseparable unity, the words as it were generating the music by an apparently invisible process, and the music in turn reflecting a new light on the words, completing their significance, and reinforcing their emotional import.[47]

Referring to tones of voice illustrates the results of this sort of experience in another case: hearing words and tone of voice as a single entity makes it the case that any emotion elicited when hearing them is elicited by the two combined. This makes clearer the implication in the case of music and words: emotions are elicited by the whole music-text entity. When words are set to music well, the music reinforces the emotional import of the words. All this will be illustrated amply in the next chapter.

Let me sum up the argument so far. Kivy claimed that music can arouse only a special 'aesthetic' emotion – from which it would follow that music can have nothing to do with eliciting emotions directed at anything other than the music. This would render false the intuitively plausible view that when works of sacred music elicit emotions directed at God or the sacred, the *musical* aspect plays a vital part. I have argued, against Kivy (and Hanslick), that music can combine with other aspects of the listener's experience to arouse fully fledged emotions with extra-musical objects – and in particular, religious objects. I have urged that this can happen in two ways. First, through the example of Mozart's 'Laudate Dominum', I showed how a musically elicited objectless affect can acquire extra-musical content, including God as the emotional object. And second, through the analogy with tones of voice, I argued that even if music fails in a particular instance to elicit *in its own right* any affective response, it can, nonetheless, combine with extra-musical factors – especially text – to elicit emotions with extra-musical objects. In both types of cases, the music contributes to the affectivity of the listener's response, and other factors (for example the text, or even just a general and fragmentary understanding of the piece's theme) give the response conceptual content, making it about something in particular. Thus, whichever kind of experience one might have in feeling a *desire* for God in response to a work of sacred music, the music has a central role to play in that desire – *contra* Kivy and Hanslick.

The reader will notice that I have not paid much attention in the foregoing to religious desire; nor have I considered the possibility of responding to 'Laudate Dominum' in the ways I describe while lacking propositional religious belief.

This may seem odd given that these topics will be the focus of the following chapters, but my purpose here was simply to demonstrate the aspects of musical response that will be important in the desiring responses I consider later. I will not labour the point by explicitly drawing out these aspects in relation to each piece discussed in the next chapter, but I trust it will become clear that they apply in each case. As I have already noted (Chapter 2), desiring something *is* possible without believing in the reality of the desire's object – including, we shall see, desiring God in response to music.

The main body of my response to Kivy is now complete. I shall end this chapter by extending the foregoing discussion in two ways, which will be relevant in the chapters that follow.

4.3 Mirroring responses and analogous affects

A key lesson of the foregoing is that we can have our affective states shaped by listening to music. One way in which this can happen is through what Ridley calls a 'mirroring response' – another name for the concept of 'emotional contagion' to which we saw Young refer earlier. In the empirical evidence I cited for music's arousing of ordinary affects, we saw especially clearly that there are times when listeners neither dispassionately note the affects of which a piece of music is expressive, nor – contrary to Kivy's view – find themselves moved by this expressiveness as an instance of purely aesthetic emotion. Rather, at these times the listener's affective state comes to reflect the affects she hears in the music[48] – or, indeed, in the music and text combined.[49] I noted earlier that changes in posture and facial expression, and proprioception of corresponding physiological changes, might plausibly be how emotional contagion occurs. However, as I explained near the start of the chapter, it does not matter how it happens, as long as it does. I should note in passing that asserting that emotional contagion can take place does not commit me to a view that Kivy rightly challenges,[50] namely that music possesses emotional properties in virtue of arousing those emotions in the listener. According to the way in which we ordinarily use emotion terms about music, to ascribe an emotional property to music is to say that the music is *expressive of* that emotion. It may also arouse that emotion, but this is not an essential part of the music's possessing the emotional property.

If my arguments are to hold in relation to the pieces I consider in the following chapters, it is of course vital for the listener to feel *some* emotion, and specifically some form of desire for God, on listening to each of those pieces. However, sometimes on listening to a piece of music the affects we feel are not exactly what we hear in the piece; and, moreover, they need not be exactly the same in order for the desiring responses considered in future chapters to have epistemic import. In the next chapter, I will discuss in more detail the issue of negative emotion in music – why such emotions, when appropriated by the listener, are not unpleasant as they are in real life – in relation to one of the pieces I consider: Purcell's *Hear My Prayer, O Lord*. I flag the issue here to reassure the reader that this issue will receive treatment insofar as it applies to my argument. We may feel only something of an emotion of which a musical work is expressive, or we may come to grasp what an emotion is about without feeling it in its entirety. Such is the response I will consider in relation to Purcell's piece in the next chapter.

4.4 Qualities of affective life

Finally, let us consider music's ability to be expressive of affects that, when appropriated by the listener, can constitute 'qualities of affective life'. Mark Wynn, following Ridley, describes these as affective senses of the world's significance that are constituted by the kinds of affective response to which one is predisposed in general.[51] Clearly, if the desires for God I shall discuss are to have any lasting significance for the desirer, then they must infuse one's general attitudes and lived experience – for only then will they shape the desirer to be open to God in a way that is more than sporadic and temporary. A key question, though, is what sorts of affective state can come to constitute a quality of affective life. One view, held by Wynn, is that the capacity to constitute a quality of affective life is a feature specifically of objectless affects: with no emotional object, an affective state can colour one's experience quite generally. Wynn is therefore focused on 'pure' or 'absolute' music (controversial though the notion is). Following Ridley and Davies, he maintains that 'absolute' music cannot be expressive of affects that are *about* anything in particular. Here the 'resemblance' theory of musical expressiveness is the underlying assumption: the movements of bodies that music must resemble in order to be expressive cannot denote any particular states of affairs.[52] Musically heard affects are thus, on this view, general moods, such as joy and sadness, rather than precise emotions such as remorse or grief. They lack any reference to particular states of affairs or narrative structures. Instead, when felt, they infuse our experience in a relatively general way;[53] and this, Wynn urges, enables them to constitute qualities of affective life.[54] The upshot is that music's ability to be expressive of and elicit affects that can constitute qualities of affective life depends on its being expressive of, and eliciting, objectless moods rather than object-directed emotions.

Wynn is right in one respect, I think, but there is an aspect of his view that I want to question. It does seem plausible that objectless affects are apt for becoming qualities of affective life. If a quality of affective life consists in the kinds of affective response to which one is generally disposed, then it will typically involve a certain affective colouring of the rest of one's experience; and this colouring may well *in itself* lack any particular object. Instead, it may be a way of experiencing whatever objects of thought one happens to have. However, I question the jump from this claim to the claim that qualities of affective life are *by nature* objectless – and, thus, that if one's affective response to a piece of music is directed at an object, then it cannot come to constitute a quality of affective life. In particular, it certainly seems possible for an object-directed desire to infuse one's experience in general. An entirely common example is romantic desire: anyone who has been in such a state knows that it colours one's experience in general, predisposing one to affective states such as excitement or joy (if the prospects seem good) or dejection (if they do not). And clearly desire for God can do similar things to one's lived experience. Witness the numerous expressions of such pervasive affective states in the Psalms. In Psalm 119, for instance, we read:

> My soul is consumed with longing for your rules at all times. ... Remember your word to your servant, in which you have made me hope. This is my comfort in my affliction, that your promise gives me life.[55]

The comfort of God's life-giving promise seems to permeate the psalmist's times of affliction in a general way: it is something to which he repeatedly returns. Moreover, this is in the context of an all-pervasive longing for God's rules – for the way of life that the psalmist believes God to have commanded. Or, again, consider Psalm 42, wherein the psalmist cries:

> My soul thirsts for God, for the living God. When shall I come and appear before God? My tears have been my food day and night, while they say to me all the day long, 'Where is your God?'

And just a little later:

> Why are you cast down, O my soul, and why are you in turmoil within me? Hope in God; for I shall again praise him, my salvation and my God.[56]

The desire and desperation here are pervasive – 'my food day and night'. But, crucially, the psalmist proceeds to urge himself to return to the hope and praise that he has previously inhabited. Such hope and praise are an affective state, directed towards God, to which the psalmist *aspires* to be disposed: in the Psalm itself, we see the conscious cultivation of a quality of affective life. As if to reinforce the point, the refrain beginning at 'Why are you cast down, O my soul' is repeated at the very end of the Psalm. This, then (assuming the Psalm was written to be set to music), is an illuminating example of the music-centred cultivation of a quality of affective life for which I want to argue.[57] In the next chapter, we will encounter musical works that (through both music and text) are expressive of, and can arouse, desire for God – a type of object-directed emotion. And these desires can very much come to constitute a quality of affective life: one directed towards God, which also infuses the desirer's lived experience in general and thereby contributes to her openness to God.

It is now time to apply the discussion of the foregoing two chapters to the central concern of this study, as we enter the heart of our argument. In the next chapter, I will apply the conclusions I have reached – about the epistemic capacity of a certain sort of desire, and about music's capacity to elicit just this sort of desire – to four examples of sacred music.

5

Sacred music and knowledge by desire: The account applied

And so the yearning strong,
With which the soul will long,
Shall far outpass the power of human telling
                From the hymn *Come Down, O Love Divine*[1]

Although the human yearning for God may 'far outpass the power of human telling', there is also a great deal that can usefully be said about it. Equipped with our conclusions regarding music and desire in general, we are now in a position to turn our attention fully to sacred music and desire for God. In this chapter, I will take the outcomes of the investigation so far and apply them to four pieces of sacred music. These are Henry Purcell's *Hear My Prayer, O Lord*, Josef Rheinberger's *Abendlied* and settings of the Nunc Dimittis by Charles Villiers Stanford and Herbert Howells. They are all settings of biblical texts: Purcell's piece contains the first verse of Psalm 102; Rheinberger sets to music a short passage of the 'road to Emmaus' story in Luke's Gospel;[2] and the Nunc Dimittis is, of course, another passage from Luke, spoken by Simeon on seeing the infant Jesus at the temple in Jerusalem.[3] The reader might wonder why I have chosen these four in particular, out of the large amount of sacred music that can be heard as expressive of desire for God.[4] I make no claim that these four pieces are in any sense among the 'best' at eliciting the sorts of desire with which I am concerned: such a claim about any piece would be impossible to justify. But, taken as a whole, the pieces here do have several features that make them apt illustrations of my general claim that sacred music can elicit knowledge-enabling desire for God.

First, they are all staples of the choral repertoire, and are therefore likely to be familiar to a good many people; this will be especially true of those who have some contact with the choral world, for example as singers, attendees at choral services, or concertgoers. *Hear My Prayer, O Lord* and *Abendlied* are classics that would be at home either in a concert setting or in liturgy – for instance, as anthems at evensong. The settings of the Nunc Dimittis by Stanford and Howells are especially well known in the Anglican Church, being established parts of the tradition of choral music composed for the Anglican liturgy – again, in this case, for evensong.

The second reason why these four pieces work well as illustrations is that there are a number of interesting comparisons to be made between the forms of desire, and hence the knowledge content, that the pieces can plausibly engender in the listener. This is most obviously the case with the two settings of the Nunc Dimittis, which are similar in some respects and significantly different in others. But as we shall see, the Purcell and Rheinberger works also have interesting comparisons and contrasts in the kinds of desire for God of which they are expressive, and in the kinds that, plausibly, they can thereby elicit.

Third, the pieces here represent a broad time span and variety of styles. Purcell (c. 1659–1695) was writing in the middle part of the baroque period, with *Hear My Prayer, O Lord* composed around 1682. Rheinberger (1839–1901) was active in the romantic era, *Abendlied* appearing in its final form in 1873. Stanford (1852–1924) spanned the latter part of the romantic era and the first part of the twentieth century: the Morning, Communion and Evening Service in G, of which the Nunc Dimittis in G discussed here is a part, appeared in 1902. Finally, Howells (1892–1983), Stanford's one-time student, was active in the twentieth century: the Evening Canticles of his *Collegium Regale*[5] service, from which the Nunc Dimittis here is taken, appeared in 1945. Thus, while these can obviously be no more than snapshots of the periods represented, and while I have missed out the Classical period entirely (though it was represented in the previous chapter), I aim to show in my examples that being expressive of desire for God is a long-standing feature of Western choral music.[6] What I say about each piece will illustrate how desire can work epistemically in a religious context, and the general epistemic components would therefore apply to many other specific forms of religious desire – including those elicited by other works of sacred music.

This chapter, then, will take the following shape. Given the subject matter of what is to come, it will first be necessary to look briefly at a concern that various parts of the church have raised in one form or another about the relationship between music and religiosity. This is that sacred music can distract from the words that are set to it, leading listeners to lose sight of the proper focus of their engagement. This worry may seem well placed given my overt focus on the emotional power of sacred music, and while there is no room here for a detailed discussion of the issue, I hope that what I say will sufficiently assuage any concerns the reader may have.

Having done this, I will turn to the four pieces mentioned above. Through a series of short musical analyses, I will point to some of the key features in virtue of which each piece can be heard as expressive of a particular form of desire for God, and can thereby elicit a particular form of desire in the listener or singer. For each of these forms of desire, I will then apply the epistemology developed in Chapter 3. It is important to be clear on what I aim to do in my accounts of possible responses to the music. These accounts are not primarily *descriptive*. If they do describe the responses that a good many people would have on listening to the pieces in question, then that is all to the good. However, each account of a possible response will be primarily two things. First, it will be a description of a conditional kind: a description of how one might plausibly respond to the piece in question *if* one were to focus on the musical features that I highlight. Second, and more fundamentally, each description will carry normative weight: each will be a *suggestion* in how to listen to the piece in question, pointing to a certain kind of value to be gained from the listening experience. I make these points so as to avoid confusion over the nature of my discussion: this is not an empirical study in how people do, in fact, respond to sacred music, but rather an exercise in highlighting how certain pieces of music have the potential to contribute to the cultivation of desire for God.

5.1 Music and religious devotion: A recurring concern in the church

Over the course of its history, the church has had a complicated relationship with music to say the least, and a worry that has reared its head repeatedly in one form or another is that sacred music can distract from the words that are set to it, making listeners lose sight of the true goal of Christian worship. Augustine, for instance, expressed concern at the possibility of 'the music mov[ing] me more than the subject of the song',[7] and the concern was echoed by Puritans more than a millennium later.[8] Moreover, with the advent of increasingly complex forms of polyphony in Roman Catholicism from the High Middle Ages onwards, ecclesiastical leaders became increasingly worried that the music was obscuring the text, rendering the latter incomprehensible.[9] This led the Council of Trent in 1562 to specify that musical settings of sacred texts should enable the words to be 'clearly understood by all', rather than giving 'empty pleasure to the ear'.[10]

Two points should suffice to defuse this worry for our purposes. The first concerns the idea that even if words which are set to music are *not* thereby obscured, one's affective response to the music can still distract from those words. This is essentially an inversion of Kivy's view, encountered in the previous chapter, that in coming to focus on extra-musical things while listening to music, one loses concentration on the music. The general worry is that it is difficult to focus simultaneously on both music and extra-musical things, such as words. I suppose some people *may* find this difficult; it seems to be something with which Augustine struggled, and Kivy after him. However, clearly much more evidence would be needed in order to claim that it is a widespread problem – widespread enough to warrant the banning of music in the church so as to prevent large numbers of people from being distracted from sacred texts by the music to which they are set. Furthermore, given the arguments of the previous chapter, there are good reasons to hold that a natural kind of response to musical settings of text is the exact opposite, that is, an affective response that is elicited by a combination of music and words. Indeed, Augustine himself acknowledged such a possibility: he claimed that 'when sacred words are chanted well', they can kindle the listener to piety more religiously, and with warmer devotion, than when they are not so sung.[11] (One is also tempted to urge Augustine not to be so hard on himself: he reports that when the music moves him more than the subject of the song, 'I confess myself to commit a sin deserving punishment'.[12] A somewhat lighter attitude would not have gone amiss.) This kind of affective power in music – involving the ability to combine with words to elicit a deeper response than the words alone would elicit – is one for which the Council of Trent also expressed its preference. It did not ban polyphony outright (so long as the words were 'clearly understood by all'), and supported certain kinds of emotional power possessed by sacred music: in particular, the power to elicit 'the desire of heavenly harmonies, in the contemplation of the joys of the blessed'.[13] It is precisely this 'combined' type of response to music and text that will be my focus when I discuss the desiring responses to the four pieces I have mentioned.

The second point to make in response to the 'musical distraction' worry concerns the possibility that occupied the Council of Trent: that texts might be obscured by the music to which they are set. The musical examples I have chosen all set their texts clearly, and thus, if the listener understands the language of each piece, her desiring responses will be shaped by her understanding of the texts. However, as I showed in the previous chapter's discussion of Mozart's 'Laudate Dominum', such 'textual shaping' does not require the listener to understand every word set to the music: one's response can be shaped even by knowing just the general theme of the text. Hence, even if one does not understand the text when one hears it set to music – either because one does not understand the language or because the text is obscured by elaborate musical polyphony – one's response can still be informed by the text's subject matter. It should be clear, then, that the responses I describe in the following discussion are not a matter of 'empty pleasure'. My whole epistemological argument depends on the possibility of responding to sacred music with a desire that is both affectively deepened by the music and conceptually nuanced by the text's subject matter. It is this sort of desire that can aid religious openness in the way I have been describing.

5.2 The epistemology applied: Desire for God in four works of sacred music

Let me very briefly recap, from Chapter 3, the kind of epistemic importance of desire that is my focus. In desiring something in some particular capacity, one can often sense what would constitute satisfaction – based on past experience at least analogous to that satisfaction. One thereby knows what the desire's object would be like in bringing about the satisfaction in question, where this knowledge involves a vivid sense of the importance that object has for oneself. The characteristics of the desire's object that one knows about through the desire are those that would bring about the projected satisfaction. Thus, if the object of desire is real and is as the desire characterizes it, then, through desiring it, one knows something about it in respect of how one perceives the characteristics in question to be personally significant. In what follows, I aim to demonstrate that desire for God can bear enough phenomenological similarity to Chapter 3's non-religious cases for there to be such a thing as desire-based knowledge about God.

In its most general guise, a religious desire might be described as a longing for 'something more' – the sense of restlessness Augustine famously captured: 'Our heart is restless until it rests in you.'[14] But this general spiritual longing cannot intrinsically include a sense of what it would take to be satisfied, since it is not precise enough. A longing for the divine could take any number of forms. One might experience something deeply beautiful that seems to hint at a greater beauty, a beauty for which one yearns but which seems to lie beyond human experience. One may long to feel loved with a love that is deeper and more perfect than any human love. Perhaps one may feel a profound need to entrust one's life and the lives of others to someone in whom those lives will find their most profound fulfilment and joy. It is certainly possible to feel the general restlessness of which Augustine wrote, and yearn for some sort of transcendence without having specified the nature of the yearning in any detail. But just as in the non-religious cases of Chapter 3, in order for religious yearning to enable the kind of knowledge about God that is our concern, one must have a sense (even if only a dim sense) of what it would take for the yearning to be satisfied. The yearning must take a particular form. In each case that follows, that form – that is, the capacity in which one desires God – is shaped by the conceptual dimension of the desire; and this, in turn, is shaped by the textual subject matter of each piece. Without further ado, then, let us finally turn to our musical examples.

5.3 Purcell's *Hear My Prayer, O Lord*

The piece and its expressiveness

Hear My Prayer, O Lord,[15] composed around 1682, is part of a larger work that Purcell apparently never completed. Nonetheless, it is remarkably powerful in its own right. The piece can be heard as *expressive of* a particular form of longing for God, thereby *eliciting* in the listener a corresponding form of longing. Based on the longing the piece elicits in her, the listener can reflect on, and form a sense of, what it may take to be satisfied in the longing of which the piece is expressive. The listener thereby vividly knows about God in the capacity of satisfying the longing she hears in the piece – a vividness of knowledge that she would lack if she merely had this longing described to her. Let us unpack each of these elements of the piece's engendering of desire-based religious knowledge.

The words of the piece are the opening of Psalm 102: 'Hear my prayer, O Lord, and let my crying come unto thee.' They paint a picture of desperation 'before the Lord':[16] a longing for God in the midst of one's distress, in the capacity of compassionately hearing and being present. 'Incline your ear to me; answer me speedily in the day when I call!'[17] the Psalm continues. Purcell's setting of the text is nothing short of extraordinary, giving the desperation in the words a profound, heart-rending depth.

The piece, which is for eight vocal parts, starts with just a single melodic line: the first altos sing 'Hear my prayer, O Lord' to a sparse, two-note melody in C minor low in their register – a lone, understated plea for help. The music unfolds and the texture thickens; the pain of the psalmist is laid bare for brief moments that are especially dissonant, a striking example of which occurs about halfway through when a G dominant seventh chord clashes with an A-flat in the top soprano line. Most of the piece passes in an uneasy ebb and flow of polyphony, with parts dropping in and out as the tension builds. Eleven bars from the end we start to approach the climax, the first basses beginning a line that moves on to a long-held dominant G, over which the other parts propel the cry towards its last, anguished moments. The piece culminates in an almost primal howl of pain heard in the very geography of the music: three bars from the end, we hear a repeat of the aforementioned dissonance consisting in a G dominant seventh chord clashing with an A-flat; but this time the A-flat is sung by one of the alto parts, leaving the top sopranos to sing an F almost three octaves above the bottom basses' low G. The sheer expanse of the chord's range conveys the sheer depth of desperation that can now be heard in those opening words of Psalm 102. The torment is further conveyed by two tritones – one of the most dissonant intervals in Western music – each between notes that are next to each other in the chord. By eliciting a desire for musical resolution, this dissonant variation on the dominant seventh theme is expressive of a desire for *religious* resolution. In the climax, then, we hear in its most *directed* form the desperation that moves through the piece as a whole. Those final moments are most clearly expressive of that aspect of the desperation that consists in a yearning for satisfaction. Here, then, can be heard especially clearly the form the desperation must take if it is to enable knowledge about God. With the final *come*, the music reaches its wits' end as the last pained, dissonant cry is wrought from the psalmist's lips, before the tension is resolved, exhausted, on to an open-fifth chord in C that dies away into silence.

Desire heard and desire aroused

Of course, *real* desperation cannot be elicited simply by a piece of music, since no piece of music can bring about the distress that is central to desperation (one would hope not, at any rate). So although this piece is *expressive of* a yearning for God in the midst of desperation, there is still the question of how it can influence the listener's affective state. The answer, I suggest, is that while Purcell's piece cannot elicit the desperation of which it is expressive, it can lead us as listeners to empathize with the psalmist, thereby recognizing our capacity for this kind of desperation. And this is true of anyone: because of the generality of the text that Purcell uses, whatever circumstances are ruled out or allowed by the shape of a listener's particular life, the depth of desperation in Purcell's piece is one that the listener has the capacity to feel, simply by being human. Moreover, at least for some listeners, the recognition of this capacity for desperation can follow the text. It is possible to recognize within oneself the capacity to reach out at certain times beyond anything encompassed in the natural world; and for the interested non-believer as described in Chapter 2, this 'something more' will likely be the God portrayed in the piece – the God of Jewish and Christian tradition.

The nature of this affective recognition of our capacity for desperation is hinted at in some remarks by Stephen Davies and Aaron Ridley on the difference between our felt responses to music and those feelings as they occur in response to life events. Both Davies and Ridley hold that the affects of which music in its own right is expressive lack material objects: they are not *about* any states of affairs.[18] As such, they are moods such as happiness and sadness, rather than emotions that require states of affairs, such as grief, relief, or desperation.[19] Feelings such as happiness or sadness *can* be directed at states of affairs, but they do not have to be. This means that if the listener feels whatever affect she hears in the music, her experience in this feeling can be abstracted from any particular state of affairs, and can thus be of a different quality to versions of those feelings that *are* directed at states of affairs. For Ridley, this helps explain why we choose to listen to sad music. Feeling sad on listening to sad music need not be an unpleasant experience, because unlike emotions such as grief, desperation or a sadness that *is* directed at some state of affairs, the sadness aroused by the music need not refer to any unpleasant circumstances in the listener's life.[20] Davies, meanwhile, notes that the affects aroused by music are 'uncluttered by the motives, desires, and the need to act that are their usual accompaniments',[21] since they lack the context that usually gives affects their action-guiding character.

How do these reflections relate to the recognition of our capacity for desperation before God that, I have suggested, Purcell's piece can elicit? This recognition does have one sort of emotional object: it is about God. It is a recognition of our capacity to feel desperation *for* God; hence, it is an emotion, and not simply an objectless mood. But it lacks another sort of emotional object: because neither Purcell's music nor the psalmist's text refers to any unfortunate circumstance, the piece provides no circumstantial context for the listener's affective response to be *about*.[22] Therefore, like the musically aroused sadness of which Ridley writes, the affective response to *Hear My Prayer, O Lord* that I am describing is not unpleasant: unlike true desperation, it is not felt about an unpleasant state of affairs in the listener's life. Moreover, Davies' description of musically aroused affects holds true here: this kind of response to Purcell's piece lacks the motives, desires and need to act that accompany real desperation.

The response I have in mind, then, is an *analogue* of desperation: by recognizing our capacity for desperation before God, we experience something of that desperation without feeling it fully. We do *not*, as Geoffrey Madell has suggested regarding unpleasant emotions in music, feel desperation and simultaneously take pleasure in feeling it.[23] The affective response to Purcell's piece I have described can be pleasurable; real desperation cannot be pleasurable. The feeling on listening to Purcell's piece is very different from real desperation. We recognize something of ourselves in the cry of the psalmist, made especially vivid and immediate in the musical ways I described. We thereby grasp enough of the nature of the psalmist's desperation to form some sense of what it would take to be satisfied were we to experience the real thing. The phenomenology of such a sense will be based on past experience of that satisfaction, or on analogous experience – the latter typically coming from interpersonal relationships in which another human being has provided comfort and support in a time of distress. This projected satisfaction, in turn, enables knowledge about the God for whom the psalmist's desperate yearning is felt, in the capacity of bringing about the satisfaction. It is to these matters that I now turn.

Satisfaction of the desperation: 'That peace which the world cannot give'

What would constitute satisfaction of the desperation before God of which Purcell's piece is expressive? Notwithstanding the aforementioned similarity with human support, we can start by noticing that there would be something profoundly misplaced about asking another human being to bear one's suffering on this sort of scale, however familiar to the sufferer or professionally well qualified he or she might be. The depth and expanse of desperation that can be heard in Purcell's piece go beyond what any human could assuage. Rather, the desperation for God would be satisfied in 'that peace which the world cannot give', to borrow from the Book of Common Prayer.[24] What might this mean, exactly? Unless we have a rather crude, nay, demonstrably false, notion of divine action in the world, we cannot expect much to change in the external state of things as a direct result of a desperate prayer. Instead, the satisfaction or assuaging of desperation before God will, if it comes, most likely consist in a *certain kind of perspective*, a certain kind of view of the situation. The peace of which Jesus, in John's Gospel, says 'Not as the world gives do I give to you'[25] must be seen as a peace arising from the conviction that no matter how painful or horrific a situation is, there is still cause for hope.

The writer Francis Spufford has recently described an especially powerful experience in this vein. At the time he was in a state of desperation of the intense kind that concerns us here – specifically, a guilt-ridden state in which 'you stop making sense to yourself'.[26] Eventually, after sitting for a while on a church pew without expecting anything in particular, he found himself enveloped by a sense of

> hav[ing] been shown the authentic bad news about myself, in a perspective which is so different from the tight focus of my desperation that it is good news in itself; I have been shown that though I may see myself in the grim optics of sorrow and self-dislike, I am being seen all the while ... with a generosity wider than oceans ... I have been enabled ... to participate a little bit in the freedom of a feeling that flows beyond, behind, beneath, around [my desperation].[27]

Spufford finds his suffering permeated by hope, a hope grounded in his being 'made unfamiliar to [him]self'.[28] That is, he sees that there are aspects of his situation – aspects of *himself* – that he had previously missed, even if he does not yet know exactly what those aspects are. This does not take away from the facts about himself that drove him to his state of confused desperation. Instead, he senses that he is generously being shown that those facts are not all that there are, and hence that there are possibilities for transformation.

Or as another, far more drastic, example of the hopeful kind of perspective that a sufferer can adopt as a result of sensing God at work, consider the case of Etty Hillesum. A young Dutch Jewish woman living in the midst of the Holocaust, Etty witnessed some of the most appalling suffering imaginable; and yet, by the religious faith and practice of silent prayer that she nurtured, she managed to retain a deep, inexhaustible joy. In one of her letters, she writes about the 'indescribable' misery in the transit camp at Westerbork, before going on to say:

> And yet, late at night ... I often walk with a spring in my step along the barbed wire. And then, time and again, it soars straight from my heart – I can't help it, that's just the way it is, like some elementary force – the feeling that life is glorious and magnificent, and that one day we shall be building a whole new world.[29]

Patrick Woodhouse observes:

> Etty Hillesum found within herself an indestructible source of life and goodness and beauty that was greater and deeper and more enduring than all the terrible death and hatred which surrounded her, and which was eventually to engulf her.[30]

She also writes of feeling, 'at unguarded moments', profoundly, maternally comforted: 'Her arms around me are so gentle and protective.'[31] In other words, Etty Hillesum, like Francis Spufford, fully recognized the 'bad news' about her situation, fully recognized the pain and suffering that it involved; and yet, like Spufford, she was able to view her situation with a peace and hope that arose from the conviction that it was not this suffering, but rather God's life and love, that would have the last word.

I should emphasize that nowhere am I making any claim as to whether or not experiences of this kind are *veridical*, revealing what they seem to reveal to those who have them. Rather, I have included these two examples in order to illustrate the sort of thing it would take to be satisfied in the desperate yearning that can be heard in Purcell's piece. This satisfaction would consist in a hope and peace that permeate the experience of, and sustain, the sufferer who is open and trusting before God. With this in mind, we can now ask: What attributes would God need in order to bring about this satisfaction? What attributes does one come to know about vividly through this desperate yearning – or through experiencing something of the yearning through music – if one has the sense I have described of what it would take to be satisfied?

The desire's characterization of God

In general terms, the source of the satisfaction's hope and peace must have unlimited resourcefulness of the kind that Rowan Williams has described: the power to '[open] the door to a future even when we can see no hope.'[32] Or, again:

> There is nowhere God is absent, powerless or irrelevant; no situation in the universe in the face of which God is at a loss ... God always has the capacity to do something fresh and different, to bring something new out of a situation.[33]

Crucial to this capacity are the ability to see reasons for hope even in a situation that looks hopeless to human eyes, and the power to convey this hope to the sufferer. While this conveying could in theory be an entirely cool and affectionless transmission of information, this is not what most of us feel the need for in desperate situations. We long to be affectionately held; we long to feel we are loved. So in conveying hope in a way that would satisfy someone who is desperate, God must intimately convey a love that holds even in the worst possible situations – the 'steadfast love' we find written about time and again in the Hebrew Bible, especially in the Psalms.[34] And in actual situations in which people have come to feel the hope and peace that satisfy desperation before God, this intimate conveying of steadfast love is, indeed, what we find. In the two cases considered, for example, the very reasons for hope are closely connected with the sufferer's sense of God's intimate love. Spufford came to feel that there were hopeful possibilities beyond his 'grim optics of sorrow and self-dislike', possibilities that existed because of the 'generosity wider than oceans' with which he sensed that God saw him 'in some wholly accurate and complete way'[35] – in the most intimate way possible. 'To be seen like that is … the essential beginning of forgiveness.'[36] And the hope with which Etty Hillesum found herself filled – encapsulated in 'the feeling … that one day we shall be building a whole new world' – seems to have stemmed at least partly from her sense of life, even in the horrors of the camp, as a 'glorious and magnificent' gift from God, given in an act of boundlessly generous love:

> My life has become an uninterrupted dialogue with You, oh God. … Sometimes when I stand in some corner of the camp, my feet planted on Your earth, my eyes raised towards Your heaven, tears sometimes run down my face, tears of deep emotion and gratitude.[37]

Her conviction that, as Woodhouse puts it, 'the beauty and gift of life … [are] so much greater than all this horror'[38] was a profoundly hopeful one, implying as it did that despite everything, there was still joy to be had and to be given. Moreover, as we have seen from her sense of maternal comfort, she experienced this source of life, goodness and beauty with great intimacy: 'No one is in their clutches who is in Your arms.'[39]

Let us bring together the strands of our discussion regarding Purcell's piece. The form of yearning of which *Hear My Prayer, O Lord* is expressive is conceptually influenced by the text: it is desperation of a general kind, with no specified context. But although the desperation in the piece lacks a context and thus a state of affairs to be about, it is experienced 'before the LORD'; and it therefore does have an object: it is desperation for God in a certain capacity. I described some of the ways in which Purcell's music can be heard to draw out the profound, heart-rending nature of the opening words of Psalm 102, before going on to discuss the kind of affective response to the music that interests us. Using the kind of response described by Davies and Ridley as a parallel, I suggested that although Purcell's music cannot elicit real-life desperation before God, it can elicit an analogue of this desperation. The analogue is an affective recognition of one's own capacity for the desperation in the piece, and thus, potentially, a recognition of one's disposition to reach out at certain times towards a realm transcending the natural world. We might say it is a yearning recognition of a deeply rooted need, a need made fully manifest in times of crisis; and through this recognition, one affectively grasps something of the nature of the psalmist's desperate longing for God, without feeling it fully.

Based on this experience, one can form a sense of what would constitute satisfaction of the desperate yearning in Purcell's piece (drawing on past experience at least analogous to that satisfaction), and arrive at some conclusions about what God would have to be like in order to bring about the satisfaction. Using the real-life narratives of Francis Spufford and Etty Hillesum as illustrations, I argued that God would need unlimited resourcefulness: specifically, the ability to see more reasons for hope in a situation than any human could ever see, and the power to convey this hope to the sufferer in intimate, steadfast love. Through responding to Purcell's piece in the way I have described, then, one's notions of attributes such as 'deeply resourceful', 'loving' and 'supportive' acquire a hue of emotional significance in light of the desire that one empathetically grasps, and one's sense of what would constitute satisfaction. One knows how those attributes matter to oneself in a religious context, and one thereby knows with a particular existential sharpness something of what God's nature would be in satisfying the yearning. Thus, if God is real and has that nature then one knows something about God through desiring him, in terms of his importance to oneself.

5.4 Rheinberger's *Abendlied*

Music, text and context

Let us now turn to the second of our pieces whose affective expressiveness can elicit desire for God. *Abendlied*[40] ('evening song') is based on a piece that Rheinberger wrote when he was about sixteen, and was eventually published in its final form in 1873. It is in F major and for six vocal parts, and its German text is from Lk. 24.29: 'Bleib bei uns, denn es will Abend werden, und der Tag hat sich geneiget' ('Stay with us, for it is towards evening and the day is now far spent'). In context, it is what the two disciples on the road to Emmaus say to the risen Christ when they do not yet recognize him. He has been expounding to them what the scriptures say about himself, and when they reach their destination they invite him to stay with them rather than leaving him to continue on his way.[41] Unlike the text of *Hear My Prayer, O Lord*, these words from Luke do not clearly depict just one form of desire. In Purcell's piece, the form of the desire conveyed is shaped in its essence by the text, while the music intensifies and deepens the expression of this desire. In contrast, the form of yearning that we can discern in *Abendlied* depends not only on the words but also on their original scriptural context, on the context in which the piece is sometimes sung and on the music itself.

When set to Rheinberger's music, perhaps the most obvious way to hear the words is as a plea for loving presence and protection throughout the night. This is especially true given that the piece is sometimes sung during Compline, and given that very similar words form part of the service's conclusion ('Abide with us, Lord Jesus, for the night is at hand and the day is now past'[42]). And extending the meaning symbolically, the words can be heard as a plea for protection in times of metaphorical darkness – in the nights we must all suffer. However, the sheer desperation of Purcell's piece is nowhere to be heard here. Instead, the music is full of long, aching phrases and rich suspensions, creating a sense of warm, tender longing.

We hear this from the very first musical phrase, in which the first sopranos climb to a high F, which they sing for three long syllables ('A-bend wer') before coming to rest temporarily in an imperfect cadence. This is achieved via a suspended fourth as they move eventually on to the E of a C major chord – only to continue their descent as they dissonantly propel the piece forward with a D sung against the second sopranos' held C. The next section largely consists of imitation between parts, including a rising and falling motif on 'denn es will Abend' sung at different pitches by all voices, until a semitone clash between the second sopranos' A and the first sopranos' B-flat leads into a rich plagal cadence in B-flat major, in which the first sopranos soar to a high G for the subdominant E-flat major chord. The music conveys a call, certainly; and there is urgency provided by the altos' appearance of the aforementioned melodic motif which drives the cadence to its resolution, before another dissonance leads to a D major chord that functions as an imperfect cadence in the new key of G minor. Yet, as well as this urgency, there is a warmth and gentleness here that would be entirely out of place in the Purcell piece. The next few bars contain more imitation between parts, this time to the words 'und der Tag hat sich geneiget'. The way the music is written allows different voices to emerge from the texture at various points, perhaps the most notable instance of which is in how the two soprano parts combine: on 'geneiget', a long G in the second sopranos ascends to a C before moving downwards again – forming, in combination with the first sopranos' held E-flat, a plaintive cry at the 'inclining' of the day towards night (a rough translation of 'geneiget'). After a return to the original key of F major and a near repeat of the first musical phrase, the piece comes round again to 'und der

Tag hat sich geneiget' as its yearning gently rises and falls in intensity – including a repeat of the small climax that finds the second sopranos emerging from the texture once more in their ascent from G to C on 'geneiget'. The piece then heads towards a *fortissimo* interrupted cadence that introduces the final phrase: 'denn es will Abend werden' is sung once more as the music, and the longing therein, relax for the final time into rest and quietness.

Desire conveyed and elicited

'The night is at hand and the day is now past': the atmosphere of Rheinberger's piece is similar to that which we find in certain settings of the Nunc Dimittis, such as those by Stanford and Howells considered a little later. There is a sense of falling into darkness – be it night, suffering or death – with confidence in the enduring presence of God's love. But if *Abendlied* conveys confidence, this should not hide the fact that the words still contain a plea. The Compline context in which the piece is sometimes sung, together with the plaintive, wistful nature of parts of the music, suggests a plea for God's enduring presence when the day ends, and in times of metaphorical darkness. However, the warmth and tenderness of the music, together with the original scriptural context of the text, suggests an additional layer to the piece's yearning. In the story of the encounter with the risen Christ on the road to Emmaus, the feelings of the two disciples suggest something like a *romantic* or *erotic* longing: the way they were captivated by Jesus, causing their 'hearts to burn within them' as they later observe,[43] sounds remarkably similar to how one might feel towards a lover (one can, perhaps, imagine making a similar plea for the person in question to stay with one throughout the evening).

I do not, of course, mean that the disciples' attraction to Jesus was straightforwardly romantic or sexual. Rather, I am referring to the long tradition in Judaism and Christianity of describing love between humans and God as being something *like* romantic desire: a strong desire that shares some of its phenomenology with the specific kind of erotic desire that is romantic and sexual, but that goes beyond the sexual in being directed towards a spiritual end.[44] In *Abendlied*, this erotic yearning is combined with the felt need for divine presence and protection in darkness, resulting in a unified emotion in the kind of divine–human relationship to which it alludes. Here we can note a connection between the forms of desire in *Abendlied* and *Hear My Prayer, O Lord*. A sense of the 'erotic' kind of divine presence is one way in which one could be satisfied in the desperate yearning of Purcell's piece, but there are also other ways: the steadfast love conveyed to the sufferer in the Purcell case may feel more like parental love, for instance. *Abendlied*, heard in the way I have described with regards to the longing it conveys, brings the notion of an erotic kind of divine presence to the forefront of the listener's awareness.

Unlike *Hear My Prayer, O Lord*, *Abendlied* can elicit in the listener the longing of which it is expressive. To feel the piece's erotic longing for God's presence in times of darkness, one need not be in any particular kind of life situation: there is none of the immediate desperation to be found in Purcell's piece. Rather, as we have seen, there can be discerned a warm intensity of longing, sharpened by the thread of wistfulness that is woven through; and these emotions can be felt at any time, since at any time we can have a sense of life's not having turned out for the best. Similarly, we all know what it is like to endure times of darkness, and one can long to feel assured of strength and protection in those times, even if one is not currently in the middle of such a time.

Projected satisfaction and its characterization of God

What would it take for this form of religious desire to be satisfied? Given the two aspects of the desire, satisfaction would seem to consist in both an analogue of erotic union and a feeling of intimate peace – indeed, a peace achieved *through* this union. In order for the satisfaction to be complete, being united with God in this sense would have to be a more complete union than one could possibly have with another human being: in Abraham Kuyper's words, 'it is [the] outshining of His life that must penetrate you and must be assimilated in the blood of your soul'.[45] If one feels as intimately loved as this, then one may well perceive things as Psalm 139 describes: 'Even the darkness is not dark to you; the night is bright as the day, for darkness is as light with you.'[46] Hence, a feeling of the most intimate peace: peace that can be had both at the *idea* (the memory or anticipation) of loss, dissatisfaction and suffering, and also in the actual, experienced midst of these things.

In order to bring about this satisfaction, there seem to be at least two attributes that God must possess – two attributes of which one can have personally significant (though inevitably incomplete) knowledge through feeling the longing I have described in *Abendlied*, provided one has the sense just outlined of what would constitute satisfaction. First, God must be able to unite himself to a human person to a greater extent than any human could. For no matter how close two human beings feel to each other, they will never reach a stage at which the life of each 'penetrates' the other and is 'assimilated in the blood of [the other's] soul'. The reasons are not far to seek. The psychotherapist Irvin Yalom has described four 'distorting prisms [that] block the knowing of the other': the non-translatability between the images of the mind and linguistic expression; our selectivity in what we choose to disclose about ourselves; our tendency to see in others our own ideas, assumptions and desires; and 'the vast richness and intricacy of each individual being'.[47] Yalom seems correct in thinking that as far as human relationships go, 'the enabling relationship always assumes that the other is never fully knowable';[48] and this, no doubt, is a large part of the 'existential isolation' he describes as 'the unbridgeable gap between self and others'.[49]

In order to satisfy fully the longing of *Abendlied*, then, God would have to see a person in the 'wholly accurate and complete way' to which we have already seen Spufford refer. However, God's intimate presence to someone must be more than just a matter of his having direct causal and cognitive access to that person's mind. As Eleonore Stump points out, direct causal and cognitive access (which, on traditional Christian doctrine, God has for every human being) would simply amount to God's knowing someone's mind 'with direct and unmediated cognition', and being able to 'communicate in a direct and unmediated way with the mind of that person'.[50] But such a relation could be entirely unilateral, with none of the reciprocity that intimacy requires. Rather, God's intimate, loving presence to someone would involve what the Christian tradition calls God's *indwelling* a person, which, on Christian doctrine, God does in virtue of the Holy Spirit.

Stump expounds this doctrine through the analogy of loving relationships between humans. Two humans in a loving relationship (possibly, but not necessarily, a romantic relationship) can be psychologically and emotionally open to each other: they can be in a state of voluntary, mutual vulnerability in which the thoughts and affects of each are available to the other.[51] In other words, such a relationship will involve mutual *mind-reading*, in which 'something of the thought, affect, or intention in the mind of one person is in the mind of another'.[52] When Paula mind-reads Jerome, 'Paula can consciously identify a mental state as within her own mind and yet somehow not hers but Jerome's' – an obvious example being empathy.[53] However, when God indwells a human person, *God himself* – rather than just his thoughts, affects or intentions – is in the mind of that person: freely accepted, and so eliciting in the person love, joy and peace.[54] Stump summarizes the idea as follows:

> In the indwelling of the Holy Spirit, God is present to a person of faith with maximal second-personal presence, surpassing even the presence possible between two human persons united in mutual love. It is a union that makes

the two of them one without merging one into the other or in any other way depriving the human person of his own mind and self.⁵⁵

Only this level of intimacy would fully satisfy the longing of *Abendlied*; and so only a personal reality with the ability to enter into intimacy of this level could fulfil the role.

Turning to the second attribute that God would need in order to fulfil *Abendlied*'s longing, we can see a convergence between the knowledge about God that Purcell's and Rheinberger's pieces enable. In being united in love with a person as completely as his indwelling would allow, and in bringing such a deep sense of peace, God would once more have the capacity to bring about a change in perspective in the one who felt loved in this way – for such love would have the capacity to transform any suffering. Indeed, this change in perspective seems to be what is being described in the passage from Psalm 139 already quoted.

In short, through desiring God in the way *Abendlied* conveys, one can come to know something of the following attributes in terms of how they are significant to oneself, which God would need in order to grant satisfaction: first, the power to indwell a person in intimate union, that is, in a more total version of the union between human lovers; and second, the capacity to bring about a change in perspective in a person through this intimate, transformative love. Once again, in having some phenomenological sense of what the satisfaction in question would be like, one might well have to draw on analogous past experience. Given the nature of the desire, this would most probably involve knowledge of what it is like to be in a relationship of intimate, mutual erotic/romantic love with another human, where that love has at times played a transformative role in how one sees a situation, or, indeed, in how one sees oneself. Such a relationship would involve the psychological and emotional openness that we saw Stump describe.⁵⁶ If one desires God in the capacity of granting a more total version of this transformative intimacy, then one can use this sort of human relationship as a basis in forming a sense of what God's fulfilment of the desire would be like.⁵⁷ The difference here, which one would glimpse in the desire but only to a limited degree, is beautifully captured in a chant from the French monastic community of Taizé: in relationship with God it would be true to say, '*all* my heart lies open to you'.⁵⁸

Even if (as Christian doctrine claims) God indwells only those people who have faith and who freely welcome him,⁵⁹ it is possible to desire intimacy of this kind without having 'come to faith'. In doing so, one can glimpse something of what God would be like if one *were* subject to his indwelling, at those times when his indwelling were manifest to one's awareness (which, I take it, would not always be the case). One thereby glimpses what it would be like for God to have the capacity to change one's perspective through this maximal, loving intimacy, making 'darkness [to be] as light'. This attribute in its 'erotic' form would be a particular manifestation of the intimate, steadfast love that the responsive listener to our previous piece, *Hear My Prayer, O Lord*, can come to know about through empathizing with that piece's desperate cry.

5.5 The Nunc Dimittis: Stanford and Howells

Text and context

I now turn to the final musical works to be considered in this chapter: two settings of the Nunc Dimittis. The Nunc Dimittis is traditionally paired with the Magnificat[60] at evensong in the Anglican Church, and is included in the evening and night services of numerous other denominations. A moving, multilayered text that has inspired a great many musical settings over the centuries, its scriptural context, as the words spoken by Simeon on seeing the infant Jesus,[61] is from the Gospel of Luke. The translation below is, as usual, from the English Standard Version Anglicized – except for the Nunc Dimittis itself, for which I have used the language of the 1662 Book of Common Prayer, to match the version used in the musical settings discussed:

> When the time came for their purification according to the Law of Moses, [Mary and Joseph] brought [the child Jesus] up to Jerusalem to present him to the Lord … Now there was a man in Jerusalem, whose name was Simeon, and this man was righteous and devout, waiting for the consolation of Israel, and the Holy Spirit was upon him. And it had been revealed to him by the Holy Spirit that he would not see death before he had seen the Lord's Christ. And he came in the Spirit into the temple, and when the parents brought in the child Jesus, … he took him up in his arms and blessed God and said,
>
> Lord, now lettest thou thy servant depart in peace according to thy word.
> For mine eyes have seen thy salvation;
> Which thou hast prepared before the face of all people;
> To be a light to lighten the Gentiles and to be the glory of thy people Israel.[62]

And of course, when Simeon's words are set to music (as dictated by the liturgical context), they have the 'Gloria' appended to them:

> Glory be to the Father, and to the Son, and to the Holy Ghost;
> As it was in the beginning, is now, and ever shall be, world without end. Amen.[63]

The words uttered by Simeon do not, perhaps, express desire for God as explicitly as the words used by Purcell or Rheinberger; nonetheless, the scriptural narrative in which they are embedded alludes to a particular kind of longing. Simeon, we are told, had been 'waiting for the consolation of Israel' – for the salvation, embodied in Jesus, which was to reach not only Israel but also 'all people'. Simeon's song, then, alludes to his longing for God's salvation, but does so through expressing the *fulfilment* of that longing. However, that is not the end of the matter, for salvation on any theological account will not simply be a static, once-and-for-all affair. Rather, as St Paul insisted, it will involve a process of sanctification, of 'being transformed [...] from one degree of glory to another' into the image of God.[64] And so, in regarding the prospect of earthly death with Simeon's peace and joy, the Nunc Dimittis can be heard as expressive of a desire for the *continued unfolding* of God's salvation – something that, on orthodox Christian doctrine, will reach its full fruition on the other side of death, when we no longer see 'in a mirror dimly', but 'face to face'.[65] The musical settings of Stanford and Howells vividly bring out this aspect of the text, so let us now turn to them both. It will help the epistemological discussion to have both in mind together, each complementing the other in the way of understanding the text on which I wish to focus.

The music

I. *Stanford in G*

As already mentioned, Charles Villiers Stanford's setting in G of the Nunc Dimittis is part of his Morning, Communion and Evening Service in G,[66] published in 1902. It is scored for bass soloist, SATB choir and organ. A short introduction in the organ presents the central melodic motif to which the piece returns a number of times, a gently falling, four-note phrase. The soloist then begins the most *cantabile* of melodies, singing 'Lord, now lettest thou thy servant' to a climbing two-note sequence, before falling on the central motif just mentioned for 'depart in peace'. The choir echoes the motif, and the soloist repeats it on 'according to thy word'. Soloist and choir proceed to sing the next phrase, 'For mine eyes have seen thy salvation, which thou hast prepared before the face of all people', the soloist dropping in and out of the texture. At this point the piece starts to open out, as the soloist sings: 'To be a light to lighten the gentiles.' But it is the choir's repetition of those words that marks the start of the music's full flourishing: F-naturals turn the music towards C major, before the word 'light' is sung *forte* by the choir on a G dominant seventh chord, resolving eventually on 'gentiles' to C major in the first inversion. The opening key of G, representing a peaceful death, now becomes in the dominant seventh a passage to something else – something visible only in light of the salvation, embodied in the infant Jesus, of which Simeon spoke. The first-inversion nature of the C major chord on 'gentiles' conveys a pause rather than a stop, raising the question of just what the 'something else' might be. We find out soon enough: the soloist sings 'and to be the glory', the word '*glory*' falling on a huge F-minor chord in the organ. The choir takes up the same words, only now the *fortissimo* 'glory' falls on D-flat major: close to F-minor but very distant from the original G major – something unfamiliar, awe-inspiring. Another chromatic shift leads to a D dominant seventh chord on a third proclamation of 'glory', before the music becomes calmer, coming to rest for the moment on a C major-seventh chord for 'Israel'.

The organ reintroduces the central, four-note motif, and the music becomes very still: the choir repeats 'Lord, now lettest thou thy servant' in unison, before singing in hushed, a cappella harmony the central motif on 'depart in peace'. The Gloria is a thing of quiet beauty. Starting with a theme that echoes the Gloria of the accompanying Magnificat, the words are sung in unison until 'ever shall be'. 'World without end' is set to a descending sequence resembling the central motif, passed down from the sopranos between all the parts before coming to rest on an A-minor first inversion. The music wants to come home, and it does so in two wonderfully understated utterances of 'Amen': two chords in the organ are answered in kind by the choir, before the central motif returns one last time, the organ joined by the choir in a final, hushed farewell.

II. Howells' **Collegium Regale**

There are a number of similarities between Stanford's Nunc Dimittis in G and Herbert Howells' *Collegium Regale* setting,[67] yet the two, composed about 45 years apart, inevitably feel very different. These 1945 settings by Howells of the Evening Canticles have become among the most celebrated of the twentieth century.[68] The overall mood of much of the Nunc Dimittis is more ethereal than Stanford's setting, the harmonies mistier, the effect one of being enveloped in mystery. Once again, the piece is scored for soloist, SATB choir and organ; the soloist this time is a tenor.

A short organ introduction leads into the soloist singing 'Lord, now lettest thou thy servant depart in peace according to thy word'. The melody hints at both B-flat major and G minor: even in light of what the piece will go on to refer to, looking to one's own death cannot help but bring a sense of introspection and vulnerability. As though to highlight that vulnerability, the first half of the phrase is sung without any accompaniment at all. The sound warms up a little on 'For mine eyes' as the choir joins the soloist in luminous quietness, the largely a cappella harmony gently moving in and out of D major – until, on the second syllable of 'salvation', the music suddenly shifts to a B-flat dominant seventh chord. Here, again, is the portrayal of something strange and mysterious through a sudden harmonic progression to a distant key; only this time, unlike Stanford's use of the same device on 'glory', the salvation itself is portrayed as possessing this strange unfamiliarity. However, the shift is anything but jarring: it is expressive of awe, a swelling of the sound, opening out on to a passage of harmonic movement that is colourful yet tranquil as the choir and soloist continue to bask in the soft light of the salvation 'prepared before the face of all people'. The music comes into full bloom at 'to be a *light*', as the sopranos ascend to a high G on a G major chord spanning nearly three octaves – a fuller version of the chord sung a few bars earlier on the word 'face'. Yet this is not a climax: a sense of continued movement is conveyed both by the first-inversion nature of the chord and by a scale motif in quick crotchets that appears around the parts, making the light shimmer. The phrase, and the enlightening of the Gentiles that it denotes, is moving towards 'the glory of thy people Israel', a phrase sung *forte* in unison as the Nunc Dimittis text of the piece reaches its most muscular musical moment, ending on a unison D over a rich D major chord in the organ. Even this is not the climax, however: coming as it does after the tonal area of G major/E minor, the final syllable of the text leaves us with the impression of an imperfect cadence, as though pausing on a cliff edge before the jump.

One is inclined to agree with composer Paul Spicer's assessment of the Gloria: 'Surely amongst the most ecstatic utterances we possess.'[69] Starting as it does in B-flat major, it combines with the end of the Nunc Dimittis to echo the harmonic sequence that appeared earlier, on the word 'salvation': here is the same sense of moving into something strange and mysterious. Now, however, the mood is one of utter triumph: the lower three parts sing in unison below a soaring, melismatic soprano descant. The momentum picks up at 'As it was in the beginning', the scale motif reappearing in the alto part, driving the doxology to its finale. But then the pace broadens once more; and the ecstatic cry of the choir on 'world without end' is an outpouring of praise, an anticipation of being caught up in the eternity of the Trinity. With two utterances of 'Amen' that are a world away from Stanford's hushed reverence, the piece is brought at last to its confident, joyful conclusion.

Affective expressiveness of the musical settings: Desire and projected satisfaction

I said earlier that both these settings bring out clearly a particular aspect of the Nunc Dimittis text, namely, a desire for the continued unfolding of God's salvation beyond earthly death. Let us now draw together the above musical analyses and see how Stanford and Howells convey this desire. Both settings start in peaceful acceptance at the prospect of death, and are therefore naturally heard as expressive of the same fulfilment that Simeon knew: fulfilment of the desire for God's salvation, 'prepared before the face of all people'. Having seen the infant Jesus, Simeon knew that such salvation was now available to all; and in that sense, his longing was satisfied. However, both the settings subsequently open out at the phrase 'to be a light': the music becomes more expansive, conveying, as it were, that expanse of possibility opened up by the light of God's salvation. Moreover, recall that there is a continued sense of movement in each setting around the word 'light', achieved by Stanford through a dominant seventh chord and use of the first inversion, and by Howells through the first inversion and fluid scale motif. In each case, the movement is towards the word 'glory', and ultimately towards the Gloria at the end. Thus, the fulfilment expressed at the beginning, through the possibility it opens up, leads to the further desire conveyed in the text and music for something more to come, for that possibility to be actualized: a desire to grow into the image of God as one's salvation comes to full fruition, until one beholds his glory face to face.

Indeed, in starting to think about the nature of the salvation for which these musical settings convey desire, we can consider how divine glory is portrayed in those settings, since (given the Pauline themes referred to on p. 102) being in the full presence of God's glory can naturally be seen as integral to the salvation prepared by God for humankind. To this issue we now turn.

I. *Divine glory*

The concept of divine glory has been given a recent analysis by John Cottingham, drawing on a number of passages from the Hebrew Bible. In Psalm 29, for instance, 'God is described as the one ... who "shakes the wilderness and strips the forests bare, while all in the temple cry 'Glory'".[70] In the Book of Exodus, God leads the Israelites out of Egypt in a 'pillar of cloud by day and [a] pillar of fire by night', and later dwells on Mount Sinai, first in a cloud and then 'like a devouring fire'.[71] These images convey 'something weighty with significance, sacred, mysterious ... something fearful that calls forth reverence and awe'. Moreover, crucial to this kind of phenomenon is that it is 'pregnant with moral significance'.[72] In Psalm 96, for instance, we read of the natural world rejoicing 'before the LORD, ... for he comes *to judge the earth ... in righteousness*'.[73] Cottingham continues:

> What is happening here is an experience where the subject is overwhelmed by the power and beauty of nature in a way that is somehow intertwined with awareness of one's own weakness and imperfection, and a sense of confrontation with the inexorable demands of justice and righteousness ... the individual feels him or herself to be checked, to be scrutinized, and to be called upon to respond and to change.[74]

The settings of the Gloria by Stanford and Howells invite us to conceive of this glory in contrasting ways. Howells, on the one hand, presents divine glory in a way that would likely come to mind naturally for many people: as magnificent and overwhelmingly powerful, like a blinding light. As divine glory is portrayed here, it is inseparable from a response of praise (that of the choir) which is itself a manifestation of that glory. In this sense it resembles the glory that Luke's Nativity narrative describes as shining around the shepherds as an angel appears to them to announce the birth of Christ: no sooner has the angel given the news, than the multitude of the heavenly host appears with its song of praise.[75] What is important for our purposes is that their praise is directed at both God's glory and God's *peace*: 'Glory to God in the highest, and on earth peace among those with whom he is pleased.' The arrival of Christ, of the salvation that the Nunc Dimittis contemplates, is centrally connected with these two things, opening the possibilities of them to humankind.

Stanford's setting of the Gloria highlights this second aspect of God's glory as it has been portrayed in the Judaeo-Christian tradition:[76] its being a source of peace, its preciousness and intimacy, its capacity to be manifest in moments of silence and calm, yet still inspire awe. In an oft-quoted passage from the First Book of Kings, God appears to the prophet Elijah not in a strong wind, an earthquake or a fire, but in a 'low whisper'.[77] Elijah's response is to wrap his face in his cloak; and, given the wider scriptural context, this carries the implication that Elijah heard in the whisper God's *glory* in particular. The inappropriateness of seeing God face to face has connotations of the divine glory being too great to behold: when in the Book of Exodus Moses requests that God show him his glory, God refuses to show Moses his face, telling him that he would not live to tell the tale.[78] In light of this connection, then, the passage from 1 Kings seems to portray God's glory taking a particular form: that of an intimate quietness that inspires reverence and wonder. It is a form of glory also conveyed in the Christian contemplative tradition, as, for instance, when Thomas Merton writes of 'love of God and wonder and adoration [swimming] up into us like tidal waves out of the depths of that peace and break[ing] upon the shores of our consciousness in a vast, hushed surf of inarticulate praise, praise and glory'.[79] Now it may be that if Stanford's Nunc Dimittis were taken in isolation, then analysing the Gloria in these terms would be to over-describe it; I leave that question open. However, hearing it in light of these aspects of the tradition is simply a case of the general phenomenon described in Chapter 4: that of music's conveying of something extra-musical in combination with extra-musical aspects of the listener's experience. When listened to in light of the portrayals of divine glory just cited, the music and text of Stanford's Gloria can, I suggest, be heard as presenting that glory in those ways: as a source of peace, intimately known, and inspiring reverence and wonder. The picture of God's glory, then, that starts to emerge – a picture involving both this characterization and the magnificence and power portrayed by Howells – is one whose essence is expressed by Henry Vaughan in a few vivid lines:

> I saw Eternity the other night
> Like a great *Ring* of pure and endless light,
> All calm, as it was bright[80]

II. Salvation in Christ: 'With unveiled face'

I have now filled in something of what the desire conveyed in these settings of the Nunc Dimittis is for: it is for the continued unfolding of God's salvation for humankind, culminating in one's beholding a glory that is at once magnificent and intimate, powerful and a source of peace. Recall, though, that divine glory as portrayed in the Hebrew Bible is often something that throws into sharp relief one's own weakness and imperfection – to such an extent that 'man shall not see me and live'. Salvation on the Christian picture must therefore involve more than simply beholding God's glory. What else might it entail, such that through it human beings might see God, 'not like Moses, who would put a veil over his face', but 'with unveiled face, … transformed … from one degree of glory to another'?[81]

Such a question is, of course, far too complex to answer comprehensively and conclusively in passing, and I have no intention of doing so. Instead, I simply wish to point to a few key themes regarding the salvation to which the Nunc Dimittis refers, and thus the desire it can be heard to convey. In order to make these themes a little more tangible, I shall provide just a small amount of theological context. Once again, these considerations will inevitably take us beyond Simeon's words themselves: the desire conveyed by Stanford's and Howells' settings acquires its content in part from the doctrinal and devotional context in which they are sung. In what follows, as elsewhere, I draw on strands of Rowan Williams' thought in filling in some of the content of the Christian world view. I take him to be a sensitive interpreter of Christian tradition, and I therefore happily defer to him in matters of doctrinal exposition. There will inevitably be disagreements over emphasis, but I try to present things in such a way that the acceptability of what I say does not depend on taking any particular stance on theologically contentious issues.

We can start by considering the language of another Gospel canticle, this time traditionally part of morning prayer in the Anglican Church: the Benedictus. Once again from Luke, the Benedictus (whose name, like those of the Magnificat and Nunc Dimittis, is the first word of the Latin Vulgate translation, meaning 'Blessed') is also known as 'The Song of Zechariah': in context, it is the prophecy spoken by the father of John the Baptist after the latter's birth.[82] Here I want to focus just on the final part. In the translation used in the Church of England's *Common Worship* liturgy, we read:

> In the tender compassion of our God
> the dawn from on high shall break upon us,
> To shine on those who dwell in darkness and the shadow of death,
> and to guide our feet into the way of peace.[83]

In sketching some of the main aspects of the salvation towards which the longing of the Nunc Dimittis is directed, I want to highlight two themes in these lines that also appear in Simeon's words: *light* and *peace*. In the Benedictus, these are more clearly connected to the nature and purpose of God's salvation than they are in the Nunc Dimittis: light is explicitly contrasted here with darkness, and hence with the state that gives rise to the need for that light, while the emphasis regarding peace is not so much on a state in which one can die satisfied, but rather a state *into* which we move if we are subject to the salvation mentioned in the text a few lines earlier, before the quoted extract.

In general terms, the longing of the Nunc Dimittis is for the sort of life that, on the Christian view, the life of Jesus of Nazareth makes possible – where both lives are characterizable in terms of 'light' and 'peace'. 'At peace with God the Father, [Jesus' life] is a life that makes peace in the human world wherever it is at work.'[84] 'Peace' here is '*not* … just the absence of rivalry and conflict; it is an active condition of loving and nurturing, giving and receiving, mutuality'.[85] In other words, Jesus concretely introduces God's 'fearlessness in giving ... within ... human exchange and interaction'.[86] Given the levels of self-deceit and self-destruction (or 'fallenness') of human beings, a life of this sort was bound to appear threatening to many – to the extent of leading to Jesus' crucifixion.[87] However, the fact remains that God's Incarnation in Jesus enables us to be freed from our 'destructive and deceitful traps'[88] – from the darkness of hatred, fear and self-absorption. In Jesus' life of self-sacrifice God concretely opens up a different way of being; and if we allow this to be infused into our own lives, by sharing in Christ's life as passed down in the Holy Spirit through the church,[89] then the light – the dawn – of God's love is shed on us. In partaking in the life of the church, we grow into Christ's intimacy with God the Father: an intimacy that is 'trustful and natural and deeply demanding'.[90] We are thereby given the security of knowing we are the object of a love that is strong enough to survive our very worst – as demonstrated, in Christian doctrine, in Christ's resurrection.[91] Such security can give us the confidence to be stripped gradually of our excuses and self-deceptions, as we '[try] to bring ourselves relentlessly out of the shadows where we hide from God and ourselves and each other':[92] a process of acclimatization to God's glory and love through sustained engagement in the life of the church.[93] By gradually having that love incorporated into us[94] – in our relationships with God, ourselves and each other – we grow into a life of peace as characterized above, a life of loving and nurturing, gift and mutuality, which liberates us to rejoice in God, who is love.[95] Beyond earthly death, this life reaches its full fruition: the culmination of our salvation.[96]

III. Summary of the desire in the Nunc Dimittis

We now have an account of the desire of which Stanford's and Howells' Nunc Dimittis settings are, together, expressive. It is a desire for the continued unfolding of God's salvation for humankind, beyond earthly death. The culmination of that salvation, if it occurs, is to be in God's presence and to behold his glory 'with unveiled face', as one is transformed into his image and likeness. The musical settings I have been considering portray that glory as at once magnificent and intimate, as both powerful and a source of peace. Moreover, we now have a theological sketch of how this might come to be, and thus of other key aspects of the salvation in question. In the Benedictus (as well as elsewhere in the New Testament, especially the Johannine texts[97]), God's love in Christ is represented as a light coming into darkness – as dawn or sunrise (in Luke's Greek, *anatolé*, ἀνατολή[98]); and as we saw, the settings of both Stanford and Howells open up on the word 'light', conveying the expanded possibilities opened up by that love – its transformative power. In this way, there is further convergence in the desires of which our musical examples are expressive: like *Hear My Prayer, O Lord* and *Abendlied*, these settings of the Nunc Dimittis are expressive of a desire that would be at least partially satisfied in a transformation of dark aspects of our lives. However, this time the transformation is explicitly linked, in its theological context, with our entire life and way of being – so much so that the love to which the Nunc Dimittis symbolically alludes, and which the music of Stanford and Howells conveys so expressively, is something to which we must become acclimatized through partaking in the life of the church – until *we ourselves* are constituted by it.[99] The more this happens, the more our salvation will be brought to fruition; and on the picture we have been considering, the final fruition in 'the life of the world to come' (to use the language of the Nicene Creed) will be to inhabit a state of peace that consists in a life of mutual love and gift in community with others, 'set in the heart of the exchange of life and joy within the Trinity',[100] in the full presence of divine glory.

Affective arousal of the settings: Desire elicited and knowledge yielded

We come at last to the question of what desire these settings of the Nunc Dimittis might plausibly elicit in the listener. Like the desire conveyed in *Abendlied*, and unlike that conveyed in *Hear My Prayer, O Lord*, the desire I have just summarized does not require one to be in any particular kind of circumstance. Regardless of what is currently happening, one can long for the full unfolding, beyond earthly death, of the transformative power of God's love in Christ as the Christian tradition sees it – freeing us from the dark aspects of how we relate to ourselves and to others, and thus freeing us to live in a state of mutual love and gift in the direct presence of God's glory. Therefore, if one were to respond to this desire in Stanford's and Howells' settings with a desire of one's own, the most natural way to do so would be to feel that desire oneself. All that remains now is to apply our epistemology to the desire and see what knowledge it could yield for the desirer.

I. Personal object and state-of-affairs satisfaction

As I made clear in Chapters 2 and 3, all the desires for God in the particular capacities considered in this study can be understood as manifestations of an underlying, non-propositional desire for God himself. Perhaps in the context of the Nunc Dimittis the underlying desire will be especially close to the surface of one's awareness: the desire I have been describing is centred on the final culmination of salvation on the Christian world view, and this involves knowing and loving God *in himself* (something I shall explore further in the next chapter). However, in addition to this, there is a desire here that fits our epistemology: a desire for God *in the capacity* of bringing about the salvation in question. Recall from Chapter 2 that even if the desire would be satisfied in a particular state of affairs, it need not be *for* that state of affairs. For the sake of brevity, I have been speaking loosely about the object of desire in this section. Still, the desire conveyed in the Nunc Dimittis, and specifically in the music of Stanford and Howells, is not simply a desire for a state of peace – at least, not when taken in the theistic context that gives it its distinctive content. Rather, it is a desire for God in the capacity of enabling us to share in *his* peace, so that we might behold 'with unveiled face' the very source of peace, of love and gift, and thus have our relationships 'fully anchored in the Trinitarian love of God and fully transparent to that love'.[101] Moreover, as we have seen, being a source of peace is one of the ways in which divine glory has been portrayed in the Judaeo-Christian tradition – and in Stanford's setting of the Nunc Dimittis specifically.

Thus, the intimate contact with God that would constitute satisfaction of the desire in the Nunc Dimittis centrally involves at least two aspects. First, one would inhabit a state of peace with other persons, and that state would be grounded in the intimate contact with God just mentioned. As a very partial analogy here, consider two people, Robert and Daniel, who find it difficult to maintain much of a conversation when alone together, but who somehow open up in the presence of a third person, Geoffrey, whom they both know. Although Geoffrey is not the source *tout court*, in the abstract, of friendly mutual attention and interest (and thus differs from God in the capacity in which we are considering him), he is at least the source of Robert and Daniel's friendly mutual attention and interest: this relationship between Robert and Daniel is 'grounded in' their shared contact with Geoffrey. God's grounding of a state of peace between persons would be, I suggest, not entirely unlike this. Of course, the Christian picture includes an extra, vital element: the relationships among those in whom salvation has been perfected would be 'fully anchored in the *Trinitarian* love of God'. I will not even attempt to provide an analogy for this, since to do so would make me a hostage to fortune in light of the theological controversies that surround the doctrine of the Trinity. Nor, perhaps, would it be appropriate to try and offer an analogy for interpersonal love being grounded in Trinitarian love; for the latter must surely remain, to a large extent, a mystery. However, I hope the above analogy sheds some small amount of light on what it might be for a relationship between two (or more) people to be grounded in their shared relationship to another person.

The second aspect of the satisfaction here would lie in what one is aware *of* in the relationship to God that grounds one's relationships of peace with others. Specifically, God's *glory* would have to be clearly present to one's awareness. Although, as we noted, the connection between glory and peace is conveyed most clearly in Stanford's setting, the implication is something we can hear in the setting by Howells: the relationships of mutual love and gift that characterize a state of peace would be revealed as having the luminosity, the magnificence, that Howells' setting of the Gloria conveys.

II. A sense of the satisfaction's phenomenology – and knowledge about God

Those, then, are two central aspects of the state of affairs that would constitute satisfaction here – satisfaction of the desire for God that is conveyed in the settings of the Nunc Dimittis by Stanford and Howells. It seems clear that in this case, any sense of what this satisfaction would be like cannot come from past experience of that very same satisfaction, since by definition it would only come to pass on the other side of earthly death. However, once again there are experiences that can offer *some* sense of what the satisfaction might be like, however vague and incomplete. I have already mentioned certain kinds of interpersonal relationships that can give us an idea of how, in the full fruition of salvation on the Christian picture, relationships to God and to other persons would be *structured*. And there are, I suggest, other kinds of experience that can offer some very partial sense of the *phenomenology* of salvation's full fruition. I do not, of course, claim that the kinds of experience I am about to cite offer anything like a comprehensive indication of what 'the life of the world to come' might be like if the Christian outlook I have been exploring is true. Nonetheless, in order for the salvation of which Christianity speaks – in particular in its full unfolding – to have any sort of appeal, it must be portrayed as resembling *some* aspects of our experience, however much it is also said to surpass them. With this in mind, consider the following.

One might, for instance, read or hear what the Gospel narratives say about the life and teachings of Jesus himself. Recall that the longing conveyed, and plausibly evoked, by the Nunc Dimittis settings we have considered would be satisfied in the sort of life that the life of Jesus makes possible on the Christian view: one characterized by a state of peace as mutual love and gift. In coming to know the Gospel accounts of, for instance, Jesus welcoming society's outcasts into his community,[102] healing the sick,[103] and preaching an ethics and theology of forgiveness and generosity,[104] it may be possible to form some sense of what it would be like to live a life that is characterized by the kinds of relationships Jesus instantiated and taught. Indeed – and this is the second sort of experience that is relevant here – that life, with any luck, will appear in certain aspects of one's life as it actually is, in relationships and people characterized by the generosity and other-centredness that the Gospels describe. Peter van Inwagen, hardly an old softie, has eloquently described the unified effect in his own life of these two kinds of experience – of familiarity with the life of Jesus as described in the Gospels, and of knowing people who instantiate this sort of life:

> There are ... Christians I know who, for all the rich individuality of their lives and personalities, are like lamps, each shining with the same dearly familiar, uncreated light that shines in the pages of the New Testament. ... When one is in the presence of this light – when one so much as listens to one of these people speak – it is very difficult indeed to believe that one is not in the presence of a living reality that transcends their individual lives.[105]

We can leave aside the question of whether or not van Inwagen is being epistemically responsible in allowing such an experience to contribute to his reasons for Christian belief. Regardless of our view on that, it is clear that what is being described is a way of living that is tangible and recognizable, with the potential to strike a profound chord of appeal in someone who witnesses or experiences it. And crucially, if one is familiar with how this sort of life is depicted in the Gospels, and is therefore able to recognize it as instantiated in one's own lived experience, then one can have some sense of what such a life is like – a fuller, more complete version of which is the sort of life that would constitute the culmination of salvation beyond death.

What about that aspect of salvation involving a clear awareness of divine glory? What could give one a sense of what *this* would be like? Again, we are necessarily speaking in very incomplete terms; yet, once again it is possible to point to certain kinds of experience that may give one something to go on. Indeed, I have already done so. The two musical settings of the Gloria I have discussed each convey different aspects of God's glory as the Judaeo-Christian tradition has portrayed it. These portrayals in the tradition are themselves often vivid depictions of divine glory, such as the accounts from the Hebrew Bible cited earlier (pp. 105–7). Moreover, it is possible to have some sense of the *connection* between glory on the one hand, and peace – with the moral elements it involves – on the other. Again, I have already alluded to this. Having in mind the Glorias of Stanford and Howells side by side, we hear the two implications of this connection: in Stanford's Gloria, divine glory is profoundly peaceful; in Howells' (listening with the connection in mind), divine peace is profoundly glorious, luminous, magnificent.

If, in response to these settings of the Nunc Dimittis, one desires God in the capacity of enabling us to share in his peace and glory after death, then it is ultimately these aspects of God that one knows about. Through the desire, and a sense – based, for instance, on the kinds of experience just canvassed – of what satisfaction may involve, one comes to know something about God's peace and glory as the Judaeo-Christian tradition has characterized them; and once again, this knowledge will be shot through with personal significance: it will involve a grasp of how that peace and glory are important to oneself as the desirer. By listening to the Nunc Dimittis, one is encouraged to look towards one's own death; through being submerged in the music's light, one glimpses something of what, according to the Christian tradition, awaits us on death's far side. This is the full unfolding of the salvation that Simeon saw, as we are 'transformed from one degree of glory to another' – until we reach a state for which the poet Richard Crashaw, in his free translation of a prayer by Thomas Aquinas, expressed his own passionate longing:

> Come love! Come LORD! and that long day
> For which I languish, come away.
> When this dry soul those eyes shall see,
> And drink the unseal'd source of thee.
> When Glory's sun faith's shades shall chase,
> And for thy veil give me thy FACE.[106]

5.6 The value of musically elicited, desire-based knowledge about God

Our musical discussions are now complete. However, before closing the chapter, we must consider two important points raised by the foregoing. The first is the question of just what the *value* is of the musically elicited religious knowledge I have been describing. In general, as we have seen, desire of the kind I have been considering can provide vivid knowledge about what we desire when we are not experiencing it directly: knowledge of what the desire's object would have to be like in order to bring about satisfaction. Again, we have seen that such knowledge, through its inherent sense of lack, gives one a deepened sense of how the object of desire is important to oneself. The desire-experience, then, can give added impetus and sustenance to the search for the desire's object if the search is a long, uncertain one, and guidance in how to be shaped to receive, eventually, the object of one's desire.

Applied to God, this may look something like the following. Through one's desires for God and the knowledge they enable, one can be drawn into a personally invested search for God, cultivating the habits and attitudes that would help one to receive him. If God turns out to be real, and somewhat similar to the way the desires characterize him, then one will be in a position to recognize him if he were eventually to become manifest in one's experience. This, in turn, will put one in a position to grow in knowledge of him – a process I will consider in depth in the next chapter. Put simply, desiring God in the general way I have been describing is one way to aid one's openness to God. What follow are brief elaborations of this idea in regard to each of the musical works I have considered. These are no more than suggestions or pointers, and are certainly not intended to exhaust the wider influence each form of desire may have on one's life. Additionally, of course, other desire-based knowledge content, stemming from desires for God in capacities other than the ones I have discussed, will feed into one's wider life in other ways.

First, then, recall the discussion of *Hear My Prayer, O Lord*. The divine attribute of which one can know something through the desire elicited here is what I called unlimited resourcefulness. Specifically, in order to satisfy the yearning that one can grasp empathetically through listening to the piece, God would need the ability to see more reasons for hope in a situation than any human could see, and the power to convey this hope to the sufferer in intimate, steadfast love. At least part of the value in having desire-based, personally significant knowledge of these divine attributes is, I suggest, that it would make one likelier to approach such a God with this knowledge in mind and heart if one were in a state of real desperation. And perhaps the more time one spent in this knowledge about God, the likelier one would be to approach God like this if one really were desperate. If such a God *is* real then this willingness to approach him in times of need is vitally important – for it seems to be an essential part of the trust in God that would lead to fullness of life in relationship with him.[107]

Next, consider the knowledge that, I argued, *Abendlied* can help the listener to acquire through desiring God. The divine attributes of which one can come to know something in this case are, first, the power to indwell a person in intimate union, and, second, the capacity to bring about a change in perspective through this intimate, transformative love. Once again, the value in such knowledge consists in its helping the knower to cultivate a relationship with such a God if he is real. If one not only conceives of God as having the capacity to be intimately and transformatively present but also reaches out through desire to a sense of what that intimate presence would be like, then one will likely be motivated to make space for that intimacy to grow. Moreover, one will know what to look for and to cultivate in one's religious practice, including any prayer life that one has (again, more on this in the next chapter).

Finally, let us return to the Nunc Dimittis. Through mirroring the forms of desire discernible in the settings by Stanford and Howells, one can glimpse – fleetingly and incompletely – what God would be like in the full unfolding of the salvation that Simeon proclaimed. I argued that as Stanford and Howells portray it, this unfolding would be centred on God's peace and glory: peace that consists in a life of love and gift in community with others, in the full presence of divine glory. And it should be clear how, in at least one respect, this desire-experience may influence one's wider life. Indeed, I touched on it earlier. In glimpsing desiringly the luminosity, the magnificence, of 'the life of the world to come', one may well be drawn into a life aimed at acclimatizing to the glory and love on which one's desire for God is focused. In a Christian context, such acclimatization is traditionally undertaken through engaging in the life of the church: its music, its liturgy, its community, its outreach. In doing so, the hope is to emerge gradually from the dark areas of one's life, and to grow into a life of peace.

5.7 Can we sense what divine satisfaction would involve without any past experience of it?

The second point raised by the foregoing is a possible objection to my argument. I have been highlighting throughout that in order to form a sense of what the satisfaction of each desire for God would be like, one may well have to draw on *analogous* past experience. For the most part, the kinds of experience I cited involved interpersonal relationships. However, in the case of the Nunc Dimittis, we saw that other kinds of experience could function in this capacity: to form some (very incomplete) sense of what a clear awareness of divine glory might be like, one might refer to how that glory has been portrayed in Jewish and Christian tradition – for instance, in textual imagery and in music. But it might be objected: Can we really have, on the basis of our worldly experience, any sense of what would constitute *divine* satisfaction, and thus knowledge of what

God would be like in granting it? In support of this attack, one might refer to what have become known as 'transformative experiences', characterizable for our purposes as experiences that effect changes in the subject – changes that, in at least some cases, could not have happened in any other way. In a recent paper, L. A. Paul has argued that one such kind of experience is that of having a child; more specifically, this is both *epistemically* and *personally* transformative.[108] That is, the experience of having a child gives a person knowledge of what it is like to have a child, knowledge unavailable to one who remains childless; moreover, it radically changes what it is like to be the person in question.[109] Importantly, there are no other experiences that would allow one to project forward with any accuracy to a sense of what it would be like to have a child of one's own. Any analogous experience (such as looking after other children) is simply not similar enough.[110]

But (the objector might continue), is an experience of God not similar in this way to that of having a child? The philosopher Thomas Morris no doubt speaks for many believers when he writes that 'the Christian faith ... has on occasion turned my little world upside down'.[111] Surely it is impossible, before experiencing God in such a radically transformative way, to know anything of what it will be like? After all, such an experience is a complete re-ordering of one's priorities, and of where one's worth as a person seems to originate (the experience will likely be *diachronic*, developing over time). It is, so to speak, the inhabiting of a different paradigm, which gives other experiences a significance they would not otherwise have had. How, then, could anything prior to such an experience of God give a clue as to what it would be like? And to round off the objection, we can situate any experience that seems to come from God – including satisfaction of the desires that I have discussed – within this understanding of what it is to experience God. If (our objector will claim) the satisfaction in each case seems to come from *God*, then it will acquire whatever significance it has from a wider conception of God's priorities and of how they relate to one's own life. But if one has not already experienced (or seemingly experienced) these things, then one cannot begin to conceive of them – and this makes it impossible to conceive of what the satisfaction of desire for God would be like in each of the cases I have discussed.[112]

To this objection I reply as follows. I do not deny that experiencing the sort of God with whom I have been concerned, in the capacity of satisfying the foregoing desires, would differ significantly from any worldly experience. Indeed, this difference is vital if the desires for God are to influence one's wider life in a way that other desires could not. I have explored elements of the difference in discussing each piece of music, and I will further address the issue in the next chapter. Nevertheless, given how God has been characterized in the Christian tradition, I maintain that it is highly implausible that an experience of God in any capacity would be *entirely* unlike our familiar, worldly experiences – such that one could not imagine anything of what a relationship with God would be like. It is entirely natural in the Christian tradition for experiences of God to be compared to worldly experiences. Jesus' parables about the 'kingdom of heaven'[113] are cases in point; another example from the New Testament is the claim in the first Johannine epistle that 'love is from God, and whoever loves has been born of God and knows God'.[114] Elsewhere in the tradition we find, for instance, Aquinas asserting that 'we know [God] … as He is represented in the perfections of creatures'.[115] And as we shall see in the next chapter, within the Christian contemplative spirituality described by Thomas Merton, there is even a similarity of sorts between certain kinds of ordinary experience and 'contemplative' knowledge of God in himself. In short, the general idea in all these places is that from certain kinds of engagement with other people and with the world in general, we can know to some extent what it would be like to relate to God. Moreover, L. A. Paul's example shows that this includes knowledge of what it is like to be personally transformed, in ways that are analogous to the transformations in the life of a believer – such as having one's priorities re-ordered and having another person at the centre of one's life. Having a child is one example, but there are, of course others, such as getting married. All this is still perfectly consistent with upholding the radical *contrast* between God and the world: we can still agree with Aquinas when he writes, in a passage immediately preceding the one quoted above, that 'we cannot know the essence of God in this life, as He really is in Himself'.[116]

When one engages with the 'live hypothesis' of God's existence within this mode of thinking, the following line of reasoning becomes apposite. From one's engagement with aspects of the world, one can know something of what certain kinds of relationship with, and experience of, God would be like. Suppose, then, that one desires God in a capacity somewhat similar to a capacity in which one has experienced aspects of the world – as is the case in each of the musical works I have considered. In this situation, based on one's experience of the partially analogous kinds of satisfaction and on one's notion of the sort of relationship with God that would be fulfilling, it is possible, through an imaginative leap, to have some sense of what it would be like for one's desire for God to be satisfied. Hence, it is possible to know with a special personal significance, albeit incompletely, something of what God would be like in satisfying that desire.[117]

Let me sum up the argument of this chapter. I have discussed four works of sacred music, in each case drawing on features of the music, text and, where appropriate, context in order to present a form of desire for God that the piece can plausibly elicit. In each example, my description of a possible desiring response on the listener's part was primarily intended to represent one natural way of hearing the piece: a way, moreover, that has the potential to bear significant fruit if one is seeking to cultivate the sort of openness to God with which I have been concerned. Each of the forms of desire I described can give the desirer knowledge about God of the kind articulated in Chapter 3; and such knowledge has the capacity to influence one's wider life in ways that can further aid openness to the God whom one desires. My musical discussions have been in-depth illustrations of my general thesis: that sacred music can elicit forms of desire for God that satisfy Chapter 3's conditions for knowledge.

Because one can desire God without believing that he is real, such desire-based knowledge is available even to an interested non-believer of the kind that is our focus. This knowledge about God can bring to life affectively for the desirer a multifaceted characterization of God. It can thus ignite, shape and sustain a journey of religious openness, framing one's religious engagement according to how it characterizes God, and giving one the energy and motivation to seek intimate love and knowledge of the God whom one desires. It is this ongoing, deepened seeking to which we must now turn, as we reach this study's final chapter.

6

Religious desire and contemplative prayer

O be mine still! still make me thine!
Or rather make no Thine and Mine!

George Herbert, 'Clasping of Hands'[1]

Up until now, the religious matters that have concerned us have been the contributions that certain forms of desire for God can make to one's religious knowledge within a broadly Christian framework. The forms of desire in question have been those that, I have suggested, can plausibly be elicited by sacred music. But there is one aspect of the religious life that, it might be urged, underpins all this engagement, giving it its proper context and full significance – namely, prayer. In this chapter, I will explore how the sort of religious engagement I have discussed so far – engagement that is possible whether or not one believes in God's reality – can enrich a life of prayer.

The kind of prayer I will discuss in this context is *contemplative* prayer: specifically, contemplative prayer as described by the twentieth-century Cistercian monk Thomas Merton. The reason for this is the one mentioned at the end of Chapter 2. Given everything said so far, there is one objection that may still be troubling the reader. Might not all this musical engagement be a self-delusional fantasy? Might not the desires I have described simply be oriented towards how one would *like* God to be, which may have little to do with what he is actually like if he is real? To defuse this charge, we must have an acceptable standard for judging what counts as a 'rightly ordered' desire for God – a desire that, if God were real, it would be in his nature to satisfy. Whether or not a desire concerning God is rightly ordered depends on what God is like. If God were maliciously vengeful, then the desire for him to wreak havoc on one's enemies would be rightly ordered. If God were lovingly compassionate, then the desire for divine compassion and for protection from total despair would be rightly ordered. We have presupposed throughout that

Christian theism is at least a 'live hypothesis'; hence, we have helped ourselves to a broadly Christian understanding of what God is like, and thus which desires for God are rightly ordered. This understanding of God was developed in the previous chapter.

However, as also noted at the end of Chapter 2, even given a multifaceted characterization of God such as we find in the Christian tradition, there is an ever-present risk of '[using] God to fill the gaps in our needs and preferences', as Rowan Williams has put it:[2] a risk of forming ideas about God based on what we *think* he ought to do for us, rather than what he would actually do for us if he were real. Christian contemplative spirituality provides a way of *purging* or *refining* one's desires for God, including the purgation that happens in 'dark nights' of ascetic detachment. This purgation is measured by how closely one's desires conform to God as he is understood in Christian contemplative tradition – that is, how closely they resemble the ideal form of contemplative desire, ordered towards God as he really is: a desire for loving union with God. As we shall see, the 'dark nights' of detachment play a key role in this, opening up the contemplative practitioner (henceforth simply the 'contemplative') to radical destabilization and change, and uprooting her from her ordinary ways of valuing the world. This is as clear an indication as any that the contemplative spirituality of which Merton is a modern proponent is *not* an exercise in wishful thinking, intended to make one 'feel better' by simply catering to one's existing desires.

Nevertheless, I will contend that the pre-contemplative desires for God of the previous chapter can, by the lights of Merton's contemplative outlook, be spiritually fruitful ways into contemplative practice. When inhabited in the right way, such desires can involve a willingness to grow in love and knowledge of God beyond whatever attracts one to him at a given time. Furthermore, we will see that the religious desires I have been exploring find their most intense form in contemplative prayer – and this contemplatively refined form of desire is supposed eventually to find its fulfilment through contemplative practice. In other words, some version of the *pre-contemplative* desires is supposed to find its fulfilment through contemplative practice; hence, one can be compelled by what these desires reveal about one's present condition to seek answers in contemplative prayer. In what follows, then, I will navigate the relationship between pre-contemplative desire for God and contemplative practice, attempting to do justice to the ways in which, and the extent to which, the former can be a fruitful influence on the latter.

I will focus specifically on Merton's descriptions of the contemplative life for two reasons. The first is the clarity and relative recentness of his writing: although he stands in a long tradition of contemplative practice and writing,[3] the cultural and linguistic filters of his work are familiar enough to make understanding him a relatively straightforward matter, without the need for detailed exegetical work. Second, his voice is often distinctive, direct and personal: even in his non-autobiographical work, one can have a strong sense of reading something emerging out of a real human life. And this means that any further reflections on his descriptions of the contemplative life, such as those contained in this chapter, will have a good chance of also being sensitive to the contours of lived experience. In what follows I will not engage with Merton's work comprehensively or systematically. I will simply use it as a springboard for arguing that contemplative prayer can be seen as a culmination of the general orientation towards God that I have been considering. To this end, I will concentrate on the descriptions of the contemplative life in Merton's *New Seeds of Contemplation*. Engaging in detail with just one of his works, and thus with his thought at a specific time, will result in a much more focused discussion than would trying to draw together the various, disparate strands of his work over many years. In *New Seeds*, one of his most mature and best-known works, we find the essence of his contemplative outlook as it had developed up until that point, written in the aforementioned direct and personal style. It is also comprehensive enough to contain discussions of all the issues I wish to raise.[4]

I will proceed by outlining the main aspects of contemplative prayer as Merton describes it. From this will emerge two challenges to incorporating contemplative prayer into the musical engagement for whose fruitfulness I have been arguing. One of these concerns contemplative prayer's relationship to ordinary experience, including desire; the other concerns its relationship to propositional belief in religious doctrine. I will address each challenge after presenting it as forcefully as possible – thereby arguing for congruence between contemplative practice and the non-doxastic religious engagement with which I have been concerned. Specifically, I shall argue that if God is real, then the musically elicited, desire-based religious knowledge discussed in the previous chapter can be a significant aspect of the further love and knowledge of God that can come through contemplative prayer. That is to say, the musically elicited knowledge is part of what can be grown and deepened through contemplative prayer.

6.1 Contemplation

What is contemplative prayer as Merton characterizes it? In the most general terms, it is the practice aimed at contemplation, and so we should first look at how Merton characterizes contemplation:

> Contemplation, by which we know and love God as he is in himself, apprehending him in a deep and vital experience that is beyond the reach of any natural understanding, is the reason for our creation by God ... a pure gift of God which no desire, no effort and no heroism of ours can do anything to deserve or obtain.[5]

Contemplation is knowledge and love of God as he is in himself, a gift from God and so not something earned. However, since God is so radically different from anything in our ordinary experience, such knowledge and love in their purest form are possible only if one is freed of one's attachments to the things of ordinary experience. Contemplative prayer is the practice by which one allows this to happen:

> If nothing that can be seen can either be God or represent him to us as he is, then to find God we must pass beyond everything that can be seen and enter into darkness. Since nothing that can be heard is God, to find him we must enter into silence. Since God cannot be imagined, anything our imagination tells us about him is ultimately misleading and therefore we cannot know him as he really is unless we pass beyond everything that can be imagined and enter into an obscurity without images and without the likeness of any created thing.[6]

But, far from being a life of complete withdrawal, the life of a contemplative will be aimed at a deepened, sanctified engagement with the world:

> Detachment from things does not mean setting up a contradiction between 'things' and 'God'. ... We do not detach ourselves from things in order to attach ourselves to God, but rather we become detached from ourselves in order to see and use all things in and for God. ... The only true joy on earth is to ... enter by love into union with the life who dwells and sings within the essence of every creature and in the core of our own souls.[7]

In particular, this contemplative engagement with the world will be manifested in one's engagement with other people – the life of contemplation has profound moral implications:

> The more we are one with God the more we are united with one another; and the silence of contemplation is deep, rich, and endless society, not only with God but

with people. Contemplatives are not isolated in themselves but liberated from their external and egoistic selves by humility and purity of heart – therefore there is no longer any serious obstacle to simple and humble love of others.[8]

This deepened moral engagement is the fruit of the love and knowledge of God that is given in contemplative prayer; it is also a *site* of such love and knowledge. In one's relationships with others (and activity more generally), the contemplative can know and love God:

> Far from being essentially opposed to each other, interior contemplation and external activity are two aspects of the same love of God. But the activity of contemplatives must be born of their contemplation and must resemble it. Everything they do outside of contemplation ought to reflect the luminous tranquillity of their interior life. To this end, they will have to look for the same thing in their activity as they find in their contemplation – contact and union with God.[9]

Indeed, loving and knowing God in one's interpersonal relationships provides a foretaste of heaven:

> The ultimate perfection of the contemplative life is not a heaven of separate individuals, all viewing their own private intuition of God; it is a sea of love that flows through the one body of all the elect. ... We do not finally taste the full exultation of God's glory until we share his infinite gift of it by overflowing and transmitting glory all over heaven, and seeing God in all the others who are there, and knowing that he is the life of all of us and that we are all one in him.[10]

Such are the main features of Merton's account that I want to highlight at this stage. I will go into more detail shortly, but it is helpful first to have in mind a general shape so that we have our bearings, and to avoid any broad misconceptions. Contemplative prayer, for Merton, is the silent practice aimed at contemplation – at knowledge and love of God for his own sake. In this practice, one attempts to allow oneself to become detached from the things of ordinary experience – detached, that is, from the desire to use things for one's own benefit, so that one may, instead, 'see and use all things in and for God'. And one also aims to become detached from one's ordinary attitudes towards God – one's conceptions, imaginings and so on – for this is a necessary part of coming to know God fully: since God is radically different from anything in our ordinary experience, we would be mistaken in identifying anything in our ordinary experience as God, including anything that conformed to our ordinary ways of thinking. The more one grows in contemplative love and knowledge of God, the more one is freed from one's own self-centredness, leading to a deepened and enriched engagement with the world and with other people in particular. Moreover, the contemplative can also know God in this engagement: such engagement is not simply a consequence of the contemplative knowledge found in prayer, but an extension of that knowledge. In this, one has a foretaste of heaven. With this overview of contemplative prayer in mind, we can now start to look at the prospects of harmonizing such a life with the kind of musical engagement that is centred on recognizing and cultivating desire for God – and in particular, this engagement in its non-doxastic form.

6.2 Contemplative prayer and 'ordinary' desire for God

Let us turn first to the issue of contemplative prayer's relationship to ordinary experience. In fact, now that I have introduced the idea of *contemplation* as that at which contemplative prayer aims, it would be more accurate to say that there is an issue concerning contemplation's relationship to ordinary experience. By 'ordinary experience' I mean the aspects of our experience that are not contemplation and do not arise out of contemplation. Much desire is part of ordinary experience, including much desire for God; indeed, there are innumerable forms of religious experience that count as 'ordinary' in this sense. Given our overall topic, it is ordinary desire for God that concerns us.

Before I highlight the potential difficulties in reconciling contemplation with ordinary desire for God, it is important to note that Merton stresses a certain kind of continuity between contemplation and many aspects of ordinary experience. We find him saying that contemplation has 'something in common' with other forms of experience – including poetry, music, art, philosophy, theology, liturgy and ordinary levels of love and belief.[11] However, alongside this assertion Merton also stresses the apparent radical *difference* between contemplation and all other experience:

> Contemplation seems to supersede and to discard every other form of intuition and experience. … This rejection is of course only apparent. Contemplation is and must be compatible with all these things, for it is their highest fulfilment. But in the actual experience of contemplation all other experiences are momentarily lost. They 'die' to be born again on a higher level of life.[12]

It is within this relationship of both continuity and discontinuity that we must approach the issue of how, within a life of contemplative prayer, to treat the musically elicited desires for God that I have been exploring. Contemplation shares something important with ordinary experience. One can draw closer to God in one's ordinary interactions with things of the world, and this is especially apt for those at a relatively early stage in the spiritual life: 'The best thing beginners in the spiritual life can do [...] is to acquire the agility and freedom of mind that will help them to find light and warmth and ideas and love for God everywhere they go and in all that they do.'[13] Ordinary experience of this sort does not merely share something with contemplation, only to be discarded when contemplation is reached; it is *fulfilled* in contemplation, its true significance recognized. But this fulfilment will not be a straightforward, seamless one: in between ordinary experience and 'the totally spiritualized purity of the saint … there lies an abyss that can only be crossed by a blind leap of ascetic detachment'.[14]

We have already seen something of why this ascetic detachment is needed: God's fundamental difference from anything in the world means that as long as one seeks the God of one's ordinary imagination and thought, one will not find God as he really is. But why should this be so? Could God not simply reveal himself in all his unfamiliarity to someone who had no experience of contemplative prayer, no experience of ascetic detachment? For one way of thinking about why God could not do this with any benefit, we can turn for a moment to Rowan Williams:

> [The contemplative life] means letting go of the emotions that we'd like to have, letting go of what we think makes us happy – not to cultivate misery but to get used to the idea that real joy might be so strange and overwhelming that we'd fail to recognize it unless we had put some distance between us and our usual comforts and re-assurances.[15]

'What we think makes us happy' includes the realm of so-called 'spiritual' experience, and so we must let go of our expectations of how God will make us feel – thus letting go of our ordinary ideas about God – as much as we must let go of how we want the world to make us feel. Hence, Merton stresses that in contemplative prayer we should wait for God's will to be done in us without hungering 'for any experience that comes within the range of our knowledge or memory, because any experience that we can grasp or understand will be inadequate and unworthy of the state to which God wishes to bring our souls'.[16]

This might all seem a little strange: in referring (as Williams does) to the state to which God wishes to bring us as 'real joy', are we not implying that it has something in common with what we usually call 'joy'? And would this not enable us to recognize real joy from our experiences of 'ordinary', or lesser, joy – as a more complete, satisfying version of those experiences? Why does one need ascetic detachment in order to recognize real joy for what it is? To answer this, we can return to a theme touched on at the start of our summary of Merton's thought: contemplation is a gift from God, not something one can earn or achieve. Therefore, it requires utter *humility* on the recipient's part – a full recognition that one's achievements and self-pride do not matter. Merton writes of an 'abyss of interior solitude [that] is a hunger that will never be satisfied with any created thing. ... Yet it is in this loneliness that the deepest activities begin. It is here that you discover ... a fulfilment whose limits extend to infinity.'[17] In order to receive God's gift of love and knowledge of himself, one needs a full recognition of one's own insufficiency, but also of the insufficiency of the world in general, for making one truly joyful – otherwise one will cling to the habit of trying to find happiness only in the world, including in one's own achievements, and not recognize the potential for joy in a life centred on something other than oneself or the world. 'God gives true theologians a *hunger born of humility* ... [that] seeks, in the humiliation of silence, intellectual solitude and interior poverty, the gift of a supernatural apprehension.'[18] In order to recognize the insufficiency of the world in general and of oneself in particular for bringing about real joy, one must stop valuing and using these things as sources of joy in their own right; instead, one must put them aside in silence without drawing on one's own resources. Merton sums up the necessity of putting aside oneself as the source of one's own happiness as follows:

> When humility delivers us from attachment to our own works and our own reputation, we discover that perfect joy is possible only when we have completely forgotten ourselves. And it is only when we pay no more attention to our own deeds and our own reputation and our own excellence that we are at last completely free to serve God in perfection for his sake alone.[19]

We come to know and love God fully when we no longer seek joy in our own achievements or in the world in general for their own sakes. And this means not seeking the sorts of experience in prayer that we are used to enjoying: since it comes from the world, including ourselves, such experience will be tainted with something or other that is symptomatic of the world's inability to give us true joy (as well as self-pride if the apparent joy comes from oneself, we can think of other things that taint our earthly experiences – impermanence or insecurity, for instance).

To sum up the foregoing: although contemplation ultimately fulfils ordinary experience, this fulfilment must come on the other side of an eventual ascetic leap in which one temporarily lets go of attachment to all experience, even that which seemed wholesome and life-giving. This is necessary for receiving God's gift of true joy that resides in knowing and loving him: in order to receive this gift one must fully appreciate the inability of the world in its own right, and specifically one's own inability, to bring true joy; and in order to come to this appreciation one must stop acting as though anything in the world *could* play this role, undertaking, instead, 'in the humiliation of silence' to 'put some distance between [oneself] and [one's] usual comforts and re-assurances'. Part of this distancing will be to let go of one's idea of what it would be like to experience, in prayer, God in himself – in his own right rather than through a filter (for example an intellectual or emotional filter) of one's own making. Only when we are freed of our expectations that we will find our fullest joy simply in our own activity or in that of the world, or, indeed, that we will find it in the sort of prayerful experience that is much like these 'ordinary' kinds of joy – only then will we be able truly to 'taste and see that the LORD is good'.[20] And when one is granted such knowledge of God, knowledge devoid of all self-centredness, the good things in the world that one knew before one's ascetic detachment will be all the clearer, untainted as they now are by one's own ego or by anything else that previously clouded one's perception. That is to say, one will find God in all things.

We can now start to see problems with incorporating the desire-based spiritual practice I have proposed into a life of contemplative prayer. For although Merton highlights the importance of 'ordinary' experience, especially at relatively early stages of the spiritual life, a main obstacle to growing in knowledge of God is the domestication of God into how one would like him to be, and the false expectations that result from this. We have already seen that Merton warns against hungering in prayer 'for any experience that comes within the range of our knowledge or memory'; and the theme of not identifying God with the object of any of our ordinary thoughts, perceptions or emotions appears time and again. For instance:

> The ordinary way to contemplation lies through a desert without trees and without beauty and without water. The spirit enters a wilderness and travels blindly in directions that seem to lead away from vision, away from God, away from all fulfilment and joy.[21]

But the musical route I have so far advocated is precisely one of identifying what God would have to be like in order to satisfy one's desire for him. The epistemology of desire that I developed in Chapter 3 and applied to sacred music in Chapter 5 crucially involves the desirer's having a sense of what would constitute satisfaction, and coming to know vividly and relationally what something would be like in bringing about that satisfaction. How can we engage in this sort of practice without forming a damagingly limited view of God that stifles our capacity to receive him as he really is?

Indeed, the problem is sharpened when we consider what Merton has to say about desire in particular. He is quite clear that we should *not*, in our spiritual lives, seek what we ordinarily (i.e. non-contemplatively) desire, no matter how spiritually worthwhile the objects of such desire might seem. Part of the reason is the aforementioned importance of letting go of what one thinks it would be like to experience God in himself – which means letting go of what one *desires* to experience when one desires God. Instead, we should '[keep] our soul as far as possible empty of desires for all the things that please and preoccupy our nature, no matter how pure or sublime they may be in themselves'.[22] But for Merton, another reason to distance ourselves from our ordinary desires is that desire as we ordinarily have it is by nature possessive – something implied by the very phrase 'to desire *x*':

> To desire God is the most fundamental of all human desires. It is the very root of all our quest for happiness. ... On the other hand, when you use the expression 'to desire God' you implicitly reduce God to the status of an 'object' or of a 'thing', as if he were 'something' that could be grasped and possessed the way we possess riches, or knowledge, or some other created entity. And though it is true that we are bound to hope for the fulfilment of our deepest needs in the vision of God, yet it is at the same time very dangerous to think of God *merely* as the satisfaction of all our needs and desires. In so doing, we tend inevitably to distort and even to desecrate his holy and infinite truth.[23]

In other words, if Merton is right then the path of religious practice I have advocated risks distorting God's nature by stressing his capacity to satisfy our desires. By cultivating specific kinds of desire for God as a key aspect of one's religious engagement, one risks assimilating him to all the other things one desires, meaning that, like those other things, God is desired possessively. Furthermore, the concepts under which we desire God, like any concept of God, '[tell] us more about ourselves than about him'.[24] Thus, being guided by our ordinary desires for God will not result in our satisfaction. As in any personal relationship, our satisfaction in relationship with God would consist in sharing in his life, and this to such an extent that we are united with him. It is this that we should desire if our desire is to lead to our satisfaction, rather than simply desiring to possess God as we do other things. And we will not share in God's life unless we let him be himself for us,[25] rather than pursuing just those aspects we think he ought to have.

6.3 Answering the challenge to 'ordinary' desire for God

How, then, are we to reconcile contemplative prayer with a path of religious practice that not only involves but is also centred on ordinary desire for God? In what follows I hope to show that cultivated in the right way, ordinary desire for God – and specifically the musically elicited forms of desire that I have been discussing – can make a valuable contribution to the path of contemplative prayer. Desire of this sort can provide impetus and direction to a journey of openness to God, contributing to the spiritual maturity that, it is hoped, will be grown in contemplative prayer and find its fullest reality in contemplative knowledge. Much of our task will be to show that ordinary desire for God can avoid the two problems described above: limiting the desirer to seeking out what she thinks God ought to be, thus preventing her from knowing him in his fullness; and reaching for God possessively, rather than seeking to share in his life.

Self-centred and other-centred emotional response

Let us start by making an observation. When one inhabits the musically elicited forms of desire I have discussed, two kinds of attitude may be present to varying degrees: on the one hand, self-regard of some sort; on the other, regard for something other than oneself that is eminently worth pursuing. This is a distinction that Eleonore Stump has discussed. Drawing on the Christian tradition at large and on Aquinas in particular, Stump describes coming closer to God as consisting in longing for the goodness that one perceives in God, which leads one progressively to surrender to God and entrust oneself to him for salvation from one's own evil.[26] Now, in being moved by sacred music's beauty, one might be moved primarily by the beauty itself in a number of ways; alternatively, one might be moved primarily by one's own response to the beauty – with pride in being sophisticated enough to appreciate the beauty, or with sentimental pleasure in being moved by the beauty.[27] And clearly, beauty will not move one closer to God – will not elicit a longing for God's goodness that leads one to trust in God – if one is focused ultimately on oneself.[28] If an affective state elicited by sacred music is to move the listener closer to God, that state's subject matter must centrally involve God or the listener's relationship to him.

What of desire in particular? Stump argues that desire called forth by beauty can help enable one to draw nearer to God in trust and surrender, which (we might add), given the vital importance of humility in coming to contemplative knowledge of God, is central to the contemplative path. In perceiving certain kinds of musical beauty, one can be moved to a hunger or restlessness with no clear object, but which is satisfiable only by God's intimate presence.[29] What Stump is getting at is perhaps something like the following. As long as we consider ourselves fairly content we will not seek anything beyond our ordinary experience, which means we will not entrust ourselves to God for salvation from our own evil. We must feel restless or unsatisfied with anything the world could provide, even if only for brief periods, in order to allow ourselves to be drawn towards God. Beauty, and musical beauty in particular, can elicit such a feeling of restless hunger; and if we come to identify this dissatisfaction with an enduring aspect of our existence in general, then we are likelier to immerse ourselves in a practice and way of life – of which contemplative prayer might be an integral part – that aims at a fulfilment transcending this world.

I think these brief considerations are enough to show that if a desire for God is 'ordinary' or 'non-contemplative', it is not automatically inimical to the contemplative life. The sort of restless yearning that Stump describes is in an important sense a desire for God: although lacking an articulable object, it would, nonetheless, be satisfied by God as classically conceived. Although the desirer may not realize it fully, the desire's subject matter centrally involves the sort of liberation or fullness that Merton and other believers in God have described. That said, it is something further to say that the forms of desire for God *that I discussed in Chapter 5* are conducive to the aims of contemplative prayer: the dangers of domestication and possessiveness remain. But we should not be too quick to dismiss Stump's insights as irrelevant to our concerns. The role I described her musically elicited, restless hunger as playing – awakening the listener to the possibility of seeking something beyond ordinary experience – can certainly also be played by the more specific kinds of desire in Chapter 5. I shall now argue that if these kinds of desire are inhabited in the outwards-facing, other-centred way I have identified, then they can lead one away from focusing ultimately on oneself – thereby avoiding the dangers of possessiveness and domestication.

Answering Merton's worries: possessiveness and domestication

I. *An analogy*

An analogy from romantic desire may help here.[30] One aspect of romantic desire is where it lies on the following spectrum. At one end, I might desire someone entirely possessively, wanting simply to have her undivided affection and loyalty. At the other end, my desire might be only for her good and to share in her life, the two of us united in our joys, sadnesses, hopes and fears.[31] Of course, most actual cases of romantic desire will lie somewhere between the two extremes; indeed, a desire's position along the spectrum may vary over time. But in thinking about the two ends of the spectrum, we can be clear on the kind of focus to which, plausibly, one should *aspire* in desiring someone romantically. Desire at the first end of the spectrum, in its possessiveness, is focused ultimately on the desirer. In wanting someone's undivided affection and loyalty and wanting nothing else as directly regards her, I do not want these things for her sake. Rather, I want them for my own sake – in all likelihood so that I can feel affirmed in some way. At the other end of the spectrum, by contrast, the desire is focused ultimately on the beloved. It is *her* good that I want, and *her* life in which I wish to share. All notion of 'having' something for myself, of acquiring something and thereby enlarging myself, is absent here. Such a desire is not possessive. Rather, in being aimed at sharing in the life of the one I love, it is aimed at my true satisfaction – a satisfaction that, paradoxically, requires me to give up thoughts of my own happiness considered in abstraction from the happiness of the beloved.

What about the other danger I identified – that of focusing just on the attributes one would like another person to have (which she may or may not actually have to some degree), resulting in an inability to be with and acknowledge that person fully? Is this mitigated by the desire's being focused on the beloved rather than on oneself? We must recognize here that as far as romantic desire is concerned, we will always be attracted to someone in virtue of attributes that they possess. Insofar as the desire is focused ultimately on the beloved, there will be some reason why I want to share in *this* person's life, want to be united to *this* person in shared joys, sadnesses, hopes and fears, want *this* person's happiness. The motivation for my desire for a particular person may be hard to articulate fully, but it will be there.[32] The question is this: If a desire is focused ultimately on the beloved, does the fact that the desirer finds some of the beloved's attributes especially attractive limit the desirer's capacity to know and love her? And the answer, we have to say, is no: this salience in the desirer's awareness of certain attractive attributes does not limit the desirer's capacity to know and love the beloved, if the desire, rather than being self-centred, is truly centred on the beloved. There is an openness to the desire to share in someone's life – an openness to discovering new things about that person and to knowing her more deeply – that is lacking in the desire merely to have someone's undivided affection and loyalty. If one has this openness, then although one will start out with an awareness of certain attributes that draw one to the other person, one's engagement with the other will not be limited by those attributes. Instead, they will be a way in – perhaps acting as foci to which one may return again and again in deeper and deeper knowledge, but not clouding one's perception of the beloved or interfering with one's coming to know her in an increasingly textured, real way.[33]

II. Desiring God without possessiveness or domestication

Although there are important dissimilarities between romantic desire and the desire for God (one of which I will broach in a moment), the above truths about romantic desire hold in at least some degree in relation to desire for God. One can desire God for possessive reasons and thus be focused ultimately on oneself (for instance, one might want to possess God's goodness so that one can feel morally superior), or one can desire him for his own sake, desire non-possessively to be united with him in a meeting of wills. Furthermore, on the picture that Merton paints, the other-centred desire for God is the one whose fulfilment would constitute the desirer's true satisfaction – just like the equivalent kind of romantic desire; and as in romantic desire, this satisfaction would require the desirer to give up thoughts of her own happiness considered in abstraction from the happiness of the beloved – that is, of God.

However, somewhat more complicated is how the 'domestication' issue in a romantic context is related to that issue in a religious context. I submit that in religious contexts, as much as in romantic ones, a desire focused on particular attributes is less limiting if it is focused ultimately on the other person rather than on oneself, and is thus constituted in part by a willingness to grow in knowledge of that person. But in the religious case, and on Merton's picture specifically, matters are complicated by the fact that the *divine* attributes to which one is attracted will differ significantly from those attributes' counterparts as one knows them from one's experience of the world (remember that, for Merton, we should not hunger in prayer 'for any experience that comes within the range of our knowledge or memory'). If I am open to growing in knowledge of a person based on my attraction to certain attributes that I find in the world, how am I to grow in knowledge of *God*, rather than growing in knowledge of an invention of mine that has attributes more or less the same as those I value in the world?

It is here that we can, for desires focused on specific attributes, recall the role played by Stump's more general restless desire, namely, awakening the desirer to the possibility of seeking something beyond ordinary experience. We have already seen that for Merton, contemplation fulfils ordinary experience – and this includes experience of the attributes in worldly contexts that one is drawn to seek in their religious forms, such as the attributes that would satisfy the desires in Chapter 5. Despite the fact that this fulfilment must come through a period of ascetic detachment, the fact remains that there must be *some* similarity between contemplation and ordinary experience. Merton attests to this in at least two ways.

First, he describes contemplation in terms of pre-contemplative experience. In one particularly striking passage he uses metaphors drawn from a variety of physical senses:

> A door opens in the centre of our being and we seem to fall though it into immense depths that, although they are infinite, are all accessible to us. ... God touches us with a touch that is emptiness and empties us. ... Our mind swims in the air of an understanding, a reality that is dark and serene and includes in itself everything. ... You have sunk to the centre of your own poverty, and there you have felt the doors fly open into infinite freedom ... the depths of wide open darkness that have yawned inside you ... are not a place, not an extent, they are a huge, smooth activity. These depths, they are love. ... There is even a whole sphere of your own activity that is excluded from that beautiful airy night. The five senses, the imagination, the discoursing mind, the hunger of desire do not belong in that starless sky. ... This is the gift of understanding: we pass out of ourselves into the joy of emptiness, of nothingness, in which there are no longer any particular objects of knowledge but only God's truth. ... This clean light, which tastes of Paradise, ... is in all and for all. It is the true light that shines in everyone, in 'every man coming into this world.' It is the light of Christ, 'who stands in the midst of us and we know him not'.[34]

'It can be suggested by words, by symbols, but in the very moment of trying to indicate what it knows the contemplative mind takes back what it has said and denies what it has affirmed'[35] – so says Merton of contemplation. It seems, then, that in the descriptive passage just quoted, Merton aims to convey very incompletely something of what contemplation is like. We just have to be sure that we do not ascribe too much similarity to that experience and the things he mentions in his metaphors. In some way that is perhaps impossible to articulate, contemplation is like falling into immense depths, being touched, swimming, spacious darkness, an airy night, the wide expanse of a starless sky, the kinds of serenity and freedom familiar to us from ordinary experience, the love we know in our ordinary relationships, a clean light. All these things can give us some hint of what contemplation is like.

A second way in which Merton implies some similarity between contemplation and ordinary experience is by reporting that when one is granted contemplative knowledge of God, one realizes that one previously had some implicit sense of what it would be like:

> The first taste of [contemplation] strikes us at once as utterly new and yet strangely familiar. Although you had an entirely different notion of what it would be like (since no book can give an adequate idea of contemplation except to those who have experienced it), it turns out to be just what you seem to have known all along that it ought to be.[36]

The choice of words here is instructive: our pre-contemplative *notion* – our abstract belief[37] – of what contemplation is like can only be entirely inaccurate, yet we somehow *know* what it ought to be like before we experience it. While it may in theory be possible to have this kind of foreknowledge without having experienced anything similar, the way Merton elsewhere speaks positively of ordinary experience strongly suggests that such foreknowledge of contemplation can be aided by ordinary experience (we have seen that he instructs spiritual beginners to 'find light and warmth and ideas and love for God everywhere they go and in all that they do').

And so we can conclude that on Merton's picture, when one's sense of what particular divine attributes would be like is based on one's experience of worldly attributes (as it may often be when one desires God in the ways described in Chapter 5), one may, indeed, glimpse in some obscure way something of those divine attributes. In light of this, we can now round out our answer to the second of Merton's worries about ordinary desire for God, namely, that it risks domesticating God, limiting one's capacity to receive him as he really is by leading one to value just some of his attributes. We saw that in romantic contexts, a desire focused on specific attributes of a person is less limiting if it is focused ultimately on the other person and not on oneself, and is thus constituted in part by a willingness to grow in knowledge of that person. Assuming that growing in knowledge of God can work in a somewhat similar way – moving from love of specific attributes to love of the person as a whole[38] – a desire focused ultimately on God that is centred on specific divine attributes can be a way into knowing God himself, beyond any focus on specific attributes. To desire in this way is, as Talbot Brewer has put it, 'to be drawn to another by a generous straining to bring into focus the goodness, hence desirability, of an as yet obscure object of desire'.[39] And the foregoing considerations suggest that in the 'attributes stage' just outlined, a desire can be focused on specific divine attributes by drawing on the desirer's experience of the world. Therefore, in desiring God as one imagines him based on one's experience of worldly attributes, one can be open to coming to know God himself – as long as the desire is focused ultimately on God and not on oneself.

III. Growing in contemplative love and knowledge of God

I now want to come from another angle at the connection between loving some of a person's attributes and loving the person – an angle that, importantly, acknowledges one's ability to undertake some of this journey into knowing and loving someone *even before being personally acquainted* with them. In Chapter 5, our overarching concern was an awareness of what God would have to be like in order to satisfy the musically elicited desires that I described. One of the most interesting aspects of the knowledge that, I argued, those desires and that awareness can give was that such knowledge is available even without the experience of satisfaction – without any experience in which God seems present (although past experience of at least something similar is needed). It is knowledge *about* God in certain respects if he exists, but not knowledge *of* God in himself. However, even this 'absent knowledge' *about* God can be understood as nascent knowledge *of* God, in the sense of being part of a process that can culminate in intimate love and knowledge of God. We can start to know someone by knowing about the characteristic aspects of that person. On eventually meeting the person we might say, 'I feel I already know you quite well': if our pre-acquaintance characterization was at least somewhat accurate, then when we eventually meet them we will be further along the path of knowing them than we would have been had we known nothing about them at all. Moreover, in the pre-acquaintance religious knowledge for which I argued in Chapter 5, there is more than just knowledge about certain divine attributes: central to the epistemic state I articulated is a grasp of what God would have to be like *in relation to oneself* were he to satisfy one's desires for him. If God really does have those attributes, then by having *this* sort of pre-acquaintance knowledge, one will make some progress along the path of knowing him not merely in a third-personal, objective way, but in a second-personal, relational way, in terms of his significance to oneself as the desirer. Having grown in this sort of knowledge about someone before meeting them, one may of course meet the person and get to know them better, perhaps growing in love of the person, in full personal relationship – even if there will always be more to know.

Let us fill in a little this journey from desire for God that is felt before contemplation, indeed before any experience in which God seems present, through contemplative growth in knowledge and love of God. One important aspect of the desires discussed in Chapter 5 was that they were for God in virtue of divine attributes that could be conceptualized. Now Merton does state that we can have a 'valid concept of the divine nature'.[40] 'The dogmas defined and taught by the Church have a very precise, positive, and definite meaning ... the understanding of dogma is the proximate and ordinary way to contemplation.'[41] This is another indication of some degree of similarity between pre-contemplative and contemplative experience. Our pre-contemplative concepts, including those that go into understanding the church's 'dogma', can only be informed by ordinary experience. And this ordinary experience can inform concepts of God that are helpful for setting one on the right track to contemplation – concepts accurate enough to give one some sense of what one is aiming at in contemplative prayer.

However, once again an assertion of Merton's on the spiritual helpfulness of ordinary experience is coupled with an important caveat. We can have a valid concept of the divine nature – and yet

> in contemplation abstract notions of the divine essence no longer play an important part since they are replaced by a concrete intuition, based on love, of God as a Person, an object of love, not a 'nature' or a 'thing', which would be the object of study or of possessive desire.[42]

But this should not be taken to mean our concepts of God must be *discarded* in contemplation. Rather, like the 'ordinary' experience that shapes them, they are *fulfilled*:

> It is not the dry formula of a dogmatic definition by itself that pours light into the mind of a ... contemplative, but the assent to the content of that definition deepens and broadens into a vital, personal and incommunicable penetration of the supernatural truth it expresses.[43]

In other words, we can have valid concepts of God and use them to guide our thoughts and affects – including our desires for God. These concepts will include that of God as a *person* so that he may be 'an object of love' for the desirer, and not an 'object of study or of possessive desire'. Eventually, in contemplation, we may come to have a fuller experiential awareness of the God alluded to in those concepts.

Earlier we saw aspects of how this fuller awareness is continuous (phenomenologically, not temporally) with ordinary experience; and it is worth ending this section by touching on how contemplation can specifically affect one's desire for God. I have argued that pre-contemplative desire can be conducive to the path of contemplative practice, but we have not seen how desire itself can be refined and deepened as one grows in contemplative knowledge and love.[44] An answer to this question will also be an answer to the charge of self-deceit, or wishful thinking, that has periodically reared its head – for, as we shall see, the contemplatively refined desire that Merton describes will not automatically be one's foremost desire for God. What we get is a description of desire that has been contemplatively 'purged' and that is therefore rightly ordered towards God by contemplative lights. Such a desire is distinct from any number of other desires that would *not* be completely rightly ordered towards God and that would therefore (to some extent) constitute wishful thinking. Hence, we have a standard for testing our desire for God: how does it measure up to what Merton describes in the passages below? On Merton's picture, the more one's desire is focused on God and not on oneself – and, therefore, the less possessive and domesticating of God the desire is – the more it will be conducive to contemplative knowledge of God. Thus, desire for God at its purest is completely untainted by any hint of self-interest:

> In the vivid darkness of God within us there sometimes come deep movements of love that deliver us entirely, for a moment, from our old burden of selfishness. … And when God allows us to fall back into our own confusion of desires and judgements and temptations, we carry a scar over the place where that joy exulted for a moment in our hearts. The scar burns us. The sore wound aches within us, and we remember that we have fallen back into what we are not, and are not yet allowed to remain where God would have us belong. We long for the place he has destined for us and weep with desire for the time when this pure poverty will catch us and hold us in its liberty and never let us go.[45]

Such desire for God, arising from moments of contemplative clarity, is characterized by a total concern for something, or rather someone, other than oneself. It is the sort of other-centred attention that one may also inhabit fleetingly in ordinary experience; indeed, such moments can be among our greatest joys – think, for instance, of easy, unselfconscious conversation with a close friend, or the triumph, shared with thousands of others, at the success of one's favourite sports team. Irvin Yalom, whom we encountered in the previous chapter, notes that such moments at their fullest can seem like moments of *union*: 'The lonely *I* ecstatically dissolving into the *we*. How often I've heard that! It's the common denominator of every form of bliss – romantic, sexual, political, religious, mystical. Everyone wants and welcomes this blissful merger.'[46] And sure enough, for Merton, contemplatively informed desire reaches its apotheosis when its satisfaction would consist in complete union with God. Let us end this section with a passage that conveys a palpable sense of this desire; moreover, in referring to the Lord's Prayer (recited at all stages of spiritual development), it acknowledges that such desire is present to a degree even in relatively nascent spirituality. Here, perhaps, is the strongest sense Merton gives of how desire can be refined and deepened by contemplative experience, central to which is detachment from one's preconceptions about God; yet this is coupled with an awareness that pre-contemplative desire – such as the desires now familiar from our discussions of sacred music – can give a foretaste of the contemplative desire for loving union with the divine:

> Where contemplation becomes what it is really meant to be, it is no longer something infused by God into a created subject, so much as God living in God and identifying a created life with his own Life so that there is nothing left of any significance but God living in God ... we are emptied into God and transformed into his joy. ... It is in this ecstasy of pure love that we arrive at a true fulfilment of the first commandment, loving God with our whole heart and our whole mind and all our strength. Therefore it is something that all those who desire to please God ought to desire – not for a minute, nor for half an hour, but forever. It is in these souls that peace is established in the world. ... They have renounced the whole world and it has been given into their possession. They alone appreciate the world and the things that are in it. They are the only ones capable of understanding joy. ... [God] does all that they want, because he is the one who desires all their desires. They are the only ones who have everything that they can desire. Their freedom is without limit. They reach out for us to comprehend our misery and drown it in the tremendous expansion of their own innocence, that washes the world with its light.
>
> Come, let us go into the body of that light. Let us live in the cleanliness of that song. Let us throw off the pieces of the world like clothing and enter naked into wisdom. For this is what all hearts pray for when they cry: 'Thy will be done.'[47]

6.4 Contemplative prayer and propositional belief

The problem

Let us now turn to the second of our issues to be addressed, namely, the relationship between contemplative prayer and propositional belief in Christian doctrine. Since our concern in previous chapters has been a *non-doxastic* form of engagement with Christian sacred music, this had better be compatible with contemplative prayer if the congruence for which I am arguing is to hold. However, once again we seem to encounter a problem. For Merton, it is clear that one must believe the teachings of the church (specifically, the Roman Catholic Church) in order to be open to the gifts God is said to give in contemplation.

We can get a better handle on this by seeing that both *understanding* and *assent* are involved in contemplative insight. Earlier I quoted Merton as saying that 'the understanding of dogma is the proximate and ordinary way to contemplation' – since 'unless [contemplation and theology] are united, there is … no substance, no meaning, and no sure orientation in the contemplative life'.[48] A degree of doctrinal understanding is available prior to any experience of contemplation, and is important to that experience. Yet contemplative experience itself is necessary for a *full* understanding of doctrine: again, we have already encountered Merton's statement that 'the assent to the content of [a dogmatic] definition deepens and broadens into a vital, personal and incommunicable penetration of the supernatural truth it expresses'. Doctrinal assent is not *negated* by contemplation, but *completed*, its full meaning coming into view. One has a partial, pre-contemplative understanding of the church's dogma; one assents to the dogma thus understood; and eventually, progressively, this assent is enriched by what one encounters in contemplation, so that one grasps more fully the meaning of the dogma – 'the supernatural truth it expresses'. And here lies the rub: for Merton, the doctrinal assent here must involve *belief*: belief in a given doctrine is necessary for the contemplatively enriched understanding of that doctrine. He writes: 'The first step to contemplation is faith; and faith begins with an assent to Christ teaching through his Church.'[49] And in case one is left in any doubt that the 'assent' in question should involve belief,

> Formulas … are means through which God communicates his truth to us. … They must be clean windows, so that they may not obscure and hinder the light that comes to us. … Therefore we must make every effort to believe the right formulas.[50]

While propositional belief may often be psychologically intertwined with other states, such as the 'belief in' a person that is akin to trust, it is at least conceptually distinct enough to be reflected on in its own right.[51]

An apparently persuasive reason for the claim that belief is necessary for contemplation is not far to seek. It seems on the face of it highly doubtful that one could undertake the contemplative journey as a whole, including the 'dark nights' of ascetic detachment, without believing that there is a point to it all that lies beyond one's present grasp of the situation. Merton understandably emphasizes that when in the 'wilderness' of ascetic detachment, it is vital to retain one's trust in God: 'A simple and faithful expectation of help from God.'[52] And a little later: 'What you most need in this dark journey is an unfaltering trust in the divine guidance, as well as the courage to risk everything for God.'[53] Does trust in God require a belief that God is real, and that he is trustworthy? It is true that nothing in the concept of personal trust (trust *in*, in contrast to trust *that*) requires a belief that the object of trust exists and is trustworthy, although clearly it does involve *some* kind of assent to these propositions.[54] I argued in Chapter 2 that for an interested non-believer, religious involvement – of which trust in God is a key aspect – can be propositionally framed by truth-normed acceptance combined with hope.[55] However, although propositional belief in the reality of whomever one trusts is not *conceptually* necessary for that trust, it may look as though propositional belief is *psychologically* necessary for trust in the context of contemplative prayer. At the very least, it is hard to see how, without any belief that God were real, it would be possible to place one's trust and expectation in God in the crisis of the 'dark nights'. Would one really be willing to risk everything for God – that is, have oneself extricated from one's ordinary ways of valuing and engaging with the world – if one lacked a belief that the risk would pay off?

Merton's talk of risking everything for God inevitably brings to mind Pascal's Wager, which we encountered in Chapter 2.[56] Pascal's argument hinges on an assessment of the comparative risks involved in wagering that Christian theism is true, and in wagering that it is false. He concludes that the risk of wagering for its truth – our loss if we are wrong – is insignificant (perhaps nothing more than some time spent in church and in prayer). The risk of wagering for its falsity is much greater: we stand to lose 'everything' if we are wrong and God turns out to be real.[57] We should therefore wager for Christian theism's truth.[58]

There is no need here to go into a detailed assessment of the argument in its various guises; instead, I simply wish to focus on how its conclusion looks in the context of contemplative prayer. Pascal assumed that wagering on Christian theism's truth does not require belief that it is true – at least not at first. One can start out by 'behav[ing] just as if [one] did believe, taking holy water, having masses said, and so on'. Eventually, one will 'believe quite naturally'.[59] In other words, the wagerer's religious involvement will be non-doxastic, at least at first. The truth-normed acceptance combined with hope that I described in Chapter 2 is a version of such involvement. However, we may well question whether, when and to what degree belief might come to someone who engages in contemplative prayer as part of the religious practice that Pascal advocates. Here we come to the crux of the matter. For the would-be contemplative, who must travel through the wilderness of the 'dark nights', there is significant risk involved: specifically, the risk of a theistic wager that turns out to be erroneous, and which does *not* bring about the belief that one might think is necessary in order to trust in God during the contemplative 'nights'. Merton describes these 'nights', or (presumably speaking of both the night of the senses and that of the spirit[60]) simply 'The Dark Night', as 'the crisis of suffering that rends our roots out of this world'.[61] If the contemplative practitioner is not convinced, somewhere in her being, that such suffering will ultimately be worthwhile, can we really expect her to enter it voluntarily? Contemplative prayer will almost certainly involve meditation of some kind;[62] and recent research has shown, unsurprisingly, that meditation can sometimes have traumatic effects, such as terror, panic or 'depersonalization' – that is, the dissolution of one's sense of identity.[63] While this is just what one might expect from a Christian perspective (and, indeed, other religious traditions, such as some of those found in Buddhism, make similar predictions[64]), to lack any framework of belief in which to place such experiences would threaten to strip them of any positive significance.

Speaking strictly according to the logic of Pascal's argument, in order for the risk of error to prevent a theistic wager from being worthwhile, it would have to be a risk of something *infinitely bad*: only then would it cancel out the infinitely good reward that one would receive if correct. And it is perhaps difficult to make the case that there would be *infinitely* negative value in the negative, frightening results of meditation both devoid of religious belief and situated within an erroneous metaphysical framework. However (and this is a shortcoming in Pascal's argument), it seems unrealistic to expect one knowingly to take this risk without much of a sense that it will pay off. Hence, Merton's insistence that belief is a necessary precondition for a life of contemplative prayer appears, on the face of it, very reasonable.

Answering the problem

We must find a way in which it would be understandable for an interested non-believer to take the plunge into a sustained commitment to contemplative prayer. As a starting point, we can consider the opposite scenario: an interested non-believer foregoes contemplative prayer, because the prospect of being uprooted from one's ordinary engagement with the world is not especially appealing. Would this, in fact, be the right thing to do? Even in Merton's thinking, there are clues that it is not so simple. The following passage introduces a caveat on the importance of belief:

> If there is no *light* of faith, no interior illumination of the mind by grace, by which one accepts the proposed truth *from God* and thereby attains to it, so to

speak, in his divine assurance, then inevitably the mind lacks the true peace, the supernatural support that is due to it. In that event there is not real faith. The positive element of light is lacking. There is a forced suppression of doubt rather than the opening of the eye of the heart by deep belief.[65]

So we should not try to force belief – that much is clear. But in that case, should we withhold from contemplative practice? One reason why this may not be such a good idea after all is something we have already encountered: the full meaning of doctrine comes into view in contemplative experience. Unless one's religious engagement has this dimension, one will be in an impoverished position to assess the truth-value of doctrinal claims, since one will not understand them fully. If fear of the 'dark nights' of contemplative prayer prevents a non-believer from engaging in the practice, then that non-believer will persist in a conception of God, and in an understanding of the more specific Christian doctrines, that are impoverished to some extent – and this may well affect whether or not she comes to believe that God is real and that those doctrines are true.[66] No doubt it is true, as I argued in the previous chapter, that before any contemplative insight, one can have knowledge about the God in question – including knowledge of how he would be important to oneself in various ways (such knowledge does not entail anything about whether God is, indeed, real). However, such a God, if he is real, is one whom humans can recognize more fully the more we 'let him be himself for us' in contemplative prayer, to return to Rowan Williams' phrase. It may therefore be to the benefit of the interested non-believer to take the plunge, for only by doing so will she be able to assess such doctrine for truth in a deeply informed way.

Be that as it may, we are still left with the question of how a non-believer might have the resolve to journey into the 'dark nights'. To be sure, the person in question might be merely curious, or be otherwise attracted to a Christian contemplative life for superficial reasons; she might, for instance, find an appeal in the 'comeliness' that a life of simplicity and prayer can have.[67] If this is the case, then there is surely no hope of having the presence of mind and resolve that are needed for the journey. However, if one follows the recommendations of the previous chapter, then one's attraction to a theistic (and specifically, in our case, a Christian) outlook will go rather deeper and be rather more informed. If, through desiring God in response to sacred music, one knows something of the divine attributes in terms of their importance to oneself as the desirer, then one will already be quite vividly aware of the inadequacies in one's life to which, we are told, there can be answers in a commitment to contemplative practice. The desire for the kind of compassionate presence that encompasses the very worst suffering we can undergo (*Hear My Prayer, O Lord*); the desire for an assurance of intimate divine protection in the dark aspects of our lives (*Abendlied*); the desire for the full unfolding, beyond earthly death, of the salvation that has purportedly been revealed in Jesus of Nazareth (Nunc Dimittis): all these find their most intense form and expression in contemplative prayer. Thus, in contemplatively refined form, these desires are supposed eventually to find their fulfilment in contemplation. In other words, the *pre-contemplative* desires, in contemplatively refined versions, are supposed to find their fulfilment in contemplation. Hence, one can be compelled by what these desires reveal about one's present condition to seek answers in contemplative prayer. If one already has the desires in some form, then that is a sign that one already has a good deal of the motivation needed for sustained contemplative practice.

Let us look at all this in a little more detail. The desires for compassionate presence in distress (Purcell) and for an assurance of divine protection in darkness (Rheinberger) are precisely those that find their strongest outworking in the contemplative 'nights'. It is important to avoid confusion here. I do not mean that these desires in their contemplative forms are desires for any particular experience – for instance, prayerful peace. This would be to make the mistake mentioned earlier: that of being attached to a certain idea of what it would be like to experience God in prayer. Nevertheless, if one is to inhabit the 'dark nights' in a way that will bear spiritual fruit, then the desire for God's compassion and protection must be central. I have noted the importance Merton ascribes to 'a simple and faithful expectation of help from God' in the wilderness of ascetic detachment. An expectation of x, where x is perceived as good, involves a desire for x. So a desire for God's help must be central to the 'dark nights'; and what could this help be if not some form of compassion, and protection from being completely 'beaten down ... by dryness and helplessness'?[68] We can conclude, then, that the desires for divine compassion and protection – versions of the desires we find in Purcell's and Rheinberger's pieces – are central to a spiritually fruitful inhabitation of the 'nights' of contemplation.

Moreover, contemplative prayer as Merton presents it will likely involve the desire that, I argued, is a natural response to Stanford's and Howells' settings of the Nunc Dimittis: a desire for God in the capacity of bringing about the full unfolding of the salvation embodied in Christ, enabling us to share fully in his peace and glory after death. Recall that the satisfaction of that desire would ultimately involve a state of peace consisting in a life of mutual love and gift with others, in the full presence of divine glory. Recall also, from our initial exposition of Merton's thought, that such a state of affairs is precisely how Merton describes the 'ultimate perfection of the contemplative life':

> A sea of love that flows through the one body of all the elect ... We do not finally taste the full exultation of God's glory until we share his infinite gift of it by overflowing and transmitting glory all over heaven, and seeing God in all the others who are there, and knowing that he is the life of all of us and that we are all one in him.[69]

In order to commit to the path of contemplative prayer, it is helpful – necessary, even – to have some sense of what one is aiming at. Moreover, once again the desire would likely (eventually) become intensified in the contemplative context, as one grew into a deepened understanding of the meaning of terms like 'love' and 'glory'. However, because one can pre-contemplatively have the desire in some form, one can have some awareness of needs and shortcomings in human life that cannot be met by the world alone – but can purportedly be met through a practice of contemplative prayer. The same goes for the desires I described as responses to Purcell's and Rheinberger's pieces – and (I would wager) for many other forms of desire for God that sacred music can elicit.

In effect, this sort of situation involves specific instances of the musical response that we saw Stump describe earlier, in which one is moved to a hunger or restlessness. When one is thus moved (either in the specific ways I have canvassed or in Stump's general way), even if one does not *believe* that those needs will ultimately find a response in God through contemplation, the prospect of doing nothing, of not engaging, starts to look less appealing. It is no longer a choice between, on the one hand, being in the world in an apparently satisfying way, and on the other, risking all this for a reward whose obtaining is far from certain. Rather, what one now has is a choice between (on the one hand) being in the world in an increasingly *unsatisfying* way as the desires in question become ever more pervasive in one's outlook, and (on the other) risking *this* for a reward whose obtaining is far from certain. The less appeal one finds in what one already has, the more compelling is the prospect of giving it up for an infinitely good reward. And if, as the desires elicited by our music suggest, what one already has turns out to be *deeply* unsatisfying, then the prospect of giving it up for a reward – even an uncertain one – that promises eventual satisfaction becomes deeply compelling.

Thus, the resolve that is needed for enduring the 'dark nights' of contemplation can come just from a shift in how one sees one's life condition, marked by desires that cannot be satisfied by anything in the world. For the interested non-believer, truth-normed acceptance combined with hope can serve as a framing for contemplative practice: belief that the ascetic undertaking will eventually find its reward is not needed in advance. But the hope will be that as one journeys further along the contemplative path, and, perhaps, ever more deeply into the contemplative 'nights', 'our certainty increases with … obscurity'.[70] And if this path eventually leads to belief, it will be belief in propositions whose meanings are contemplatively enriched in the way I have already referred to. Such enrichment will flow from the fact that 'one not only assents to propositions revealed by God, … but one assents to God himself. … One fully accepts the statement not only for its own content, but for the sake of him who made it.'[71]

6.5 Conclusions

In this chapter I have examined Merton's characterization of the Christian contemplative life, arguing that it can be enriched by musically elicited desire for God such as those discussed in Chapter 5. Merton warns against what I called 'possessiveness' and 'domestication' in desiring God: wanting to possess God as one possesses other, worldly things; and focusing only on those attributes that one would like God to have. In addressing this challenge, I drew on Eleonore Stump's work and distinguished two forms a desire may take: self-centred or other-centred. I argued that if a desire for God is centred on God rather than on oneself, then it is not possessive; rather, it is a desire to be united with him in a meeting of wills. Similarly, a God-centred desire can avoid the danger of domestication – even if it is focused on specific divine attributes, as are the desires of the previous chapter. As such, these kinds of desire need not be an obstacle to growing in love and knowledge of God through contemplative practice. Indeed, they can be part of what is grown, reaching their apotheosis in the desire for total union with God.

I then turned to the issue of non-doxastic engagement in contemplative prayer. Using the conceptual apparatus of Pascal's Wager, I articulated an apparently compelling reason to agree with Merton in taking propositional belief in Christian doctrine as a necessary precondition to contemplative prayer. Given the potential trauma of the contemplative 'nights' – a trauma sometimes mirrored in secular meditation – it would seem to be an act of folly to risk what one has (one's present way of engaging with and valuing the world), and enter into contemplative prayer without a framework of belief that gives positive significance to such experiences. Moreover, if the prayer turns out to be based on erroneous metaphysical assumptions, then the trauma will, it seems, have been for nothing. In response to this challenge, I showed that the musically elicited desires of Chapter 5 find a central place in contemplative prayer. One can therefore be guided by those desires into a sustained commitment to contemplative practice, since the 'stakes' (to use Pascal's terminology) are different given the desires in question. One now perceives oneself to have less to lose, since the desires reveal a deep dissatisfaction that cannot be met by anything the world has to offer, but which can purportedly be met in contemplation. Hence, propositional belief in religious doctrine is not, after all, needed in order for a commitment to contemplative prayer to make sense – even given the risks involved.

We see, then, that the musically elicited desires for God discussed in Chapter 5, and the non-doxastic religious engagement they can shape, are deeply consonant with the Christian contemplative life as Merton presents it. Cultivating those desires, and others, through exposure to sacred music is one way to be receptive to what, according to Merton, are those ultimately important things grown in contemplative practice: love and knowledge of God as he is in himself. If the God in question is real, then responding to sacred music by desiring him can give the desirer this love and knowledge in a nascent form. The hope is that it will then gradually flourish in contemplative prayer: the heart of one's involvement in a religious life.

7

General conclusion

This study has analysed in depth a phenomenon that a good many people will find familiar: the experience of being moved by sacred choral music in a way that does not depend on believing in the reality of God, or in the truth of specific religious doctrines. In the foregoing chapters, I have argued for one way in which such deep enjoyment of sacred music can be focused on cultivating openness to God, as he is characterized in the Christian devotional context I have been examining. This is an undertaking that believers and interested non-believers alike will want to take seriously, and my focus on desire for God has made the path I have advocated eminently available to non-believers.

The overall argument has taken in a range of topics: the phenomenology and conditions of interested non-belief; the nature and variety of non-doxastic, propositional attitudes; the philosophies of emotion, desire and music. It is my hope that the conclusions reached in these areas will be interesting in their own right. However, these conclusions were ultimately geared towards the discussions of sacred music and contemplative prayer in the final two chapters. Only Chapter 5 discussed both sacred music and desire for God in detail: there I examined four pieces of music, in order to give three in-depth examples of how knowledge-by-desire in response to sacred music can work. However, the interface between these two topics has been my overall focus. Chapters 2–4 were aimed at establishing claims that gave Chapter 5's arguments their context and significance, and which undergirded those arguments. Chapter 6, meanwhile, opened out Chapter 5's content onto wider considerations of religious life and practice. The desiring responses to sacred music described in Chapter 5, and, indeed, other responses to sacred music that are of the same general kind, are not limited in their significance to the chapel or concert hall. Rather, because they are consonant with Christian contemplative spirituality, at least as Merton presents it, these responses can be taken up into contemplative prayer, thus infusing one's wider religious involvement – and, by extension, the rest of one's life.

In all this, I have developed in a particular direction a religious 'epistemology of involvement'. I explained the general idea in the Introduction and in Chapter 2: it is a form of epistemology based on the recognition that religious understanding must require openness and receptivity, and that these, in turn, presuppose involvement in religious practice and the cultivation of certain patterns of affective response. In particular, I have aimed to exploit the possibility of non-doxastic religious engagement that such an epistemology leaves open. Cultivating desires for God that yield personally significant knowledge of the kind I have described – knowledge of what God would be like in satisfying the desires – can help a non-believer grow in openness to God. That is, such desires can help a non-believer grow in her capacity to receive and live out the inestimable benefits that are available if God is real, central to which are knowing and loving God in himself. Engaging with sacred music is an especially good way to cultivate the desires in question: because of its capacity to combine with other aspects of the listener's experience, including text and wider devotional context, such music can elicit desires with the conceptual content necessary for yielding knowledge of the kind that has been my concern. It should go without saying that there are also other elements of religious practice in which a non-believer can engage if she seeks to cultivate openness to God. Liturgical participation is a clear example; indeed, regular involvement in liturgy can provide structure and context to the experience of sacred music. However, for the sake of focus I have simply developed one, musical, strand of how a religious epistemology of involvement could look: a strand that could no doubt be combined with others.

John Cottingham, who (as we saw in Chapter 2) has developed the idea of an epistemology of involvement in detail, describes the *theist's* situation as 'less like that of one who has items of doxastic baggage carefully secured and stowed prior to the voyage, than of one who embarks on a journey of hope'.[1] Whether or not we agree with this assessment of what it is to be a theist, the description is an apt summary of the path I have been recommending for the interested non-believer. By allowing ourselves to be shaped by the richness and beauty of sacred music in the Western classical tradition, our desires for God can be trained on the kinds of satisfaction to which the musical works allude. By taking the fruits of this practice into contemplative prayer, we can risk the darkness and confusion therein, even in a state of unbelief. If we do these things, we let ourselves be guided by the hope that all this involvement might find a response. As our opening epigraph said, there is no promise that it will be easy, and there is no guarantee of the outcome. But for some, as long as the music of our human longing calls us, there will be no other path we can with integrity follow.

Notes

Chapter 1

1 Jonathan Arnold, *Sacred Music in Secular Society* (Farnham: Ashgate, 2014), xiv.
2 David Pugmire, 'The Secular Reception of Religious Music', *Philosophy* 81, no. 1 (2006): 65.
3 See, for instance, Simon Jenkins, 'Why Cathedrals Are Soaring', *The Spectator*, 8 October 2016, accessed 16 October 2016, http://www.spectator.co.uk/2016/10/why-cathedrals-are-soaring/; and John Bingham, 'Looking for Britain's Future Leaders? Try Evensong', *The Telegraph*, 1 March 2016, accessed 16 October 2016, http://www.telegraph.co.uk/news/ religion/12176998/Looking-for-Britains-future-leaders-Try-evensong.html.
4 Existing literature, and the place of the present study in relation to it, will be fully described in the main body as appropriate. Here I simply introduce the study's themes and motivation.
5 John Cottingham, *Philosophy of Religion: Towards a More Humane Approach* (New York, NY: Cambridge University Press, 2014), 22–3.

Chapter 2

1 John Cottingham, *Why Believe?* (London: Continuum, 2009), 170.
2 From Alf Gabrielsson, *Strong Experiences with Music: Music Is Much More than Just Music*, trans. Rod Bradbury (Oxford: Oxford University Press, 2011), 186–9 (slightly abridged). The student who wrote the account is anonymous; I have given her a name to lend the story extra narrative force. That she is based in Sweden is also not explicitly stated, although it is strongly implied by the context of the book as a whole, which contains accounts taken from interviews conducted in Sweden. Other than these details, the story is true.
3 I should say at the outset that, contrary to what an analytic-philosophical readership might have taken our opening vignette to imply, this study will not be a contribution to the 'epistemology of religious experience' as that phrase has come to be used: that is, the enquiry into whether religious experiences (however they are

construed) can be evidence for religious belief. For arguments on the theistic side of that debate, see, for instance, Richard Swinburne, *The Existence of God*, 2nd edn (Oxford: Clarendon Press, 2004), chap. 13; William P. Alston, *Perceiving God: The Epistemology of Religious Experience* (Ithaca, NY: Cornell University Press, 1991); and Caroline Franks Davis, *The Evidential Force of Religious Experience* (Oxford: Oxford University Press, 1999). For work on the atheistic side, see, for instance, Michael Martin, *Atheism: A Philosophical Justification* (Philadelphia, PA: Temple University Press, 1990), chap. 6; and J. L. Mackie, *The Miracle of Theism* (Oxford: Oxford University Press, 1982), chap. 10.

4 By 'theistic content in Christian doctrine', I simply mean the content that could not be understood without reference to God. Most Christian doctrinal content is of this kind, though not all: the claim in the Apostles' Creed that Jesus 'suffered under Pontius Pilate, was crucified, died, and was buried' can be understood at least in some minimal way without reference to God. However, understood in such a way, it would lack the religious layers of significance that it has in the credal context.

5 The phrase 'North Atlantic world' I have taken from Charles Taylor, *A Secular Age* (Cambridge, MA: Harvard University Press, 2007), 1. For more on the sort of secularity I have in mind, see my engagement with Taylor on pp. 9–11.

6 Thus, I shall be concerned with how one's experience of sacred music may play out in the rest of one's life. The connection between music and the wider religious life is something on which others have also written, albeit not focused specifically on *desire* for God, or on sacred music in the life of a non-believer. For instance, Mark Wynn has examined how music can be religiously suggestive and affect one's wider life. Included in Wynn's suggestions are that music can help to inculcate certain qualities of affective life, including those encouraged by faith traditions; that insofar as musical affects lack action-guiding content, they may foster a religiously valuable transcending of an egocentric perspective; and that musical affects may be indispensable for a full articulation of a faith perspective, considered in terms of the affectively informed attitude towards the world that such a perspective includes. See Mark Wynn, 'Musical Affects and the Life of Faith: Some Reflections on the Religious Potency of Music', *Faith and Philosophy* 21, no. 1 (2004): 25–44. The last point in the list has also been taken up by John Cottingham, who discusses both music's ability to lead one into a deep, emotionally toned understanding of the significance of the Christian world view, and its capacity to show the nature of the life of faith in a way that escapes full verbal articulation. See, respectively, John Cottingham, *The Spiritual Dimension: Religion, Philosophy, and Human Value* (Cambridge: Cambridge University Press, 2005), 80–4; and Cottingham, *Why Believe?* 168–70.

7 In this, I am developing one strand of a wider movement in analytic religious epistemology, namely, an expansion in the kinds of religious understanding analytic philosophers have explored. Until recently, the focus was largely on

showing propositional theistic belief to be epistemically meritorious. Two prominent cases have been Richard Swinburne's work, for example, *The Existence of God*; and the 'reformed epistemology' of William Alston, Alvin Plantinga and Nicholas Wolterstorff. For the latter, see Plantinga and Wolterstorff, eds., *Faith and Rationality: Reason and Belief in God* (Notre Dame, IN: University of Notre Dame Press, 1983); Plantinga, *Warranted Christian Belief* (Oxford: Oxford University Press, 2000); Alston, *Perceiving God*; and Wolterstorff, *Practices of Belief: Selected Essays, Volume 2*, ed. Terence Cuneo (Cambridge: Cambridge University Press, 2010). However, philosophers have increasingly been exploring the roles of the *emotions* in religious understanding. For instance, Mark Wynn's *Emotional Experience and Religious Understanding: Integrating Perception, Conception and Feeling* (Cambridge: Cambridge University Press, 2005) is a book-length exploration of this topic; and John Cottingham has also written on the emotions in the context of religious adherence (see pp. 19–20). I argue in Chapter 3 that the desires that interest us are emotions; hence, this study is an application to desire of the thought that the emotions have a role to play in religious epistemology.

8 Note, then, that I do not say the desire is *evidence* for God's reality; rather, it is a way of non-doxastically knowing about God *if* he is real.

9 For two, somewhat similar, reflections on what it is for music to be 'sacred', see Arnold, *Sacred Music in Secular Society*, 8–11; and Albert L. Blackwell, *The Sacred in Music* (Louisville, KY: Westminster John Knox Press, 1999), 13, 15–17. Both Arnold and Blackwell hold that sacredness in music can go beyond having an explicitly religious subject matter and/or context. Arnold suggests that 'music … is "sacred" to the degree that it directs us away from the ego, and … speaks to a humanity united by shared frailty, doubt, and a desire to admire something transcendent'; Blackwell, meanwhile, holds that music is sacred whenever it 'has potential to bear sacramental meaning', which may be understood broadly in terms of 'echoing transcendent beauty, … communicating divine blessing'.

10 Pugmire, 'The Secular Reception of Religious Music', 65.

11 Pugmire, 'The Secular Reception of Religious Music'.

12 Daniel Putman, 'Can a Secularist Appreciate Religious Music?' *Philosophy* 83, no. 325 (2008): 393–4.

13 Ibid., 394.

14 I shall argue in Chapter 3 that, contrary to what some have claimed, desire should be counted as an emotion.

15 I have avoided the term 'agnostic', instead going for 'interested non-believer' to refer to the sort of situation that interests me. This is because there is a blurry line between agnosticism and what Anthony Flew has called 'negative atheism', which is simply the state of not being a theist, rather than the positive assertion that there is no God (the latter is 'positive atheism' in Flew's parlance). The interested non-believer may call herself either an agnostic or a negative atheist; what is

important is that she sees theism as likely enough to be taken seriously. See Antony Flew, 'The Presumption of Atheism', *Canadian Journal of Philosophy* 2, no. 1 (1972): 30.

16 'If one no longer believes in … God …, nothing is left to the music except a lingering emotional attachment and a revivifying of emotions *which one now knows have no object*' (Putman, 'Can a Secularist Appreciate Religious Music?' 394, my emphasis).

17 Arnold, *Sacred Music in Secular Society*, xiv, 11.

18 Taylor, *A Secular Age*, 3. The other two kinds of secularity are as follows. First, writes Taylor, the connection that religious adherence once had with public institutions and practices (most obviously the state) has largely been severed. Second, there is 'the falling off of religious belief and practice, in people turning away from God, and no longer going to Church'. See ibid., 1–2.

19 The characterizations that follow are taken from ibid., 4–20.

20 Jn 10:10.

21 For instance, in Kantian moral lawmaking, cool, disengaged reason, or romantic inner depths of feeling (*A Secular Age*, 8–10).

22 William James, 'The Will to Believe', in his *The Will to Believe and Other Essays in Popular Philosophy* (New York, NY: Longmans Green and Co, 1897), 2.

23 Ibid., 2–3.

24 Ibid., 9.

25 Blaise Pascal, *Pensées*, trans. A. J. Krailsheimer, revised edn (London: Penguin, 1995), 121–5, no. 418. Rather than just one 'wager', there are actually the seeds of several distinct arguments to be found in Pascal's textual fragment entitled '*Infinite – nothing*'. See Jeff Jordan, *Pascal's Wager: Pragmatic Arguments and Belief in God* (Oxford: Oxford University Press, 2006), 19–25, cited in Michael Rota, *Taking Pascal's Wager: Faith, Evidence and the Abundant Life* (Downers Grove, IL: IVP Academic, 2016), 23, n. 3. The different arguments one might construct need not concern us here, since I simply want to use James' treatment of Pascal to highlight a key aspect of what it is to be a live hypothesis.

26 James, 'The Will to Believe', 6.

27 For a statement of the many gods objection, see Mackie, *The Miracle of Theism*, 203. For attempts at replies, see, for instance, Rota, *Taking Pascal's Wager*, 65–9; and Jeff Jordan, 'The Many-Gods Objection', in *Gambling on God: Essays on Pascal's Wager*, ed. Jeff Jordan (Lanham, MD: Rowman & Littlefield, 1994), 101–13, referenced in Alan Hájek, 'Pascal's Wager', in *The Stanford Encyclopedia of Philosophy*, ed. Edward N. Zalta, Winter 2012, sec. 5, n. 8, accessed 6 August 2016, http://plato.stanford.edu/archives/win2012/entries/pascal-wager/.

28 John Cottingham, *How to Believe* (London: Bloomsbury, 2015), chap. 4, sec. 2.

29 Ibid., 84.

30 For this notion of 'shaping and channelling', see ibid., 91.

31 There is, of course, plenty of recent philosophical work that argues for or against theism in general or Christian theism more specifically. See, for instance, Richard Swinburne, *The Christian God* (Oxford: Oxford University Press, 1995); Peter van Inwagen, *God, Knowledge & Mystery: Essays in Philosophical Theology* (Ithaca, NY: Cornell University Press, 1995); Mackie, *The Miracle of Theism*; Martin, *Atheism*. See also nn. 3 and 7 above. A recent, different approach can be found in Michael Rota's *Taking Pascal's Wager*. Rota aims to show that a version of Pascal's Wager lowers the bar for natural theology: if Christianity has at least a 50 per cent chance of being true, then it is rational to commit to living a Christian life. He then goes on to argue that Christianity does have at least a 50 per cent chance of being true, and hence, that it is rational to commit to living a Christian life. As such, Rota's book can be viewed as an attempt to address the sort of problem with the wager that we saw James observe earlier. The book aims to make Christianity a live hypothesis for the reader, and thus one on which she *could* wager; and it uses a version of the wager argument to persuade the reader to go ahead and commit.

32 'Bart the Lover', *The Simpsons*, dir. Carlos Baeza (first broadcast in USA: Fox Network, 13 February 1992).

33 For an example of this view, see L. W. Sumner, *Welfare, Happiness, and Ethics* (Oxford: Clarendon Press, 1996), 124. For further instances, see the sources cited in Talbot Brewer, 'Three Dogmas of Desire', in *Values and Virtues: Aristotelianism in Contemporary Ethics*, ed. Timothy Chappell (Oxford: Clarendon Press, 2006), 260, n. 1.

34 See Plato's comments in the *Symposium*, trans. C. J. Rowe (Warminster: Aris & Phillips, 1998), 200a6–201a1. While Plato grants that one may desire the future continuation of some current state of affairs, he denies that one can desire something that already obtains.

35 Robert Audi, 'Belief, Faith, and Acceptance', *International Journal for Philosophy of Religion* 63, no. 1 (2008): 88. Audi distinguishes between two ways in which belief-about locutions may function: *objectually* (believing a property to attach to something) and *topically* (holding beliefs about something more generally). He goes on to claim that objectual belief entails not only a *commitment* to the reality of its object but also the object's actual reality: 'We cannot believe the sky to be threatening unless there really *is* a sky *of* which we believe this.' This seems wrong. There is no clear distinction between objectual and topical belief: a belief about the relationship between two fictional characters could be (indeed, would probably be) a belief that the relationship has certain properties. It follows that objectual belief, as well as topical belief, entails neither a commitment to its object's reality nor the object's actual reality: one can believe something fictional to have certain (fictional) properties while knowing it is fictional.

36 See p. 17 for more on 'fictionalism': the view either that we do, or that we should, engage with a given area of discourse as a fiction, that is, non-doxastically in some way.

37 Audi, 'Belief, Faith, and Acceptance', 93; for the term 'fiducial faith', see, for example, 96.
38 William P. Alston, 'Belief, Acceptance, and Religious Faith', in *Faith, Freedom, and Rationality*, ed. Jeff Jordan and Daniel Howard-Snyder (Lanham, MD: Rowman & Littlefield, 1996), 12.
39 Heb 11:1, quoted in Alston, 'Belief, Acceptance, and Religious Faith', 12.
40 Audi, 'Belief, Faith, and Acceptance', 93.
41 Ibid., 99.
42 Alston, 'Belief, Acceptance, and Religious Faith', 8–12. In recognizing the distinction between acceptance and belief, Alston acknowledges his debt to L. Jonathan Cohen's *An Essay on Belief and Acceptance* (Oxford: Clarendon Press, 1992): see 'Belief, Acceptance, and Religious Faith', 3.
43 Alston, 'Audi on Nondoxastic Faith', in *Rationality and the Good: Critical Essays on the Ethics and Epistemology of Robert Audi*, ed. Mark Timmons, John Greco and Alfred R. Mele (Oxford: Oxford University Press, 2007), 133.
44 Christopher Jay, 'The Kantian Moral Hazard Argument for Religious Fictionalism', *International Journal for Philosophy of Religion* 75, no. 3 (2014): 209–10. The 'is' and 'should' formulations denote what Jay calls 'hermeneutic fictionalism' and 'revolutionary fictionalism', respectively (211–12). Cf. Natalja Deng, 'Religion for Naturalists', *International Journal for Philosophy of Religion* 78, no. 2 (2015): 197, for a similar formulation. There are many areas of discourse about which it is possible to be a fictionalist. Richard Joyce, in *The Myth of Morality* (Cambridge: Cambridge University Press, 2001), 186, cites the work of Hans Vaihinger, who was 'an enthusiastic proponent of the fictionalist stance – for morality, ... infinity, freedom, absolute space, atoms, substance, abstract and general concepts, force, infinitesimals, and much more besides'; see Vaihinger, *The Philosophy of 'As If'*, trans. C. K. Ogden (London: Routledge and Kegan Paul, 1949). It is implied by Joyce that Vaihinger was a revolutionary fictionalist about these areas of discourse, though this is not made clear.
45 Joyce, *The Myth of Morality*, 189.
46 Ibid., 194–8.
47 Robin Le Poidevin, *Arguing for Atheism: An Introduction to the Philosophy of Religion* (London: Routledge, 1996), chap. 8; Deng, 'Religion for Naturalists', esp. 202–3.
48 Audi, 'Belief, Faith, and Acceptance', 99. Audi follows Alston in his use of the term 'acceptance', at least to an extent; see ibid., 91. However, the extent to which he does so is not important to us, since the point he makes about the compatibility of acceptance and hope fully applies to acceptance of the kind I have appropriated from Alston.
49 For this phrase specifically, see Cottingham, *Philosophy of Religion*, 22–3.
50 Cottingham, *The Spiritual Dimension*, 12.

51 As well as drawing on Pascal's work (discussed here), the thinkers and practices to which Cottingham refers include the 'spiritual exercises' both of St Ignatius of Loyola (*The Spiritual Dimension*, 4, 12), and of the Stoics (4–5, 7–8). Of the latter kinds of exercise, he writes that their aim 'was not merely intellectual enlightenment, or the imparting of abstract theory, but a transformation of the whole person, including our patterns of emotional response … [that is,] *metanoia*' (5). Cottingham uses the term 'spiritual' 'to cover forms of life that put a premium on certain kinds of intensely focused moral and aesthetic response, or on the search for deeper reflective awareness of the meaning of our lives and of our relationship to others and to the natural world' (3). One could, of course, also cite William James as defending a religious epistemology of involvement: 'We feel … as if [religious] evidence might be forever withheld from us unless we met the hypothesis half-way' ('The Will to Believe', 28). James' approach aligns with the one developed here in other ways, too: the voluntary aspect of choosing a hypothesis is, for him, a willingness to act (ibid., 3, 6, 27); and such willingness tends to be driven by desire (9).

52 Pascal, *Pensées*, 124–5, cited in *The Spiritual Dimension*, 7–8.

53 No doubt it was Pascal's view that growth in morality and in knowledge of God are linked: as Christ says in Matthew's Gospel, 'Blessed are the pure in heart, for they shall see God' (Mt 5:8). As for self-deception, I will return to this shortly.

54 Pascal, *Pensées*, 125.

55 Cottingham, *Why Believe?* 105.

56 Ibid., 106–7.

57 Ibid., 108–9.

58 John Cottingham, 'What Difference Does It Make? The Nature and Significance of Theistic Belief', *Ratio* 19, no. 4 (2006): 418–19.

59 Ibid., secs 3–4.

60 Ibid., 411. Some examples of such expressions are the following (page references are to Cottingham, 'What Difference Does It Make?'): for humility, Pss 100:3, 49:6, 40:17, 70:5, 52:8 (cited on 408); for hope, Pss 43:5, 130:5–7, Rom 4:18, 8:38 (cited on 408–9); for awe, Ps 19 (cited on 412–14); for thankfulness and praise, the liturgy of morning and evening prayer (referred to on 415).

61 Cottingham, 'What Difference Does It Make?' 415–16.

62 Ibid., 419. For another account of how religious practice can cognitively and affectively shape participants in a way that encourages spiritual receptivity, see Terence Cuneo, 'Liturgy and the Moral Life', in *Ritualized Faith: Essays on the Philosophy of Liturgy* (Oxford: Oxford University Press, 2016), 89–105. Cuneo discusses Christian liturgy's capacity to lead participants into an awareness of character traits shared by all, such as deep and regrettable fragilities and frailties. His case study involves activities performed by those participating in Eastern Orthodox liturgy – specifically, identifying with biblical characters who display

certain traits, and coming to see oneself in the process as having those traits. Thus, the liturgy can lead participants into a shared awareness of some need that is purportedly met through living a Christian life. For instance, by identifying with the Prodigal Son, the participants in the Orthodox liturgy are made aware of their wrongdoing and their need for forgiveness.

63 Cottingham, 'What Difference Does It Make?' 420.
64 James, 'The Will to Believe', 18–19, 27.
65 Pascal, *Pensées*, 123, 125.
66 Cottingham, *How to Believe*, 110.
67 Bede Griffiths, *The Golden String* (London: Fount, 1979), 9. Cited in Taylor, *A Secular Age*, 5.
68 I have not broached the thorny topic of *which* interpretation of Christian doctrine and practice one might find oneself drawn to – for it is clear that within Christianity there are significant differences in theological and moral outlook, style of worship and even some basic assumptions. While the differences cannot be neatly divided between denominations and do not all map onto each other, we can get an idea of what is at stake by considering the following example. A theologically and morally conservative evangelical community that holds the Bible to be an infallible source of authority will look very different in its world view and practice from a liberal Anglican church that places the sacraments at the centre of its worship, or a community of contemplative spirituality such as Taizé or the World Community for Christian Meditation. For an interesting study of how some of these divisions are currently manifesting themselves in the Church of England, see Harriet Sherwood, 'As Traditional Believers Turn Away, Is This a New Crisis of Faith?' *The Guardian*, 13 August 2016, accessed 16 August 2016, http://www.theguardian.com/world/2016/aug/13/church-of-england-evangelical-drive. My own theological emphases and presuppositions will emerge in Chapters 5 and 6 as I discuss several works of sacred music and the practice of contemplative prayer. That said, I will not attempt to offer anything like a comprehensive interpretation of the general Christian world view found in the canonical creeds: there is not enough room, and in any case, I do not have one to offer.
69 James, 'The Will to Believe', 27.
70 Ibid., 19.
71 Pascal, *Pensées*, 124–5.
72 See Cottingham, *Philosophy of Religion*, 22–3.
73 I do not mean to imply that such psychological fragmentation is *inconceivable*: if one has intellectual misgivings over a given religious world view, then there is surely some risk involved in openly engaging with that world view. The emotions and the intellect may pull in opposite directions, leading to no small amount of strife; and in extreme cases, this may lead one to 'compartmentalize' one's attitudes, so that one comes to believe the world view out of wishful thinking, despite strong reservations

over its plausibility. I take it that such a state can never be upheld with integrity; one will never be fully at home in a religious world view in this sort of case. A certain amount of vigilance is no doubt required, then, in the form of religious engagement that I advocate for the interested non-believer.

74 Brewer, 'Three Dogmas', sec. 2, including citations to those who have subscribed to the 'dogmas' in question.
75 Ibid., 264; Sumner, *Welfare, Happiness, and Ethics*, 124.
76 Brewer, 'Three Dogmas', 264.
77 Ibid.
78 'To love another is to be drawn to another by a generous straining to bring into focus the goodness, hence desirability, of an as yet obscure object of desire' (ibid., 280).
79 Ibid., 275, 279.
80 Ibid., 280.
81 Ibid., secs 5–6.
82 Ibid., 260–1.
83 Ibid., 265.
84 Plato, *Symposium*, 202d8–e1.
85 See Rowe's introduction to the *Symposium*, 5.
86 Plato, *Symposium*, 204a1–b5.
87 Ibid., 204b1–b5.
88 Ibid., 209e5–212b4. See also Frisbee C. C. Sheffield, *Plato's Symposium: The Ethics of Desire* (Oxford: Oxford University Press, 2006), 60.
89 See Brewer, 'Three Dogmas', sec. 5 for an overview of these sources. For a more detailed account of the development of Christian mysticism, including the role of desire for God in this development, see Andrew Louth, *The Origins of the Christian Mystical Tradition: From Plato to Denys*, 2nd edn (Oxford: Oxford University Press, 2007).
90 Rowan Williams, *Tokens of Trust: An Introduction to Christian Belief* (London: Canterbury Press Norwich, 2007), 157.
91 My thanks go to Sameer Yadav and Sarah Coakley for raising this objection.

Chapter 3

1 *The Journals of Arnold Bennett*, ed. Frank Swinnerton (London: Penguin, 1954), entry for 18 March 1897.
2 John Deigh, 'Cognitivism in the Theory of Emotions', *Ethics* 104, no. 4 (1994): 827.
3 Ibid., 828.
4 Ibid., 827.

5 C. D. Broad, *The Mind and Its Place in Nature* (New York, NY: Harcourt Brace, 1925), 574–5; and 'Emotion and Sentiment', in *Broad's Critical Essays in Moral Philosophy*, ed. D. R. Cheney (London: Allen & Unwin, 1971), 286. Both cited in Deigh, 'Cognitivism in the Theory of Emotions', 828.
6 G. F. Stout, *A Manual of Psychology*, 4th edn (London: University Tutorial Press, 1929), 363–4. Cited in Deigh, 'Cognitivism in the Theory of Emotions', 828.
7 H. H. Price, *Thinking and Experience* (Cambridge, MA: Harvard University Press, 1953), 152. Cited in Deigh, 'Cognitivism in the Theory of Emotions', 828.
8 Deigh, 'Cognitivism in the Theory of Emotions', 828.
9 Ibid., 829.
10 Robert Solomon and Martha Nussbaum, for instance, *identify* emotions with judgements. See Robert C. Solomon, 'Emotions and Choice', in *What Is an Emotion? Classic and Contemporary Readings*, ed. Robert C. Solomon, 2nd edn (New York, NY: Oxford University Press, 2003), 224–35; Martha Nussbaum, 'Emotions as Judgements of Value and Importance', in the same volume, 271–83; Nussbaum, *Upheavals of Thought: The Intelligence of Emotions* (Cambridge: Cambridge University Press, 2001). Other theorists have introduced further elements, an example of whom is William Lyons, who has described emotions as affect-laden judgements. See William Lyons, *Emotion* (Cambridge: Cambridge University Press, 1980). See also Ronald de Sousa, 'Emotion', in *The Stanford Encyclopedia of Philosophy*, ed. Edward N. Zalta, Spring 2014, sec. 3, accessed 16 May 2014, http://plato.stanford.edu/archives/spr2014/entries/emotion/.
11 Deigh, 'Cognitivism in the Theory of Emotions', 841.
12 Ibid., 842.
13 Broad, 'Emotion and Sentiment', 286, cited in Deigh, 'Cognitivism in the Theory of Emotions', 831–2.
14 Justin Oakley, *Morality and the Emotions* (London: Routledge and Kegan Paul, 1992), 11.
15 We must distinguish between different kinds of feeling that can form part of an emotional experience. As well as affective feelings, there are physiological feelings: feelings of an increased heart rate, butterflies in the stomach and so on. William James famously identified emotions as just cases of these feelings when they occur in response to the thought, or perception, of an exciting object: see William James, *The Principles of Psychology*, vol. 2 (New York, NY: Dover, 1950), 449, cited in Deigh, 'Cognitivism in the Theory of Emotions', 829. James' theory, then, is a non-cognitive theory of emotion, in that while James recognized that emotional experience as a whole includes some cognition, he defined the emotion as only part of this experience – a part lacking any cognitive content. But there is an obvious problem with this theory: a given physiological change can occur with different emotional experiences, or with no emotional experience at all. My increased heart rate might be because I am frightened, or it might be because I have been running.

Also, as Robert Solomon has pointed out, the physiological feelings that accompany an emotional episode do not subside as soon as the emotion subsides. If I am angry with you for stealing my car, but I then realize that you did not steal it, my anger disappears as soon as I realize this – yet the physiological feelings (such as flushing) remain a while longer (Solomon, 'Emotions and Choice', 227). Physiological feelings, then, cannot be emotions.

16 Mark Wynn brings out this aspect of emotional affective *feelings* as we ordinarily talk about them: 'What is distinctive about emotional feelings is that we can take them to have a subject matter, and can therefore ask questions such as: what are you feeling triumphant about?' See Wynn, *Emotional Experience and Religious Understanding*, 91. Meanwhile, Jeremy Begbie notes that according to 'the way the word "emotion" is commonly used ... emotion is by its nature object-oriented'. See his 'Faithful Feelings: Music and Emotion in Worship', in *Resonant Witness: Conversations between Music and Theology*, ed. Jeremy S. Begbie and Steven R. Guthrie (Grand Rapids, MI: Wm. B. Eerdmans Publishing Co., 2011), 332, n. 23. Ronald de Sousa distinguishes three kinds of emotional objects, towards at least one of which an emotion will be directed: propositional objects or states of affairs (I am angry that you betrayed me); concrete particulars or targets (a parent takes joy in his or her children); and attentional focuses (I love a particular aspect of a friend, such as his steadfast support). As well as these, every emotion has a *formal object*, which is simply a property ascribed to its focus, concrete target, or propositional object in virtue of which the emotion is *this* emotion and not *that*. For instance, if I am frightened of a dog, the formal object of my fear will be the property of being frightening. See de Sousa, 'Emotion', sec. 3.
17 Wynn, *Emotional Experience and Religious Understanding*, 93, n. 5.
18 Begbie, 'Faithful Feelings', 332; de Sousa, 'Emotion', sec. 3.
19 As Peter Goldie notes, the difference between emotions and moods is a matter of degree. See his *The Emotions: A Philosophical Exploration* (Oxford: Oxford University Press, 2000), 17–18.
20 Ibid., 4.
21 Geoffrey Madell, 'What Music Teaches about Emotion', *Philosophy* 71, no. 275 (1996): 77 (original emphasis).
22 The example is from Jesse Prinz, 'Emotion, Psychosemantics, and Embodied Appraisals', *Royal Institute of Philosophy Supplement* 52 (2003): 80.
23 There are, of course, a whole host of complex conditions that are required for this intentional feeling to have been possible. For instance, as well as my realization that ten years had passed, my life needed to have had a particular narrative, and I needed to see myself in a particular way (for example, as not having undergone any seismic changes in those ten years – hence the surprise that was a part of my feeling unsettled). But these things, although necessary conditions of the emotion of being unsettled and of emotions in general, are not part of the emotion itself; they are

not themselves part of what we typically call an emotion – just as, for instance, a certain background picture of the world is necessary in order for any belief to be intelligible, but is not itself part of what we call the belief.

24 Madell, 'What Music Teaches about Emotion', 81.
25 Nussbaum, 'Emotions as Judgements of Value and Importance', 283.
26 Ibid., 282.
27 Ibid.
28 Ibid., 281.
29 Ibid., 275.
30 It is worth noting that this concept of emotion applies equally to *non-occurrent* emotions. I have said that emotions sometimes do, and sometimes do not, include their own cognitive content – and that in either case an emotion is an intentional affect. The same can be said of emotions that are not felt. We can expand on the earlier example of non-occurrent anger: I may be angry with my friend without being consciously aware that I am, and my thoughts and perceptions of him might be coloured and shaped accordingly; for instance, I might have a heightened awareness of things about him that irritate me, or feel weighed down at the sight or thought of him. My non-occurrent anger is about some thought content (regarding certain aspects of my friend and our friendship, including something he has done of which I disapprove), and it colours the thoughts that have this content even if I am unaware of its doing so. I leave open the question whether anger incorporates cognitive content of its own (disapproval, for instance, which includes the thought of wrongdoing). But regardless of whether it does, and, indeed, of whether there are any non-occurrent emotions that are also cognitive, the description 'intentional affect' is just as fitting when used of non-occurrent emotions as it is when used of occurrent ones.
31 Melinda Vadas, 'Affective and Non-Affective Desire', *Philosophy and Phenomenological Research* 45, no. 2 (1984): 276.
32 Ibid., 276–7 (original emphasis).
33 Ibid., 277 (original emphasis).
34 Ibid.
35 Ibid., 278.
36 I will discuss all this more fully in Chapter 6. As an example of the contrast between apparent and real happiness in Thomas Merton's work, through which I will engage with the Christian contemplative tradition, see, for instance, his *New Seeds of Contemplation* (London: Burns & Oates, 1999), 169–70: 'You were not created for pleasure: you were created for spiritual JOY ... Pain, which is the contrary of pleasure, is not necessarily the contrary of happiness or of joy ... [God's] work in your soul demands the sacrifice of all that you desire and delight in, and, indeed, of all that you are.'
37 Oakley, *Morality and the Emotions*, 27.

38 Goldie, *The Emotions*, 78–9.
39 Madell, 'What Music Teaches about Emotion', 78.
40 Wynn, *Emotional Experience and Religious Understanding*, 106–7 (my emphasis).
41 The analogy between hungering for food and desiring God is highlighted at certain points in the Bible. In the Hebrew Bible, see, for instance, Am 8:11: "'Behold, the days are coming,' declares the Lord GOD, "when I will send a famine on the land – not a famine of bread … but of hearing the words of the LORD …"." And in the New Testament, John's Gospel is especially noteworthy for its language of hunger and food regarding God. See Jesus' 'I am the bread of life' address in Jn 6:22–59, which recapitulates and extends the theme, from the book of Exodus, of the bread that comes from heaven.
42 A. A. Milne, *The House at Pooh Corner*, reissue edn (New York, NY: Penguin, 1991), 124.
43 Leo Tolstoy, *Anna Karenina*, trans. Richard Pevear and Larissa Volokhonsky, revised edn (London: Penguin, 2003), 596.
44 Frank Jackson, 'Epiphenomenal Qualia', *Philosophical Quarterly* 32 (1982): 130.
45 Wynn, *Emotional Experience and Religious Understanding*, 94.
46 Ibid.
47 Ibid., 96.
48 Ibid., 95–6.
49 Goldie, *The Emotions*, 59–60. The ice example is originally from Michael Stocker, 'Psychic Feelings: Their Importance and Irreducibility', *Australasian Journal of Philosophy* 61 (1983): 21.
50 Goldie, *The Emotions*, 60.
51 Ibid., 59.
52 Wynn, *Emotional Experience and Religious Understanding*, 145.
53 Eleonore Stump, *Wandering in Darkness: Narrative and the Problem of Suffering* (Oxford: Oxford University Press, 2010), 52–3.
54 In other words, a romantic relationship is a particular 'office of love', as Eleonore Stump has used the phrase. See ibid., 97ff. for an analysis. In brief, the offices of love are differing kinds of loving relationships, each of which 'shapes the sort of sharing and closeness suitable in that relationship and … delimits the sort of love appropriate within [it]' (97–8).
55 To take just one example, there is evidence that the quality of early attachment relationships is correlated with the quality of later development in aspects such as dependency levels, the capacity to tolerate vulnerability and intimacy in romantic relationships and self-esteem. See L. Alan Sroufe, 'From Infant Attachment to Promotion of Adolescent Autonomy: Prospective, Longitudinal Data on the Role of Parents in Development', in *Parenting and the Child's World: Influences on Academic, Intellectual, and Social-Emotional Development*, ed. John G. Borkowski, Sharon Landesman Ramey and Marie Bristol-Power, eBook edn (Mahwah, NJ: Lawrence

Erlbaum Associates, 2009), 189–90. If, for instance, one has had anxious early attachments and subsequently suffers from low self-esteem, then one will likely seek out romantic relationships in which one is constantly reassured of one's worth in the face of self-doubt. On the other hand, if one's early attachments have been secure, then one will likely seek romantic relationships in which vulnerability and intimacy are central. A prospective romantic partner would need different attributes in order to be the partner in each of these kinds of relationship.

56 For example, David Efird and Daniel Gustafsson have recently argued that Christian art, including music, 'is best conceived as iconic, such that it is an occasion for, and a mode of, experiencing God'. See their 'Experiencing Christian Art', *Religious Studies* 51, no. 3 (2015): 431–9.

57 I thank Tim Crane for raising this objection.

58 For a discussion of standing and occurrent desires, see Tim Schroeder, 'Desire', in *The Stanford Encyclopedia of Philosophy*, ed. Edward N. Zalta, Summer 2015, sec. 2.4, accessed 27 August 2016, http://plato.stanford.edu/archives/sum 2015/entries/desire/.

59 St Augustine, *Homilies on the First Epistle of John*, ed. Boniface Ramsey, Daniel Doyle, and Martin Thomas, trans. Boniface Ramsey (Hyde Park, NY: New City Press, 2008), IV.6.

60 At least, one must believe in such things as abstract relations, even if not instantiated in any particular instance. However, it is doubtful that one could come to desire the resolution to the tonic unless one had heard such a resolution before; hence, it seems that one must believe in the existence of concrete instances of the resolution – at least the ones that one has heard – in order to desire a particular instance of it.

61 I pointed out in Chapter 2 that we can experience what we take to be portrayals of someone's character without believing in that person's existence. We can add that one need not even believe in the existence of the *kind* of thing that person is. I might experience what I take to be a portrayal of Legolas from Tolkien's *The Lord of the Rings*, even though I do not believe in elves. Similarly, one can experience what one takes to be a portrayal of aspects of God, even if one lacks belief in anything of God's kind.

Chapter 4

1 St Augustine, *Confessions*, trans. Henry Chadwick, reissue edn (Oxford: Oxford University Press, 2008), X. xxxiii (49).

2 James Young, following Peter Kivy and Stephen Davies, has distinguished between music's *expressing* an affective state and its *being expressive of* such a state. To express an affective state is to make manifest some affect of the composer or performer

(whether or not at the time of composing or performing). To be expressive of an affective state is to have properties that resemble human expressive behaviour; and, if music can possess these properties at all, it can possess them even if it does not express any affect of the composer or performer. Young persuasively argues that our attributions of affective properties to music cannot be primarily a matter of saying that music *expresses* those affects, since we can hear music as affective in certain ways without knowing whether the composer or performer ever felt those affects. See James O. Young, *Critique of Pure Music* (Oxford: Oxford University Press, 2014), 5–7. A more plausible understanding of such attributions is that the music calls to mind affective properties quite apart from whether we believe that it expresses those affects as felt by the composer or performer. Moreover, this is so regardless of *how* we think music does this – and specifically, regardless of whether we think it does so by resembling human expressive behaviour. Henceforth in this and future chapters, then, I will refer to the phenomenon of an affect's being audible in a piece of music as the music's being expressive of that affect – even though this is a wider use of the phrase than Young's – or, sometimes, as the music's *conveying* that affect. These two phrases I use synonymously.

3 The Pythagoreans saw musical rhythms as signs or expressions of character, giving music a capacity unique among the arts to shape the human soul – by improving and healing or by depraving and sickening. See Frank Burch Brown, 'Music', in *The Oxford Handbook of Religion and Emotion*, ed. John Corrigan (Oxford: Oxford University Press, 2008), 204. Both Plato and Aristotle took up this theme in discussing music's capacity to shape the listener by being expressive of, and thereby eliciting, various character traits, a number of which are affectively toned. See Plato, *The Republic*, trans. Desmond Lee, 2nd edn (London: Penguin, 2003), 398e–99d; and Aristotle, *The Politics*, trans. Ernest Barker, revised edn (Oxford: Oxford University Press, 2009), bk. VIII. 5. Both Plato and Aristotle thus gave an important role to music in shaping the listener *morally* by inculcating character traits as habitual.

4 Alan Macfarlane, 'John Rutter Interviewed by Alan Macfarlane 28th January 2009', accessed 10 September 2014, http:// www.alanmacfarlane.com/DO/filmshow/rutter1_fast.htm.

5 Burch Brown, 'Music', 208–9.

6 Ibid., 209.

7 Another proponent of this sort of view is Jonathan Arnold, who also maintains that sacred music's ability to have its most profound effects does not depend on the composer's intentions: 'Truly great music, then, whatever the intentions of the composer …, is "sacred" to the degree that it directs us away from the ego, and … speaks to a humanity united by shared frailty, doubt, and a desire to admire something transcendent.' See Arnold, *Sacred Music in Secular Society*, 11.

8 For the name 'resemblance theory', see Young, *Critique of Pure Music*, 7; and see 15–26 for an array of psychological evidence in support of the theory.

9. Aaron Ridley, *Music, Value and the Passions* (Ithaca, NY: Cornell University Press, 1995), chap. 4. For a discussion, see Wynn, 'Musical Affects and the Life of Faith', 26–9.
10. Stephen Davies, *Musical Meaning and Expression* (Ithaca, NY: Cornell University Press, 1994), 228. Again, Wynn references this view ('Musical Affects and the Life of Faith', 30).
11. It is no part of my argument that some pieces of music are better suited to the purpose than others, but this does not mean I hold no view on the matter. I take it as obvious that some music can elicit affective responses that are deeper and more nuanced, and that take in a greater range of human experience, than the responses that other music can elicit. This applies not only to music in general but also to Christian music in particular. For instance, take works that are expressive of, and can thereby elicit, *praise*. I am quite certain that Brenton Brown's Christian rock number *Lord, Reign in Me* – uplifting though it undoubtedly is to many – lacks anything like the purity and radiance of Mozart's 'Laudate Dominum' from his *Vesperae Solennes de Confessore*, or the depth and nuance of Bruckner's *Ave Maria*. That said, this is no reason to be snobbish. Indeed, I am aware that my own tastes may be on the wrong end of some aesthetic judgements. I have never been able to get much out of Bach, and this may well be a shortcoming on my part; perhaps some Bach lovers would turn their noses up at the aforementioned pieces by Mozart and Bruckner. In general, on the matter of musical taste as it applies to religious music, I agree with Eleonore Stump: listeners need to be *moved* by religious music, and it must therefore meet them where they are. 'But because a greater beauty has more power to move a person once that person is able to perceive it, there is some real point in a person's learning to perceive, and so learning to enjoy, the greater beauty, if the gifts of wealth, leisure, opportunity, and talent make such training possible. … Insofar as beauty is a road to God, greater beauty will be a better road.' See Eleonore Stump, 'Beauty as a Road to God', *Sacred Music* 134, no. 4 (2007): 20–1.
12. Peter Kivy, *Music Alone: Philosophical Reflections on the Purely Musical Experience* (Ithaca, NY: Cornell University Press, 1990), 159–60.
13. Ibid., 171.
14. Ibid., 161.
15. Peter Kivy, 'Mood and Music: Some Reflections for Noël Carroll', *Journal of Aesthetics and Art Criticism* 64, no. 2 (2006): 280. Quoted in Young, *Critique of Pure Music*, 57.
16. Kivy, *Music Alone*, 148–52, 157, 159–61.
17. Ibid., 161.
18. See Eduard Hanslick, *On the Musically Beautiful: A Contribution Towards the Revision of the Aesthetics of Music*, reproduced in John Andrew Fisher, *Reflecting on Art* (Mountain View, CA: Mayfield Pub. Co., 1993), 284, referenced in turn in Wynn, 'Musical Affects and the Life of Faith', 26.
19. Kivy, *Music Alone*, ix.

20 See Begbie, 'Faithful Feelings', 339; also Nicholas Cook, *Analysing Musical Multimedia* (Oxford: Clarendon Press, 1998), 86–92, whom Begbie cites.
21 Young, *Critique of Pure Music*, 8, 137.
22 Kivy's example is of Uncle Charlie, who arouses Kivy's anger by continually and untruthfully blaming Aunt Bella for his failure in business. Kivy describes the facts about the Uncle Charlie situation that can be used in a common-sense explanation for his anger as *why* and *how* Uncle Charlie makes him angry, and who he is angry at. See Kivy, *Music Alone*, 148.
23 Ibid., 150.
24 Or at least anyone of a given cultural formation, if the affect in question is culturally dependent.
25 Kivy, *Music Alone*, 167.
26 Young, *Critique of Pure Music*, 61.
27 I am aware that the present explanation of music's arousal of objectless affects by 'contagion', in depending on music's resemblance to human expressive behaviour, depends on something I have not firmly established, and which I said did not need to be established for our purposes. While I find plausible both the notion that music bears this resemblance, and the present explanation of how music arouses objectless affects by 'contagion', the 'how' of this arousal is not as important for our purposes as the fact that it happens. Thus, even if the present explanation of how it happens is false – for instance, because music does not, in fact, resemble expressive behaviour – there is still compelling evidence that it happens, to which I will turn shortly.
28 Young, *Critique of Pure Music*, 62.
29 Kivy, *Music Alone*, 167–8.
30 Young, *Critique of Pure Music*, 42.
31 Davies, *Musical Meaning and Expression*, 271.
32 Young, *Critique of Pure Music*, 40.
33 See, respectively, ibid., 48–58 and 137–42.
34 Ibid., 48–9, 52–3. Kivy voiced this worry in his 'Critical Study: Deeper than Emotion', *British Journal of Aesthetics* 46, no. 3 (2006): 306. Cited in Young, *Critique of Pure Music*, 48.
35 C. L. Krumhansl, 'An Exploratory Study of Musical Emotions and Psychophysiology', *Canadian Journal of Experimental Psychology* 51, no. 4 (1997): 336–53. Cited in Young, *Critique of Pure Music*, 48.
36 Young, *Critique of Pure Music*, 49–50.
37 Ibid., 54–6.
38 Ibid., 55–6.
39 S. Omar Ali and Zehra F. Peynircioğlu, 'Songs and Emotions: Are Lyrics and Melodies Equal Partners?' *Psychology of Music* 34, no. 4 (2006): 511–34. Cited in Young, *Critique of Pure Music*, 138.
40 Young, *Critique of Pure Music*, 137–8.

41 Ibid., 138–9.
42 Kivy is here responding to the possibility as raised by Peter Mew, in 'The Expression of Emotion in Music', *British Journal of Aesthetics* 25, no. 1 (1985): 34. See Kivy, *Music Alone*, 166.
43 Kivy, *Music Alone*, 168.
44 For more on this, see Begbie, 'Faithful Feelings', 349–51.
45 K.339. A recording conducted by Christopher Hogwood with Emma Kirkby, Winchester Cathedral Choir and the Academy of Ancient Music can be heard here: 'Emma Kirkby – "Laudate Dominum" K 339 Mozart', *YouTube*, accessed 4 October 2016, https://www.youtube.com/watch?v=sUrcLzk5oKE.
46 Williams, *Tokens of Trust*, 8–9.
47 R. G. Collingwood, 'Words and Tune', in his *The Philosophy of Enchantment: Studies in Folktale, Cultural Criticism, and Anthropology*, ed. David Boucher, Wendy James and Philip Smallwood (Oxford: Clarendon Press, 2005), 3.
48 Ridley, *Music, Value and the Passions*, 128–9; see also Wynn, 'Musical Affects and the Life of Faith', 28–9, 34–5.
49 Unsurprisingly, experiments show that listeners respond to a musical setting of text by feeling a given affect most intensely if both the music and the text are expressive of that affect. See Young, *Critique of Pure Music*, 138.
50 Kivy, *Music Alone*, 162.
51 Ridley presents the notion of the quality of an affective life in *Music, Value and the Passions*, 160; see Wynn, 'Musical Affects and the Life of Faith', 33.
52 Wynn, 'Musical Affects and the Life of Faith', 27. See Ridley, *Music, Value and the Passions*, 112; and Davies, *Musical Meaning and Expression*, 227.
53 Wynn, 'Musical Affects and the Life of Faith', 28.
54 Ibid., 34.
55 Ps 119:20, 49–50.
56 Ps 42:2–3, 5–6, 11.
57 The first part of Psalm 42 has been put to music in a well-known setting by Herbert Howells. I shall not be discussing this piece in the following chapters, although no doubt the general structure of the arguments I develop in those chapters could be fruitfully applied to it.

Chapter 5

1 *The New English Hymnal*, full music edn (Norwich: Canterbury Press Norwich, 1986), 309, final stanza. Original Italian text by Bianco da Siena, trans. R. F. Littledale. Set to the tune 'Down Ampney' by R. Vaughan Williams.
2 From Lk. 24.29.
3 Lk. 2.29–32.

4 J. S. Bach's *Komm, Jesu, Komm* is an obvious example, as are Howells' *Like as the Hart* and William Henry Harris' *Bring Us, O Lord God*, both composed over 200 years later. There are also many congregational hymns in this vein, such as *Lo! He Comes with Clouds Descending* (traditionally sung at Advent), and the great Pentecost hymn *Come Down, O Love Divine*, quoted in this chapter's epigraph.

5 Composed originally for the Choir of King's College, Cambridge.

6 To be sure, this feature predates the baroque period. For instance, Thomas Tallis' exquisite and otherworldly *O Nata Lux* (1575) is expressive of desire for God, with its plea for Christ to hear the praise and prayer of his people (*Dignare clemens supplicum / Laudes precesque sumere*), and for him to knit the assembled into his mystical body, the Church (*Nos membra confer effici / Tui beati corporis*).

7 St Augustine, *Confessions*, X. xxxiii (50). See also Burch Brown, 'Music', 206.

8 Quentin Faulkner, *Wiser than Despair: The Evolution of Ideas in the Relationship of Music and the Christian Church* (Westport, CT: Greenwood Press, 1996), 136–7.

9 Burch Brown, 'Music', 207.

10 Faulkner, *Wiser than Despair*, 140.

11 St Augustine, *Confessions*, X. xxxiii (49).

12 Ibid., X. xxxiii (50).

13 Faulkner, *Wiser than Despair*, 140–1.

14 St Augustine, *Confessions*, I. i (1). There may be differences in 'general' religious desire across different religious traditions. Is there, for instance, even such a thing as Buddhist desire, general or otherwise, if desire or craving is seen as the root of suffering? And if there is, can it take the form of a desire for 'something more'? Would it not, instead, be a desire for Nirvana – for the end of all desires and the suffering that they cause (itself a desire that one would have to transcend in order to attain Nirvana)? See Peter Harvey, *An Introduction to Buddhism: Teachings, History and Practices* (Cambridge: Cambridge University Press, 1990), 53, 60–1. However, these considerations need not concern us, for if, indeed, there is no such thing as a general desire for 'something more' to be found in all religious mind-sets, then we can at least talk about this sort of desire as a religious longing for something of a certain description (roughly, a realm transcending the material world in which lies our ultimate fulfilment), a description satisfied by the theistic God.

15 Z.15 in the Zimmerman catalogue of Purcell's works. A recording conducted by Jeremy Summerly with Oxford Camerata can be heard here: 'Henry Purcell – ' Hear My Prayer, O Lord', *YouTube*, accessed 4 October 2016, https://www.youtube.com/watch?v=y2D67ybXGz0.

16 The Psalm's heading reads, 'A Prayer of one afflicted, when he is faint and pours out his complaint before the LORD.'

17 Ps. 102.2.

18 Ridley, *Music, Value and the Passions*, 110–13; Davies, *Musical Meaning and Expression*, 227. See Wynn, 'Musical Affects and the Life of Faith', 27.

19 Wynn, 'Musical Affects and the Life of Faith', 28.
20 Ridley, *Music, Value and the Passions*, 168; see Wynn, 'Musical Affects and the Life of Faith', 32.
21 Davies, *Musical Meaning and Expression*, 271; see Wynn, 'Musical Affects and the Life of Faith', 30, 32.
22 The wider context of the view shared by Ridley and Davies, that music cannot intrinsically refer to any specific circumstance, is the 'resemblance' theory of how music can be expressive of affective states, mentioned in Chapter 4. If music is expressive by resembling human expressive behaviour, then, since no expressive behaviour that can resemble musical movement can intrinsically refer to any specific circumstance, music cannot intrinsically refer to any specific circumstance either. See Wynn, 'Musical Affects and the Life of Faith', 27, 31. However, regardless of whether or not one endorses the resemblance theory, it is hard to see how Purcell's music, or any other music, could intrinsically refer to any particular kind of circumstance; and, given that the text of the piece does not do so either, the piece as a whole cannot refer to any unfortunate circumstance.
23 Madell, 'What Music Teaches about Emotion', 82.
24 See the Church of England webpage cited in n. 63.
25 Jn 14.27.
26 Francis Spufford, *Unapologetic* (London: Faber and Faber, 2012), 50.
27 Ibid., 65.
28 Ibid.
29 Etty Hillesum, *Etty: The Letters and Diaries of Etty Hillesum 1941–1943, Complete and Unabridged*, ed. Klaas A. D. Smelik, trans. Arnold J. Pomerans (Grand Rapids, MI: Wm. B. Eerdmans Publishing Co., 2002), 616. Quoted in Patrick Woodhouse, *Etty Hillesum: A Life Transformed* (London: Continuum, 2009), 127–8.
30 Woodhouse, *A Life Transformed*, 128.
31 *The Letters and Diaries of Etty Hillesum*, 386, quoted in Woodhouse, *A Life Transformed*, 49.
32 Williams, *Tokens of Trust*, 44.
33 Ibid., 16.
34 See, for instance, Pss. 5.6-7; 6.3-5; 13.3-6; 31.15-16; 51.1; 100.4-5; 143.7-8. Many more examples could be given.
35 Spufford, *Unapologetic*, 63.
36 Ibid., 64.
37 *The Letters and Diaries of Etty Hillesum*, 640, quoted in Woodhouse, *A Life Transformed*, 119.
38 Woodhouse, *A Life Transformed*, 120.
39 *The Letters and Diaries of Etty Hillesum*, 489, quoted in Woodhouse, *A Life Transformed*, 52.

40 Op. 69, No. 3. A recording conducted by John Rutter with The Cambridge Singers can be heard here: 'Rheinberger – Abendlied – The Cambridge Singers', YouTube, accessed 4 October 2016, https://www.youtube.com/watch?v=TGc__HGwdxk.
41 Lk. 24.13-35.
42 The version I have in mind is the one in contemporary language that is intended for use at any time of the year, from the Church of England's *Common Worship: Daily Prayer* (London: Church House Publishing, 2005), 337–43.
43 Lk. 24.32.
44 This kind of longing is prevalent in Hebrew tradition, especially in the Psalms (e.g. 84.2; 63.1; 42.1-2; 119.131). But the description I gave could also be a description of the Greek concept of *erōs* – a theme that features centrally in, for instance, Plato's *Symposium* (see Chapter 2, pp. 27-8 of the present study for more on this). Hence, one can discern a convergence of sorts between the Hebrew and Greek traditions in the kind of erotic longing at issue here: a convergence expressed in the work of early Christian writers such as Origen and Gregory of Nyssa, who drew extensively on another Hebrew text, the Song of Songs, in their mystical theology. For detailed discussions of Origen and Gregory, see Louth, *The Origins of the Christian Mystical Tradition*, chaps 4–5. See also Plantinga, *Warranted Christian Belief*, chap. 9, sec. 4 for a discussion of erotic longing in the wider Christian tradition, in such diverse figures as St Augustine, St Francis of Sales, John Donne, and (even) Puritans such as Jonathan Edwards, Henry Scougal and Samuel Willard. One could also, of course, cite St John of the Cross in this capacity, notably in his *Dark Night of the Soul*, ed. T. N. R. Rogers, trans. E. Allison Peers (Mineola, NY: Dover, 2003). See the Prologue for the poem itself, with its remarkable physical imagery of erotic love.
45 Abraham Kuyper, *To Be Near Unto God*, trans. John Hendrik de Vries (Grand Rapids, MI: Wm. B. Eerdmans Publishing Co., 1925), 675. Quoted in Plantinga, *Warranted Christian Belief*, 314.
46 Ps. 139.12.
47 Irvin D. Yalom, *Love's Executioner and Other Tales of Psychotherapy*, reprint edn (London: Penguin, 1991), 180–6.
48 Ibid., 185.
49 Ibid., 10.
50 Eleonore Stump, 'Omnipresence, Indwelling, and the Second-Personal', *European Journal for Philosophy of Religion* 5, no. 4 (2013): 46.
51 Ibid., 50.
52 Ibid., 41.
53 Ibid., 48. Stump discusses mind-reading further in her *Wandering in Darkness*, chap. 4.
54 Stump, 'Omnipresence, Indwelling, and the Second-Personal', 46, 50–1. For Paul's list of the 'fruit of the Spirit', in which love, joy and peace are the first three, see Gal 5:22–3.

55 Stump, 'Omnipresence, Indwelling, and the Second-Personal', 51.
56 As I argued in Chapter 3, it is possible to know something of what a romantic relationship would be like even if one has had no such experience – based on experience of relationships that are partially analogous to the romantic, and on what one knows about the sort of love appropriate to romantic relationships. Thus, even if one had had no experience of an erotic/romantic relationship, one could still form a sense – third hand, as it were – of what it would be like for *Abendlied*'s desire to be satisfied. Such a sense would be based on one's sense of what a romantic relationship would be like, in turn based on one's knowledge of what analogous human relationships are like. However, it is probably the case that the more 'levels' are involved in one's sense of what the satisfaction of a desire would be like, the more diluted that sense will be.
57 The view that erotic love can give us a clue as to what relationship with God would be like is also voiced by biblical scholar Ellen Davis, who brings it to bear on her commentary on the Song of Songs. She states: 'The experience of healthy sexual desire can help us imagine what it might mean to love God truly.' See Ellen F. Davis, *Proverbs, Ecclesiastes, and the Song of Songs* (Louisville, KY: Westminster John Knox Press, 2000), 233.
58 The words are from the English translation of a chant originally in Lithuanian, a direct quotation from Jn 21.17: *Viešpatie, tu viską žinai. Tu žinai, kad tave myliu* – literally, 'Lord, you know everything. You know that I love you.' The English version sometimes used by the community runs: 'All my heart lies open to you, and you know, Lord, that I love you'. A recording of the Lithuanian version can be found at 'Viešpatie, Tu Viską Žinai', *YouTube*, accessed 1 October 2016, https://www.youtube.com/watch?v=vWSCosT5gVE. A recording of the English version can be found at 'Taizé – All My Heart Lies Open to You', *YouTube*, accessed 1 October 2016, https://www.youtube.com/watch?v=GlzYz4RDJw.
59 Stump, 'Omnipresence, Indwelling, and the Second-Personal', 46, 50.
60 Mary's song of praise at Lk. 1.46-55.
61 The title consists of the opening words of the Vulgate Latin translation, meaning 'Now you dismiss'.
62 Lk. 2.22-32.
63 The Church of England's website contains the Book of Common Prayer liturgy for Evening Prayer, including the Nunc Dimittis and Gloria: 'Worship – Book of Common Prayer – the Order for Evening Prayer', accessed 16 September 2016, https://www.churchofengland.org/prayer-worship/worship/book-of-common-prayer/the-order-for-evening-prayer.aspx.
64 2 Cor. 3.18.
65 1 Cor. 13.12.
66 Op. 81. A recording of the Nunc Dimittis conducted by Christopher Robinson with the Choir of St John's College, Cambridge can be heard here: 'Charles Stanford

– Evening Service in G (Op. 81) - Nunc Dimittis', *YouTube*, accessed 4 October 2016, https://www.youtube.com/watch?v=IILfUJi2cpg.
67 A recording of Howells' setting conducted by Stephen Layton with the Choir of Trinity College, Cambridge can be heard here (starting at 4:53): 'Howells' "Collegium Regale" (Mag & Nunc)', *YouTube*, accessed 4 October 2016, https://www. youtube.com/watch?v=jlOwVE_JYrU.
68 Paul Spicer, liner notes to *Howells: Choral Music*, Wells Cathedral Choir and Malcolm Archer, Hyperion, CDA67494, CD, 2014.
69 Ibid.
70 Cottingham, *How to Believe*, 115, quoting Ps. 29.8-9.
71 Ex. 13.21-2; 24.15-17.
72 Cottingham, *How to Believe*, 115.
73 Ps. 96.11-13 (my emphasis). See Cottingham, *How to Believe*, 114.
74 Cottingham, *How to Believe*, 115–16, 120.
75 Lk. 2.8-14.
76 I am told by Sarah Coakley that the term 'Judaeo-Christian tradition' is sometimes considered politically incorrect, taken to imply that the Jewish roots of Christianity, important though they were, were a precursor to the 'main event'. Although I do not use the term to mean this, I must admit my inability to see how such a view could be peculiarly upsetting. The view in question is something with which many, if not most, Christians would agree, being first and foremost the claim that something of monumental importance occurred in the history of the Jewish people, the culmination of all that had gone before, of which non-Christian Jews fail to take full account. In other words, the situation is a particular case of religious disagreement, an entirely common phenomenon. But in any case, as I say, the 'precursor' view of pre-Christian Judaism is not one I wish to defend. I simply use the term 'Judaeo-Christian' to highlight the continuity between the Christian tradition and the Judaism out of which it arose, and which continues to play a prominent role in shaping the thought and practice of Christianity – not least in the various uses of the Hebrew Bible in Christian liturgy.
77 1 Kgs. 19.9-13.
78 Ex. 33.18-23.
79 Thomas Merton, *New Seeds of Contemplation* (London: Burns & Oates, 1999), 153.
80 Henry Vaughan, 'The World', in *Eight Metaphysical Poets*, ed. Jack Dalglish (Harlow: Heinemann, 1961), 81, ll. 1–3.
81 See 2 Cor. 3.12-18.
82 Lk. 1.68-79.
83 See, for instance, *Common Worship: Daily Prayer*, 118.
84 Williams, *Tokens of Trust*, 84.
85 Ibid., 102. An obvious worry here is the saying, attributed to Jesus, that he had 'not come to bring peace, but a sword', such that a person's enemies would be 'those of

his own household' (Mt. 10.34-9; see also Lk. 12.49-53). I will not settle the question here of how this passage should be interpreted. Suffice it to say that in light of the other accounts of Jesus' acts and teachings in the gospels, in which he is portrayed as promulgating an ethics of peace and reconciliation (see e.g. nn. 102–4), it seems clear that some special interpretation of the passage is required. Given the context, one natural interpretation is that Jesus was stressing the potential cost of a life of discipleship: one must be prepared to break off one's closest relationships if necessary (see also the story of the rich young man, Mt. 19.16-30). However, the key fact for my purposes is simply that on the theological picture on which I am drawing, and in at least much of Christianity, Jesus is remembered and interpreted as having introduced the possibility of peace as defined in the Rowan Williams passage just quoted. This is all I need in order to flesh out the longing of the Nunc Dimittis in light of the doctrinal and devotional context in which it is sung.

86 Williams, *Tokens of Trust*, 83.
87 Ibid., 84–8.
88 Ibid., 88.
89 Ibid., 92–4.
90 Ibid., 94.
91 Ibid., 91; see also 158–9.
92 Ibid., 99.
93 Ibid., for example 99–100. This can include – indeed, for Williams, it *must* include – *contemplative* practice, of the kind that Chapter 6 will examine: see ibid., 154–5.
94 For the language of God's love being 'in' us, see, for instance, 1 Jn 2.5; also Williams, *Tokens of Trust*, 145.
95 See 1 Jn 4.8.
96 Williams, *Tokens of Trust*, 141–4, 155.
97 See, for instance, Jn 1.1-9; 1 Jn 2.8.
98 Lk. 1.78.
99 Williams, *Tokens of Trust*, 101–2; see also n. 94.
100 Williams, *Tokens of Trust*, 155.
101 Ibid., 141.
102 For instance, inviting 'tax collectors and sinners' to eat with him and his disciples (Mt. 9.9-13).
103 For instance, Mk 1.21-45.
104 For instance, the parables of the unforgiving servant (Mt. 18.21-35), the labourers in the vineyard (Mt. 20.1-16) and the prodigal son (Lk. 15.11-32).
105 Peter van Inwagen, 'Quam Dilecta', in *God and the Philosophers: The Reconciliation of Faith and Reason*, ed. Thomas V. Morris (New York, NY: Oxford University Press, 1995), 57–8.
106 Richard Crashaw, 'The Hymn of Saint Thomas in Adoration of the Blessed Sacrament', in Dalgish (ed.), *Eight Metaphysical Poets*, 64–5, ll. 51–6. The original

prayer by Aquinas is 'Adoro Devote', in *The Oxford Book of Medieval Latin Verse*, ed. F. J. E. Raby (Oxford: Clarendon Press, 1959), 403–4.
107 'It is trust that sets you right' (Williams, *Tokens of Trust*, 159).
108 L. A. Paul, 'What You Can't Expect When You're Expecting', *Res Philosophica* 92, no. 2 (2015): see esp. 153–62.
109 Ibid., 156–7.
110 Ibid., 161.
111 Thomas V. Morris, 'Suspicions of Something More', in Morris (ed.), *God and the Philosophers*, 8–9.
112 I thank Joshua Cockayne and Amber Griffioen for raising this objection.
113 See, for instance, the passages cited in n. 104 above.
114 1 Jn 4.7.
115 Thomas Aquinas, *Summa Theologica*, trans. Fathers of the English Dominican Province, online (Kevin Knight, 2016), I, Q13, A2, ad 3, accessed 2 October 2016, http://www.newadvent.org/summa/index.html.
116 Ibid.
117 This mirrors the way, for which I argued in Chapter 3, in which one can know something of what a romantic relationship would be like even if one has had no such experience. See n. 56.

Chapter 6

1 In *A Choice of George Herbert's Verse*, ed. R. S. Thomas (London: Faber and Faber, 1967), 68, final two lines.
2 Williams, *Tokens of Trust*, 157.
3 See the Author's Note in Merton, *New Seeds of Contemplation*, where Merton refers to some of his main influences, including the Rule of St Benedict, St Bernard of Clairvaux and St John of the Cross.
4 That *New Seeds of Contemplation* can be read as a mature summary of Merton's thought is attested to by Merton scholar William Shannon, who has grouped Merton's main works into early, transitional and mature stages. In the early group he places *What Is Contemplation?*, *Seeds of Contemplation* and *The Ascent to Truth*; *The Inner Experience* he identifies as a transitional work; and the mature works listed are *New Seeds of Contemplation*, *Contemplative Prayer* and *Zen and the Birds of Appetite*. See William H. Shannon, *Thomas Merton's Paradise Journey: Writings on Contemplation* (Tunbridge Wells: Burns & Oates, 2000), 17.
5 Merton, *New Seeds of Contemplation*, 150, 153.
6 Ibid., 94.
7 Ibid., 25, 27.

8   Ibid., 52.
9   Ibid., 130–1.
10 Ibid., 51–2.
11 Ibid., 13–14.
12 Ibid., 14.
13 Ibid., 145.
14 Ibid., 141.
15 Williams, *Tokens of Trust*, 156.
16 Merton, *New Seeds of Contemplation*, 158–9. This corresponds to the two 'nights' of contemplative prayer described by St John of the Cross: that of the senses and that of the spirit. In the night of the senses, one is purged of one's desires for worldly, material things. In the night of the spirit, one is denied even those experiences that were felt to be spiritually satisfying, as one is prised from one's established, self-centred ways of relating to God. See St John of the Cross, *The Ascent of Mount Carmel*, trans. David Lewis (London: Aeterna Press, 2015), bks I (night of senses) and II–III (night of spirit); also his *Dark Night of the Soul*, ed. T. N. R. Rogers, trans. E. Allison Peers (Mineola, NY: Dover, 2003), bks I (night of senses) and II (night of spirit). Roughly speaking, *Ascent* deals with the 'active' nights – the aspects of the process that we can help to bring about in cooperation with God; *Dark Night*, meanwhile, deals with the 'passive' nights – 'the actual experiential level of God's purifying activity'. For a discussion of the 'nights', see Rowan Williams, *The Wound of Knowledge*, 2nd edn (London: Darton, Longman and Todd, 1990), 165–76 (the description of the passive nights just quoted is on 170). I am grateful to Sam Hole for helping with the elucidation of these aspects of John's work.
17 Merton, *New Seeds of Contemplation*, 61.
18 Ibid., 104, my emphasis.
19 Ibid., 47.
20 Ps 34.8.
21 Merton, *New Seeds of Contemplation*, 156.
22 Ibid., 153.
23 Ibid., 125–6.
24 Ibid., 22.
25 See Williams, *Tokens of Trust*, 157.
26 Stump, 'Beauty as a Road to God', 17.
27 Ibid., 21–2.
28 Ibid., 22.
29 Ibid., 23.
30 For more on the analogy between romantic/erotic desire and desire for God, including examples of how this analogy has been used in Jewish and Christian tradition, see Chapter 5, p. 97, esp. n. 44. See also n. 57 of that chapter, where I cited Ellen Davis, in her commentary on the Song of Songs, voicing the view that erotic

love can give us a clue as to what relationship with God would be like. It is worth seeing some of the context of the passage I quoted there, since it echoes some of what I say in this section about the romantic/religious analogy: 'Fundamental to both is a desire to transcend the confines of the self for the sake of intimacy with the other ... the experience of healthy sexual desire can help us imagine what it might mean to love God truly. ... Like the love of God, profound love of another person entails devotion of the whole self.' See Davis, *Proverbs, Ecclesiastes, and the Song of Songs*, 233.

31 In this more positive characterization of romantic desire, I am drawing partly on Aquinas' account of love as presented by Stump, in her *Wandering in Darkness*, chap. 5, esp. 90ff. As Stump explains, Aquinas thought that love involves two interconnected desires: a desire for the good of the beloved, and a desire for union with the beloved.

32 This is a problem for 'volitional' accounts of love, such as Harry Frankfurt's, which characterize love as necessarily *generating* the beloved's value in the eyes of the lover, and as *not* necessarily being *grounded* in the perceived value of the beloved. See Harry Frankfurt, *The Reasons of Love* (Princeton, NJ: Princeton University Press, 2004), chap. 2, secs 3–4. This may be true of certain kinds of love, such as parental love; but it is not true of romantic love. While romantic love does, indeed, generate for the lover a special kind of value in the beloved, clearly such love *is* also necessarily grounded in the beloved's attractiveness to the lover: in answer to the beloved's question 'Why do you love me?' we would expect the lover's response to involve *something* about the beloved.

33 This observation should be enough to forestall any worry that I am committed to a naïve 'responsiveness' account of love, according to which love is simply 'a response of the lover to qualities he perceives and values in the beloved' (Stump, *Wandering in Darkness*, 86). See, for example, Gabriele Taylor, 'Love', *Proceedings of the Aristotelian Society* 76 (1976): 147–64; and J. David Velleman, 'Love as a Moral Emotion', *Ethics* 109, no. 2 (1999): 338–74. A key objection to this account is that it has the counterintuitive result of making the beloved substitutable: the substitute need only have the same valued characteristics as the beloved (Stump, *Wandering in Darkness*, 86). But given what I have said in the context of romantic desire, as one grows in knowledge of one's beloved, one's attitude towards her will increasingly be defined by more than just an attraction to some of her attributes. And so, even if in the early stages of a relationship one is mainly attracted to attributes that one might just as well have found in someone else, as the relationship develops the beloved will (if things go well) become unsubstitutable.

34 Merton, *New Seeds of Contemplation*, 151–2, 154.
35 Ibid., 13.
36 Ibid., 150.
37 Merton elsewhere uses 'notions' to refer to abstract thoughts, which he distinguishes from 'concrete intuition'. See ibid., 20, note.

38 For examples of such a focus on specific divine attributes, we need look no further than the many mentions of those attributes in the Psalms. See, for instance, Ps 103.8, 13, 17, in which God is praised in virtue of his mercy, graciousness, slowness to anger, steadfast love, compassion and righteousness.
39 Brewer, 'Three Dogmas', 280.
40 Merton, *New Seeds of Contemplation*, 20, note.
41 Ibid., 104.
42 Ibid., 20, note.
43 Ibid., 103.
44 Does the notion of desire for God that is born of contemplation imply that there is no final fulfilment, but rather an endless journey into ever-deeper knowledge and love of God? After all, if knowing God elicits further desire for him, what could ultimately satisfy it? It is debatable as to whether Merton thought final fulfilment possible; certainly, in *New Seeds*, he denied that the culmination of the spiritual life is the experiential high point in comparison with other experiences (183–5). The question in its Christian form goes back at least to the church fathers. Origen arguably held that final fulfilment is possible, consisting in contemplative knowledge of God that divinizes the knower. See his *Commentary on the Gospel according to John*, trans. Ronald E. Heine (Washington DC: Catholic University of America Press, 1989), bk. II, sec. 23 and bk. XXXII, sec. 338. Gregory of Nyssa, meanwhile, denied that final satisfaction is possible – only a never-ending ascent to God consisting in desire for God that is constantly fulfilled, yet thereby constantly intensified. See his *The Life of Moses*, trans. Abraham J. Malherbe and Everett Ferguson (Mahwah, NJ: Paulist Press, 1978), bk. II, secs 231–9; also his *Homilies on the Song of Songs*, trans. Richard A. Norris Jr. (Atlanta, GA: Society of Biblical Literature, 2012), 389 (hom. XII). There are discussions of Origen and Gregory in Louth, *The Origins of the Christian Mystical Tradition*, chaps 4–5. We need only remark that the notion of contemplative desire for God does not entail any view on whether final fulfilment is possible. If it is not, then contemplative desire for God is always intensified as it is fulfilled. But if final fulfilment *is* possible then there may be contemplative knowledge of God to an intermediate degree, resulting in a desire for deeper knowledge.
45 Merton, *New Seeds of Contemplation*, 154.
46 Yalom, *Love's Executioner and Other Tales of Psychotherapy*, 39.
47 Merton, *New Seeds of Contemplation*, 184, 186–7.
48 Ibid., 167.
49 Ibid., 103.
50 Ibid., 93.
51 For a discussion of the relationship between propositional belief and personal trust in a religious context, see Nicholas Wolterstorff's introduction to Plantinga and Wolterstorff, eds, *Faith and Rationality*. Here Wolterstorff focuses on how these

two attitudes feature in the biblical account of how we ought to relate to God. As Wolterstorff explains, in the Bible – and in the New Testament in particular – belief is one of the authentic manifestations of trust: the one who trusts in God and Jesus believes what they say. Thus on this picture, there are some propositional religious beliefs that presuppose personal trust. The discussion below is on whether there are also propositional religious beliefs that are psychologically *necessary* for personal trust in God, in the context of contemplative prayer.

52 Merton, *New Seeds of Contemplation*, 159.
53 Ibid., 160.
54 Robert Audi makes both these points in 'Belief, Faith, and Acceptance', 93.
55 Thus I cannot accept Audi's claim that trust implies 'certain cognitive attitudes stronger than hope' (ibid.).
56 Pascal, *Pensées*, 121–5, no. 418.
57 Ibid., 123.
58 As mentioned in Chapter 2, n. 25, there are several distinct arguments to be found in Pascal's text, only one of which I have briefly reconstructed here.
59 Pascal, *Pensées*, 125.
60 See n. 16 of this chapter.
61 Merton, *New Seeds of Contemplation*, 142.
62 Ibid., 144–7.
63 See, for instance, Jolyon Jenkins, 'Seriously – Is Mindfulness Meditation Dangerous? – BBC Radio 4', *BBC*, accessed 24 April 2016, http://www.bbc.co.uk/programmes/articles/2nB1psRz3JFQpzDh6J2Z6xl/is-mindfulness-meditation-dangerous.
64 Ibid.
65 Merton, *New Seeds of Contemplation*, 95.
66 The point here is similar to one that John Cottingham has made about the importance of familiarity with a religious world view if we are to evaluate its truth claims. See Cottingham, *The Spiritual Dimension*, 83: 'In so far as the gospel story carries metaphysical implications, ... these will not begin to have any real significance for the hearer (and hence will not even be candidates for serious evaluation) unless ... two main components [are in place]: first, a certain kind of emotional dynamic, and second, a [multilevelled response to the] layered structure of mutually resonating symbols and narratives' (the idea of a multilevelled response is found in ibid., 88). I have argued that contemplative prayer can combine fruitfully with one kind of pre-contemplative emotion, that is, desire; more generally, emotional response and contemplative experience are two convergent examples of how a rich grasp of Christianity's doctrinal claims depends on lived involvement in its way of life.
67 Merton, *New Seeds of Contemplation*, 165.
68 Ibid., 158.

69 See p. 125 above.
70 Merton, *New Seeds of Contemplation*, 96.
71 Ibid., 92.

Chapter 7

1 Cottingham, 'What Difference Does It Make?' 420.

Bibliography

Ali, S. Omar and Zehra F. Peynircioğlu. 'Songs and Emotions: Are Lyrics and Melodies Equal Partners?' *Psychology of Music* 34, no. 4 (2006): 511–34.

Alston, William P. 'Audi on Nondoxastic Faith'. In *Rationality and the Good: Critical Essays on the Ethics and Epistemology of Robert Audi*, edited by Mark Timmons, John Greco and Alfred R. Mele, 123–38. Oxford: Oxford University Press, 2007.

Alston, William P. 'Belief, Acceptance, and Religious Faith'. In *Faith, Freedom, and Rationality*, edited by Jeff Jordan and Daniel Howard-Snyder, 3–27. Lanham, MD: Rowman & Littlefield, 1996.

Alston, William P. *Perceiving God: The Epistemology of Religious Experience*. Ithaca, NY: Cornell University Press, 1991.

Aquinas, Thomas. 'Adoro Devote'. In *The Oxford Book of Medieval Latin Verse*, edited by F. J. E. Raby, 403–4. Oxford: Clarendon Press, 1959.

Aquinas, Thomas. *Summa Theologica*. Translated by Fathers of the English Dominican Province. Online. Kevin Knight, 2016. http://www.newadvent.org/summa/index.html.

Aristotle. *The Politics*. Translated by Ernest Barker. Revised edn. Oxford: Oxford University Press, 2009.

Arnold, Jonathan. *Sacred Music in Secular Society*. Farnham: Ashgate, 2014.

Audi, Robert. 'Belief, Faith, and Acceptance'. *International Journal for Philosophy of Religion* 63, no. 1 (2008): 87–102.

Baeza, Carlos. 'Bart the Lover'. The Simpsons. USA: Fox network, 13 February 1992.

Begbie, Jeremy S. 'Faithful Feelings: Music and Emotion in Worship'. In *Resonant Witness: Conversations between Music and Theology*, edited by Jeremy S. Begbie and Steven R. Guthrie, 323–54. Grand Rapids, MI: Wm. B. Eerdmans Publishing Co., 2011.

Bennett, Arnold. *The Journals of Arnold Bennett*, edited by Frank Swinnerton. London: Penguin, 1954.

Bingham, John. 'Looking for Britain's Future Leaders? Try Evensong'. *The Telegraph*, 1 March 2016. http://www.telegraph.co.uk/news/religion/12176998/Looking-for-Britains-future-leaders-Try-evensong.html.

Blackwell, Albert L. *The Sacred in Music*. Louisville, KY: Westminster John Knox Press, 1999.

Brewer, Talbot. 'Three Dogmas of Desire'. In *Values and Virtues: Aristotelianism in Contemporary Ethics*, edited by Timothy Chappell, 257–84. Oxford: Clarendon Press, 2006.

Broad, C. D. 'Emotion and Sentiment'. In *Broad's Critical Essays in Moral Philosophy*, edited by David R. Cheney, 283–301. London: Allen & Unwin, 1971.

Broad, C. D. *The Mind and Its Place in Nature*. New York, NY: Harcourt Brace, 1925.

Burch Brown, Frank. 'Music'. In *The Oxford Handbook of Religion and Emotion*, edited by John Corrigan, 200–22. Oxford: Oxford University Press, 2008.

Cohen, L. Jonathan. *An Essay on Belief and Acceptance*. Oxford: Clarendon Press, 1992.

Collingwood, R. G. 'Words and Tune'. In R. G. Collingwood, *The Philosophy of Enchantment: Studies in Folktale, Cultural Criticism, and Anthropology*, edited by David Boucher, Wendy James and Philip Smallwood, 3–17. Oxford: Clarendon Press, 2005.

Common Worship: Daily Prayer. London: Church House Publishing, 2005.

Cook, Nicholas. *Analysing Musical Multimedia*. Oxford: Clarendon Press, 1998.

Cottingham, John. *How to Believe*. London: Bloomsbury, 2015.

Cottingham, John. *Philosophy of Religion: Towards a More Humane Approach*. New York, NY: Cambridge University Press, 2014.

Cottingham, John. *The Spiritual Dimension: Religion, Philosophy, and Human Value*. Cambridge: Cambridge University Press, 2005.

Cottingham, John. 'What Difference Does It Make? The Nature and Significance of Theistic Belief'. *Ratio* 19, no. 4 (2006): 401–20.

Cottingham, John. *Why Believe?* London: Continuum, 2009.

Crashaw, Richard. 'The Hymn of Saint Thomas in Adoration of the Blessed Sacrament'. In *Eight Metaphysical Poets*, edited by Jack Dalglish, 63–5. Harlow: Heinemann, 1961.

Cuneo, Terence. 'Liturgy and the Moral Life'. In Terence Cuneo, *Ritualized Faith: Essays on the Philosophy of Liturgy*, 89–105. Oxford: Oxford University Press, 2016.

Davies, Stephen. *Musical Meaning and Expression*. Ithaca, NY: Cornell University Press, 1994.

Davis, Caroline Franks. *The Evidential Force of Religious Experience*. Oxford: Oxford University Press, 1999.

Davis, Ellen F. *Proverbs, Ecclesiastes, and the Song of Songs*. Louisville, KY: Westminster John Knox Press, 2000.

De Sousa, Ronald. 'Emotion'. In *The Stanford Encyclopedia of Philosophy*, edited by Edward N. Zalta, Spring 2014. http://plato.stanford.edu/archives/spr2014/entries/emotion/.

Deigh, John. 'Cognitivism in the Theory of Emotions'. *Ethics* 104, no. 4 (1994): 824–54.

Deng, Natalja. 'Religion for Naturalists'. *International Journal for Philosophy of Religion* 78, no. 2 (2015): 195–214.

Efird, David and Daniel Gustafsson. 'Experiencing Christian Art'. *Religious Studies* 51, no. 3 (2015): 431–9.

Faulkner, Quentin. *Wiser than Despair: The Evolution of Ideas in the Relationship of Music and the Christian Church*. Westport, CT: Greenwood Press, 1996.

Fisher, John Andrew. *Reflecting on Art*. Mountain View, CA: Mayfield Pub. Co., 1993.

Flew, Antony. 'The Presumption of Atheism'. *Canadian Journal of Philosophy* 2, no. 1 (1972): 29–46.

Frankfurt, Harry. *The Reasons of Love*. Princeton, NJ: Princeton University Press, 2004.

Gabrielsson, Alf. *Strong Experiences with Music: Music Is Much More than Just Music*. Translated by Rod Bradbury. Oxford: Oxford University Press, 2011.

Goldie, Peter. *The Emotions: A Philosophical Exploration*. Oxford: Oxford University Press, 2000.

Gregory of Nyssa. *Homilies on the Song of Songs*. Translated by Richard A. Jr Norris. Atlanta, GA: Society of Biblical Literature, 2012.

Gregory of Nyssa. *The Life of Moses*. Translated by Abraham J. Malherbe and Everett Ferguson. Mahwah, NJ: Paulist Press, 1978.

Griffiths, Bede. *The Golden String*. London: Fount, 1979.

Hájek, Alan. 'Pascal's Wager'. In *The Stanford Encyclopedia of Philosophy*, edited by Edward N. Zalta, Winter 2012. http://plato.stanford.edu/archives/win2012/entries/pascal-wager/.

Harvey, Peter. *An Introduction to Buddhism: Teachings, History and Practices*. Cambridge: Cambridge University Press, 1990.

Herbert, George. 'Clasping of Hands'. In *A Choice of George Herbert's Verse*, edited by R. S. Thomas, 68. London: Faber and Faber, 1967.

Hillesum, Etty. *Etty: The Letters and Diaries of Etty Hillesum 1941-1943, Complete and Unabridged*, edited by Klaas A. D. Smelik. Translated by Arnold J. Pomerans. Grand Rapids, MI: Wm. B. Eerdmans Publishing Co., 2002.

Jackson, Frank. 'Epiphenomenal Qualia'. *Philosophical Quarterly* 32 (1982): 127–36.

James, William. *The Principles of Psychology*. Vol. 2. 2 vols. New York, NY: Dover, 1950.

James, William. 'The Will to Believe'. In William James, *The Will to Believe and Other Essays in Popular Philosophy*, 1–31. New York, NY: Longmans Green and Co, 1897.

Jay, Christopher. 'The Kantian Moral Hazard Argument for Religious Fictionalism'. *International Journal for Philosophy of Religion* 75, no. 3 (2014): 207–32.

Jenkins, Jolyon. 'Seriously - Is Mindfulness Meditation Dangerous? - BBC Radio 4'. BBC. Accessed 24 April 2016. http://www.bbc.co.uk/programmes/articles/2nB1psRz3JFQpzDh6J2Z6xl/is-mindfulness-meditation-dangerous.

Jenkins, Simon. 'Why Cathedrals Are Soaring'. *The Spectator*, 8 October 2016. http://www.spectator.co.uk/2016/10/why-cathedrals-are-soaring/.

Jordan, Jeff. *Pascal's Wager: Pragmatic Arguments and Belief in God*. Oxford: Oxford University Press, 2006.

Jordan, Jeff. 'The Many-Gods Objection'. In *Gambling on God: Essays on Pascal's Wager*, edited by Jeff Jordan, 101–13. Lanham, MD: Rowman & Littlefield, 1994.

Joyce, Richard. *The Myth of Morality*. Cambridge: Cambridge University Press, 2001.

Kivy, Peter. 'Critical Study: Deeper than Emotion'. *British Journal of Aesthetics* 46, no. 3 (2006): 287–311.

Kivy, Peter. 'Mood and Music: Some Reflections for Noël Carroll'. *Journal of Aesthetics and Art Criticism* 64, no. 2 (2006): 271–81.

Kivy, Peter. *Music Alone: Philosophical Reflections on the Purely Musical Experience*. Ithaca, NY: Cornell University Press, 1990.

Krumhansl, C. L. 'An Exploratory Study of Musical Emotions and Psychophysiology'. *Canadian Journal of Experimental Psychology* 51, no. 4 (1997): 336–53.

Kuyper, Abraham. *To Be Near Unto God*. Translated by John Hendrik de Vries. Grand Rapids, MI: Wm. B. Eerdmans Publishing Co., 1925.

Le Poidevin, Robin. *Arguing for Atheism: An Introduction to the Philosophy of Religion*. London: Routledge, 1996.

Louth, Andrew. *The Origins of the Christian Mystical Tradition: From Plato to Denys*. 2nd edn. Oxford: Oxford University Press, 2007.

Lyons, William. *Emotion*. Cambridge: Cambridge University Press, 1980.

Macfarlane, Alan. 'John Rutter Interviewed by Alan Macfarlane 28th January 2009'. Accessed 10 September 2014. http://www.alanmacfarlane.com/DO/filmshow/rutter1_fast.htm.

Mackie, J. L. *The Miracle of Theism*. Oxford: Oxford University Press, 1982.

Madell, Geoffrey. 'What Music Teaches about Emotion'. *Philosophy* 71, no. 275 (1996): 63–82.

Martin, Michael. *Atheism: A Philosophical Justification*. Philadelphia, PA: Temple University Press, 1990.

Merton, Thomas. *New Seeds of Contemplation*. London: Burns & Oates, 1999.

Mew, Peter. 'The Expression of Emotion in Music'. *British Journal of Aesthetics* 25, no. 1 (1985): 33–42.

Milne, A. A. *The House at Pooh Corner*. Reissue edn. New York, NY: Penguin, 1991.

Morris, Thomas V. 'Suspicions of Something More'. In *God and the Philosophers: The Reconciliation of Faith and Reason*, edited by Thomas V. Morris, 8–18. New York, NY: Oxford University Press, 1995.

Nussbaum, Martha. 'Emotions as Judgements of Value and Importance'. In *What Is an Emotion? Classic and Contemporary Readings*, edited by Robert C. Solomon, 2nd edn, 271–83. New York, NY: Oxford University Press, 2003.

Nussbaum, Martha. *Upheavals of Thought: The Intelligence of Emotions*. Cambridge: Cambridge University Press, 2001.

Oakley, Justin. *Morality and the Emotions*. London: Routledge and Kegan Paul, 1992.

Origen. *Commentary on the Gospel according to John*. Translated by Ronald E. Heine. Washington DC: Catholic University of America Press, 1989.

Pascal, Blaise. *Pensées*. Translated by A. J. Krailsheimer. Revised edn. London: Penguin, 1995.

Paul, L. A. 'What You Can't Expect When You're Expecting'. *Res Philosophica* 92, no. 2 (2015): 149–70.

Plantinga, Alvin. *Warranted Christian Belief*. Oxford: Oxford University Press, 2000.

Plantinga, Alvin and Nicholas Wolterstorff, eds. *Faith and Rationality: Reason and Belief in God*. Notre Dame, IN: University of Notre Dame Press, 1983.

Plato. *Symposium*. Translated by C. J. Rowe. Warminster: Aris & Phillips, 1998.

Plato. *The Republic*. Translated by Desmond Lee. 2nd edn. London: Penguin, 2003.

Price, H. H. *Thinking and Experience*. Cambridge, MA: Harvard University Press, 1953.

Prinz, Jesse. 'Emotion, Psychosemantics, and Embodied Appraisals'. *Royal Institute of Philosophy Supplement* 52 (2003): 69–86.

Pugmire, David. 'The Secular Reception of Religious Music'. *Philosophy* 81, no. 1 (2006): 65–79.

Putman, Daniel. 'Can a Secularist Appreciate Religious Music?' *Philosophy* 83, no. 325 (2008): 391–5.

Ridley, Aaron. *Music, Value and the Passions*. Ithaca, NY: Cornell University Press, 1995.

Rota, Michael. *Taking Pascal's Wager: Faith, Evidence and the Abundant Life*. Downers Grove, IL: IVP Academic, 2016.

Schroeder, Tim. 'Desire'. In *The Stanford Encyclopedia of Philosophy*, edited by Edward N. Zalta, Summer 2015. http://plato.stanford.edu/archives/sum2015/entries/desire/.

Shannon, William H. *Thomas Merton's Paradise Journey: Writings on Contemplation*. Tunbridge Wells: Burns & Oates, 2000.

Sheffield, Frisbee C. C. *Plato's Symposium: The Ethics of Desire*. Oxford: Oxford University Press, 2006.

Sherwood, Harriet. 'As Traditional Believers Turn Away, Is This a New Crisis of Faith?' *The Guardian*, 13 August 2016. http://www.theguardian.com/world/2016/aug/13/church-of-england-evangelical-drive.

Solomon, Robert C. 'Emotions and Choice'. In *What Is an Emotion? Classic and Contemporary Readings*, edited by Robert C. Solomon, 2nd edn, 224–35. New York, NY: Oxford University Press, 2003.

Spicer, Paul. Liner notes to *Howells: Choral Music*. Wells Cathedral Choir and Malcolm Archer. London: Hyperion, CDA67494. CD. 2014.

Spufford, Francis. *Unapologetic*. London: Faber and Faber, 2012.

Sroufe, L. Alan. 'From Infant Attachment to Promotion of Adolescent Autonomy: Prospective, Longitudinal Data on the Role of Parents in Development'. In *Parenting and the Child's World: Influences on Academic, Intellectual, and Social-Emotional Development*, edited by John G. Borkowski, Sharon Landesman Ramey and Marie Bristol-Power, EBook edn, 187–202. Mahwah, NJ: Lawrence Erlbaum Associates, 2009.

St Augustine. *Confessions*. Translated by Henry Chadwick. Reissue edn. Oxford: Oxford University Press, 2008.

St Augustine. *Homilies on the First Epistle of John*, edited by Boniface Ramsey, Daniel Doyle and Martin Thomas. Translated by Boniface Ramsey. Hyde Park, NY: New City Press, 2008.

St John of the Cross. *Dark Night of the Soul*, edited by T. N. R. Rogers. Translated by E. Allison Peers. Mineola, NY: Dover, 2003.

St John of the Cross. *The Ascent of Mount Carmel*. Translated by David Lewis. London: Aeterna Press, 2015.

Stocker, Michael. 'Psychic Feelings: Their Importance and Irreducibility'. *Australasian Journal of Philosophy* 61 (1983): 5–26.

Stout, G. F. *A Manual of Psychology*. 4th edn. London: University Tutorial Press, 1929.
Stump, Eleonore. 'Beauty as a Road to God'. *Sacred Music* 134, no. 4 (2007): 13–26.
Stump, Eleonore. 'Omnipresence, Indwelling, and the Second-Personal'. *European Journal for Philosophy of Religion* 5, no. 4 (2013): 29–53.
Stump, Eleonore. *Wandering in Darkness: Narrative and the Problem of Suffering*. Oxford: Oxford University Press, 2010.
Sumner, L. W. *Welfare, Happiness, and Ethics*. Oxford: Clarendon Press, 1996.
Swinburne, Richard. *The Christian God*. Oxford: Oxford University Press, 1995.
Swinburne, Richard. *The Existence of God*. 2nd edn. Oxford: Clarendon Press, 2004.
Taylor, Charles. *A Secular Age*. Cambridge, MA: Harvard University Press, 2007.
Taylor, Gabriele. 'Love'. *Proceedings of the Aristotelian Society* 76 (1976): 147–64.
The New English Hymnal. Full music edn. Norwich: Canterbury Press Norwich, 1986.
Tolstoy, Leo. *Anna Karenina*. Translated by Richard Pevear and Larissa Volokhonsky. Revised edn. London: Penguin, 2003.
Vadas, Melinda. 'Affective and Non-Affective Desire'. *Philosophy and Phenomenological Research* 45, no. 2 (1984): 273–9.
Vaihinger, Hans. *The Philosophy of 'As If'*. Translated by C. K. Ogden. London: Routledge and Kegan Paul, 1949.
Van Inwagen, Peter. *God, Knowledge & Mystery: Essays in Philosophical Theology*. Ithaca, NY: Cornell University Press, 1995.
Van Inwagen, Peter. 'Quam Dilecta'. In *God and the Philosophers: The Reconciliation of Faith and Reason*, edited by Thomas V. Morris, 31–60. New York, NY: Oxford University Press, 1995.
Vaughan, Henry. 'The World'. In *Eight Metaphysical Poets*, edited by Jack Dalglish, 81–2. Harlow: Heinemann, 1961.
Velleman, J. David. 'Love as a Moral Emotion'. *Ethics* 109, no. 2 (1999): 338–74.
Williams, Rowan. *The Wound of Knowledge*. 2nd edn. London: Darton, Longman and Todd, 1990.
Williams, Rowan. *Tokens of Trust: An Introduction to Christian Belief*. London: Canterbury Press Norwich, 2007.
Wolterstorff, Nicholas. *Practices of Belief: Selected Essays, Volume 2*, edited by Terence Cuneo. Cambridge: Cambridge University Press, 2010.
Woodhouse, Patrick. *Etty Hillesum: A Life Transformed*. London: Continuum, 2009.
'Worship – Book of Common Prayer – the Order for Evening Prayer'. *Church of England*. Accessed 16 September 2016. https://www.churchofengland.org/prayer-worship/worship/book-of-common-prayer/the-order-for-evening-prayer.aspx.
Wynn, Mark. *Emotional Experience and Religious Understanding: Integrating Perception, Conception and Feeling*. Cambridge: Cambridge University Press, 2005.
Wynn, Mark. 'Musical Affects and the Life of Faith: Some Reflections on the Religious Potency of Music'. *Faith and Philosophy* 21, no. 1 (2004): 25–44.
Yalom, Irvin D. *Love's Executioner and Other Tales of Psychotherapy*. Reprint edn. London: Penguin, 1991.
Young, James O. *Critique of Pure Music*. Oxford: Oxford University Press, 2014.

Index

Abendlied (Rheinberger)   83, 84, 95–101
   desire conveyed and elicited   97–8
   music, text and context   95–7
   projected satisfaction and
      characterization of God   98–101
absolute music   65, 66, 68, 80
acceptance
   non-truth-normed   16, 17
   truth-normed   16–17
adagios   72
aesthetic emotion   66, 77
   arousal of   69, 71
aesthetic essence of mood   62
aesthetic love for music   67–8
affective desire   38–9, 40, 46
affectivity of emotion   66
Alfvén, Hugo   72
Alston, William   15–16, 153 n.7
analogues   68
anger   34, 68
Anglican liturgy   84
Anna Karenina (Tolstoy)   45
anxiety   68, 69
Aquinas, Thomas   28, 118, 131
Aristotle   61
Arnold, Jonathan   1, 9, 151 n.1, 153 n.9
ascetic detachment   21
attitudes in composing   62
attunement   19
Audi, Robert   15–16, 18, 155 n.35
Augustine   28, 55, 85, 87

baroque era, music   62
Beethoven, Ludwig van   74
belief   56
Bennett, Arnold   31
Blackwell, Albert L.   153 n.9
brainwashing. *See* self-deception
Brewer, Talbot   24–5, 48
   dogmas   27–8
Broad, C. D.   33
Brown, Brenton   166 n.11

'cast forwards'   43
Chaucer's *Canterbury Tales*   12
choral music   1, 8, 9
choral services   1
Christ   10
Christian
   contemplative tradition   6
   framework   121
   prayer   5
   theism   12, 21
   worship   13
Christian God, The (Swinburne)   155 n.31
Christianity   7, 155 n.3
   doctrinal content   18
   hypothesis of   12, 52
   tradition in   97
   truth   21
Christian tradition   28
   cultural heritage of   5
   interpreter of   108
   Judaeo-Christian tradition   106, 114
   strands of   19
cognitive theory of emotions   65–6
Collegium Regale   84
Collingwood, R. G.   78
Come Down, O Love Divine   83
consummation   42–3
contemplation   124–6
contemplative prayer   121, 126–30
   and propositional belief   140–7
contemplative spirituality   21
Cottingham, John   2, 3, 12, 18, 19, 22, 150, 151 n.5, 152 n.6
Council of Trent   86
Critique of Pure Music (Young)   165 n.2
cultural associations   72
cultural heritage   13
   of Christian tradition   5

dark night   21, 122, 141–6, 143
Davies, Stephen   63, 80

degrees of confidence 1
Deigh, John 32, 33, 47
Deng, Natalja 17
depression 69
desire(s) 23–4. *See also* emotions
   affective desire 38–9, 40, 46, 147
   characterization of God 93–5
   defined 38
   desirer's knowledge 53–5
   developing the account 43–4
   food 44–6
   for God 1–2, 5, 23, 40, 57–9, 84
   for God and theological framework 28–30
   as having mind-to-world fit 27–8
   interpersonal 25
   k-desire 56–7
   kinds of 31, 38–41
   to kneel and pray 4
   knowledge about 42–3, 56–7
   musical resolution 46–8
   musical tension 42–3
   non-affective desire 38, 39–40
   object-directed desire 81
   for persons and for states of affairs 24–7
   pre-contemplative desires 145
   religious desire 1–2, 3–4
   romantic desire 32, 48–53
   satisfaction 6
   state-of-affair desires 25, 26
   union with God 29
   un-self-centred desire 29
   'Wynn-Madell' account 42–3
desiring responses 64
despair 34
devotional feelings 1, 8
dishonesty 13
dissatisfaction 5, 6
distress 36
divine attributes 58
divine satisfaction 116–19
domestication 132–40, 147
dominant-to-tonic resolution 57

Efird, David 164 n.56
emotions. *See also* desire(s)
   affectivity of 66
   classification 33
   cognitive 32

   cognitive theory of 65–6
   non-cognitive 32
   pathological emotion 68–9
   philosophy of 31
   thought and affect 32–8
emotional affects 34
emotional arousal 65
emotional contagion 63, 70, 79–80
emotional well-being 39–40
epistemology of involvement 2, 18, 19, 150
erōs in the *Symposium* (Plato) 24, 27
evensong 1, 84, 101
excitement 34
extra-musical associations 68
extra-musical emotion, Peter Kivy on 64–7
   extra-musical subject matter 67–8
   music and extra-musical factors 73–9
   objectless versions of everyday affects 68–73
extra-musical objects 73

faith 16. *See also* belief
fear
   and hope 11
   object of 33
feeling towards 34
fictionalism 17
fiducial faith 15

Gabrielsson, Alf 3, 151 n.2
'garden-variety' affect 76
generalised spirituality 62
God
   characterization of 98–101
   of Christian doctrine 5
   contemplative love and knowledge of 137–40
   desire concerning 121
   desire's characterization of 93–5
   framework for seeking 7
   loving and worshipping 10
   musically elicited, desire-based knowledge 114–16
   ordinary desire for 132
   portrayal of God's character 14
   reality 7
   tradition's conception of 29
Goldie, Peter 34, 41

Index

Gregorian chant 3–4, 5, 12
Gregory of Nyssa 28
grief 36
Gustafsson, Daniel 164 n.56

habituation 19
half-believer 5
Hanslick, Eduard 65
happiness 34, 68
Harvey, Peter 169 n.14
Hear My Prayer, O Lord (Purcell) 80, 83, 84
   desire heard and desire aroused 89–91
   desire's characterization of God 93–5
   piece and expressiveness 88–9
   satisfaction of desperation 91–3
heavenly harmonies 86
Herbert, George 121
Hillesum, Etty 92, 93
hope 18, 34
Howells, Herbert 83, 84, 101–14
humanism 10
human vulnerability 5
humility 128
hunger 39
hunger born of humility 128

imaginative engagement 8
imitation and partisanship 11
infant Jesus 83
interested non-belief 30
interested non-believer 1
   and Christian theism 4, 7
interpersonal desire 25
intimacy 51
Introduction to Buddhism, An: Teachings, History and Practices (Harvey) 169 n.14

Jackson, Frank 45
James, William 11–13, 22, 160 n.15
Jamesian 'live hypothesis' 11
Jay, Christopher 156 n.44
jealousy 34
Jenkins, Simon 151 n.3
John's Gospel 10, 91, 163 n.41
joy 68
Joyce, Richard 17

k-desire 56–7
Kivy, Peter on extra-musical emotion 64–7
   aesthetic emotion 68
   extra-musical subject matter 67–8
   music and extra-musical factors 73–9
   neutralizing arguments 68–71
   objectless versions of everyday affects 68–73
Krabappel, Edna 14

Laudate Dominum 74–5, 76, 78
Le Poidevin, Robin 17
lived conditions 10
Lord, Reign in Me (Brown) 166 n.11
love, sense 36

Madell, Geoffrey 34, 42–3
Mahdi 11, 12
'many gods' objection to Pascal's Wager 12
Mars 72
Merton, Thomas 6, 29, 121–3, 128–30
Midsommarvaka (Alfvén) 72
Milne, A. A. 44
mind-to-world direction 27
mirroring responses 79–80
mood 34
Morris, Thomas 117
Mozart 74–5, 76
music. *See also* sacred music
   'aesthetic' emotion 78
   affective responses 72
   baroque and romantic eras 62
   combined affective response 73–9
   emotional arousal 68
   and emotions 65
   religious associations 68
   and religious devotion 85–7
musical affectivity 61. *See also* sacred music
   affective responses 63–4
   composer and listener 61–2
   expressive of and arouses affective state 63
   extra-musical emotion, Peter Kivy 64–79
   mirroring responses and analogous affects 79–80
   qualities of affective life 80–2

musical arousal of emotion   69
'musical distraction'   86
musical expressiveness   63
musical resolution   46–8
musical tension   42–3
music's capacity   6
music-text entity   78
Myth of Morality, The (Joyce)   17

New Seeds of Contemplation
  (Merton)   123
Night on Bare Mountain
  (Mussorgsky)   72
non-absolute music   66
non-affective desire   38, 39–40
non-believer   1, 5
non-believing religious involvement   2
  secularity and phenomenology
    9–11
non-doxastic acceptance   17
non-doxastic involvement   23
non-doxastic religious engagement   7,
  148, 150
non-musical physiological states   72
non-occurrent anger   162 n.30
non-propositional desire   56
non-rational factors   12
non-truth-normed acceptance   16, 17
Nunc Dimittis   83, 84, 101–2
  affective arousal   110
  affective expressiveness of musical
    settings   105–10
  divine glory   105–7
  Howells' *Collegium Regale*   103–4
  salvation in Christ   107–9
  Stanford in G   102–3
  summary of desire   109–10
Nussbaum, Martha   33, 36, 37,
  160 n.10

Oakley, Justin   41
object-directed desire   81
object-directed emotions   81, 82
openness to God   5
'ordinary' desire for God   126–30
  possessiveness and domestication
    132–40
  self-centred and other-centred
    emotional response   130–2
ordinary emotions   65, 68

Pascal, Blaise   11, 19, 23, 142, 154 n.25
Pascal's Wager   11–12, 19, 142–3, 147,
  154 n.25, 155 n.31
pathological emotion   68–9
Paul, L. A.   117, 118
Pensées (Pascal)   11
personal object and state-of-affairs
  satisfaction   110–12
personal transformation   19
phenomenon of pervasiveness   12
physiological states   72
Pilate, Pontius   152 n.4
Planets (Holst)   72
Plantinga, Alvin   153 n.7
Plato   24, 27, 61, 155 n.34
polyphony   86
possessiveness   132–40, 147
prayer, practice of   6
pre-Christian Judaism   173
pre-contemplative desires   122, 145,
  146
pre-contemplative religious orientation
  21
prejudice and passion   11
Price, H. H.   33
propositional attitudes   149
propositional attitudes and interested
  non-belief
  acceptance   16–17
  belief and desire   14–15
  epistemology of involvement
    17–21
  hoping acceptance   17–21
  propositional faith   15–16
Psalm
  117   74
  119   81
  42   81
  102   83, 88
  139   98
psychoanalytic untangling   69
Pugmire, David   1, 8, 151 n.2
Purcell, Henry   80
  Hear My Prayer, O Lord   83, 88–95
pursuit of human flourishing   10
Putman, Daniel   8
Pythagoras   61

reformed epistemology   153 n.7
regret   34

religious desire 1–2, 3–4, 121–3
   contemplation 124–6
   contemplative prayer 126–30
   contemplative prayer and propositional belief 140–7
   epistemology 6, 7
   'ordinary' desire for God 126–30
religious emotion 75
religious emotional object 74
religious faith 2–4
religious hypothesis 12
religious praxis 19
religious truth 20
Rheinberger, Josef 84
   Abendlied 83, 84, 95–101
Ridley, Aaron 63, 80
Roman Catholic Church 141
Roman Catholicism 85
romantic desire 32, 58
   affective and conceptual elements 48–50
   and desire for God, similarities 50–3
romantic era, music 62
romantic love 55
romantic relationship 48, 52

Sacred in Music, The (Blackwell) 153 n.9
sacred music 3–4, 61
   ability 6
   defined 8
   desire for God and theological framework 28–30
   desire for God in 87–8
   emotional response to 8
   listener 73
   non-believing openness 4–7
   and non-believing religious involvement 2, 8–9
   religious desire 3–4
   Western classical tradition 5
Sacred Music in Secular Society (Arnold) 153 n.9, 165 n.7
sacred vocal music 76
sadness 34, 68
satisfaction's phenomenology 112–14
Secular Age, A (Taylor) 9–10
secular society 9
self-centredness 129
self-deception 7, 13, 19, 21–3
self-delusional fantasy 121
self-esteem 4

self-knowledge 4, 5
self-sufficient humanism 10
sexual desire 177 n.30
The Simpsons 14
sin deserving punishment 86
Solomon, Robert 160 n.10, 161 n.15
Song of Zechariah 108
sorrow 36
spiritual experience 127
spiritual growth 58
spiritual traditions 18
Spring (Vivaldi) 72
Spufford, Francis 92
'stakes' 148
Stanford, Charles Villiers 83, 84, 101–14
state-of-affair desires 25, 26
state of affairs 56
Stout, G. F. 33
Strong Experiences with Music (Gabrielsson) 3
Stump, Eleonore 50, 99, 131, 147
Swinburne, Richard 155 n.31

Taylor, Charles 9–11
theistic and secular outlooks 10
theistic religions 20
tones of voice 78
truth-normed acceptance 16–17
   and hope 17–18

union with God 29
un-self-centred desire 29

Vadas, Melinda 38
value-ascription 37
Vesperae Solennes de Confessore (Mozart) 74, 166 n.11
Violin Concerto 74

weak epistemic position 16
Williams, Rowan 29, 75, 121, 127
Winnie-the-Pooh (Milne) 44
wishful thinking 28–30
Wolterstorff, Nicholas 153 n.7
Woodhouse, Patrick 92
'Woodrow' 14
Wynn, Mark 42–3, 80, 81, 152 n.6
'Wynn-Madell' account 42–3

Young, James O. 63, 70, 71, 79, 165 n.2

www.ingramcontent.com/pod-product-compliance
Lightning Source LLC
Chambersburg PA
CBHW052045300426
44117CB00012B/1976